BALANCING BLESSINGS
and Obtaining Order

BALANCING BLESSINGS
and *Obtaining Order*

11 STEPS TO BALANCING YOUR LIFE,
ORGANIZING YOUR POSSESSIONS, AND
Walking in the Spirit of God

REVISED AND UPDATED

Sandra Miller

ByB e-Fublishers, LLC
Woodbridge, VA 22191

Balancing Blessings and Obtaining Order

Copyright © 2022, 2009, 2008, by Sandra Miller

Third Edition, Paperback
ISBN-13: 978-0-9800093-7-8
ISBN-10: 0-9800093-7-5

Library of Congress Catalog Card Number: 2021924146

All rights reserved. No part of this publication may be reproduced, stored in a retrieval system, or transmitted in any form or by any means—electronic, mechanical, photocopy, recording, or any other—except for brief quotations in printed reviews, without the prior permission of the author.

Reasonable care and consideration has been taken in ensuring the clarity and accuracy of this book; therefore the publisher and author assume no responsibility for damages resulting from the use of the information contained herein.

The web site addresses recommended throughout this book are offered as a resource to you. These web sites are not intended in any way to be or imply an endorsement on the part of the author, nor does she vouch for their content for the life of the book.

Unless otherwise noted, all verses are taken from the New King James Version, Copyright © 1982 by Thomas Nelson, Inc. Used by Permission. All rights reserved.

Scripture quotations marked AMP are taken from The Amplified Bible, Old Testament, Copyright © 1971 by Tyndale House Publishers, Inc., Wheaton, Illinois. All rights reserved.

Verses marked NIV are taken from the HOLY BIBLE, NEW INTERNATIONAL VERSION ®. Copyright © 1973, 1978, 1984 by International Bible Society. Used by permission of Zondervan Publishing House. All rights reserved.

The "NIV" and "New International Version" trademarks are registered in the United States Patent and Trademark Office by International Bible Society. Use of either trademark requires the permission of International Bible Society.

Cover design by: Book Creatives

Printed in the United States of America

1000126001-2000123

In Loving Memory of:

My friend, Christine Baity (1964 to 2007).
I am so blessed to have known you.
Your graciousness, your strength, and your
positive attitude will always be a living
example to me, of what a virtuous woman is;

and to:

All the beautiful women in Christ Jesus,
I am honored that you have selected this book.
I have prayed for you and have asked God to
bless your efforts in balancing your blessings,
and in obtaining and maintaining order in
your daily life.

Let all things be done decently and in order.
—1 Corinthians 14:40

Let all that you do be done with love.
—1 Corinthians 16:14

Table of Contents

Acknowledgments	9
Preface: Hold Up!	11

Part 1

Introduction: Don't Step without God	19
Step 1: Getting Geared Up	29
Step 2: Establishing Proper Priorities	49
Step 3: Prayerfully Planning Ahead	65
Step 4: Exercising and Eating Healthy	93
Step 5: Conquering Your Clutter	115
Step 6: Evolving through Productive Pursuits	151

Part 2

Step 7: Reviving Your Relationships	187
Step 8: Making Your Ministry Matter	225
Step 9: Getting Financially Focused	245
Step 10: Being Divine by Design	279
Step 11: Caring for Your Castle	299
Conclusion: Bringing It Home!	320

Appendix A: Forms and Worksheets   *321*
    Combination To-Do List   322
    Fitness Vision Profile   323
    Clutter Analysis Worksheet   324
    Identify Your Passion(s) Worksheet   325
    Goal Setting Worksheet   327
    Monthly Household Budget Worksheet   328
    Characteristics of the Proverbs 31 Woman   330

The Proverbs 31 Woman Index   *331*

Bibliography   *332*

Acknowledgments

Lord, I am beyond humbled that you would put the desire to write this book in my heart. It is a blessing and a privilege to be able to aid women in finding and maintaining order in their daily lives. Thank you, Lord, for your grace and mercy and for helping me to get what was in my heart out.

To my family, thank you for your patience and encouragement and for fueling my focus to rediscover my passion.

To all the ladies who have allowed me to share their testimonies, taken the time to edit my work, or helped out in other ways, thank you.

Preface: Hold Up!

*L*et me forewarn you: this book is not a book that you can merely sit back and read. Then again, neither is the Bible, yet at times we have a tendency to sit back and read the Bible without being compelled to do what has been required of us.

The purpose of this book is to take you on a step-by-step journey of examining and organizing every aspect of your life—in the light of God's Word and will. You will identify and conquer hindrances in your home, within yourself, and in your processes that have distracted you from focusing on your God-given priorities and from fulfilling God's divine plan for your life.

That said, I believe God has blessed me with a heart for women and the struggles that most of us have in getting and maintaining balance in the different facets of our lives. I have fought this battle for years, and like a runner running a long-distance race, this is a race I continue to run—knowing that how I handle the complexities of life will increase or decrease my effectiveness for God.

So it's no surprise to me that in writing this book, my heart began to ache as I thought of not only myself, but single and married women—those I know and those I do not know—who have so much potential; Christian women who are not living life to its fullest, and grabbing a hold of all that God has in store for them. They may feel as if the weight of the cross—or life's responsibilities and challenges—is bearing down on them. Their finances are out of control, making it difficult to sleep at night. Their weight is beyond what would be considered healthy—putting them at risk for heart disease and diabetes. Their husbands, children, passions, and talents are being neglected in some form or fashion because they lack the skills to balance and properly manage their time, homes, careers, and relationships. Women who are living in depression because the clutter—in their homes and in their lives—has become so overwhelming, or their desires to rise out of poverty, be their own bosses, or be stay-at-home moms have not come to fruition. I am referring to women desperately seeking balance and order in their daily lives.

If this is you, this book is designed to help you get some level of balance and order in every aspect of your life. So, I hope you are okay with my forthrightness throughout this book. I am speaking from a deep longing to see Christian women who never thought they were leaders, become leaders; who never thought they could have order, have order; and who never thought their relationship with Christ could be better, be better.

Although this book covers an array of subjects, I am by no means a licensed expert in any of them; I can only give you what I've gleaned from formal education, personal experience, research, and the Spirit of God as I prayed and identified areas in my own life that needed overhauling.

Book Layout

This book is laid out in eleven specialized chapters, including chapter one—which prepares you for the journey ahead. The chapters that follow focus on getting order in these key areas of your life:

- your priorities,
- your prayer life,
- your health,
- your possessions,
- your passions,
- your relationships,
- your ministry,
- your finances,
- your self-worth, and
- your attitude within your home.

As you venture through this book, I will address—in one form or another—four fundamental questions:

- Why have order?
- What is not having order?
- How do you get order?
- When do you have order?

Let me also add that most of what will be shared with you in this book has been expressed and stated in various forms and in various books. Solomon put it well when he said: "What has been will be again, what has been done will be done again; there is nothing new under the sun" (Ecclesiastes 1:9, NIV).

What this book offers you are simplified guidelines, spiritually based reasons, and specific steps for: purging, pruning, planning, preparing, and purposely redefining your life with the help and prayers of friends; through the counsel of the Word of God; and through the grace and presence of God in your life.

The chapters are organized so that you can quickly jump to a step that interests you, or is a source of frustration and concern in your life. Be sure, however, to complete the introduction and step one, which provides preparation for the journey ahead.

Chapter Layout

Occasionally, throughout this book, you will be flagged (🏳) to meditate on a question that will challenge you to look within yourself and beyond your circumstances to grasp God's wisdom for your life. At the end of each step you will find a section called "Your Daily Call to Order," which will consist of:

- **Chapter Comments**. The principles and tools in this section are designed for you to meditate on or apply; they can also be used to spur group discussions.
- **Chapter Questions.** These questions are designed to help reinforce and clarify what you have read and aid you in applying biblical principles to your life. Keep your answers in a journal, which can also be used to record your thoughts, experiences, and prayers.
- **Chapter Assignments.** This is your master task list—prompting you to do more than just read but to take steps in transforming your life. Try to complete each challenge before moving on to the next step. Pace yourself by trying to complete at least one or two challenges daily, depending on whether you meet with your accountability partner or small group weekly or biweekly. The extreme and group challenges are optional—compelling a few brave souls to go beyond what is required.

Forms, worksheets, and additional resources are available in Appendix A and at: balancingblessings.org.

Small Group Study

Though this journey can be completed alone, I highly encourage you to use this book in a small group with no more than ten women. Meet weekly or biweekly (preferred) for 1½ to 2½ hour sessions. Try to discuss one chapter per session to give the participants time to work on the assignments. In addition, make a conscientious effort to pray earnestly for each other and to frequently check on one another to ensure that your sisters in Christ do not lose heart.

Designate a facilitator for each session to keep the class focused on the chapter topic or meeting agenda. The introduction and step one should be read before the first meeting. Your meeting goal is to start and end on time, having encouraged, empowered, and edified your sisters to do all things to God's glory.

Create *Your* Reading Plan

Although this book covers an array of subjects, my intent is not to overwhelm you. To allow this book to effectively minister to you, scrap the idea that you have to read this book from cover to cover; focus on getting balance and order in those areas of your life in desperate need of it.

Start by thinking about the areas in your life that need overhauling. Jot these areas down on a piece of paper, then read through each step's summary on pages 26-27 under "Create *Your* Reading Plan" and place a check by the steps you are interested in going through. Next, sift through your selections and prioritize the steps in order of importance to you. After reading the required sections, begin reading the book based on your defined needs.

If you are working through this book with a partner, sit down with your partner and put a check by the steps that are important to *both* of you. Then, organize the steps according to which steps are most vital to helping you *both* get balance and order.

My Prayer for You

May God bless you on your journey to *Balancing Blessings and Obtaining Order*. My prayer for you is the same prayer that Paul so graciously prayed for the saints who were in Ephesus and to the faithful in Christ Jesus:

> [May] the God of our Lord Jesus Christ, the Father of glory,... give to you the spirit of wisdom and revelation in the knowledge of Him, the eyes of your understanding being enlightened; that you may know what is the hope of His calling, what are the riches of the glory of His inheritance in the saints, and what is the exceeding greatness of His power toward us who believe, according to the working of His mighty power which He worked in Christ when He raised Him from the dead and seated Him at His right hand in the heavenly places, far above all principality and power and might and dominion, and every name that is named, not only in this age but also in that which is to come. And He put all things under His feet, and gave Him to be head over all things to the church, which is His body, the fullness of Him who fills all in all (Ephesians 1:17-23, emphasis added).

Part 1

It is easy to imagine that we will get to a place where we are complete and ready, but preparation is not suddenly accomplished, it is a process steadily maintained

Oswald Chambers

Introduction: Don't Step without God

*J*ust as a mother rejoices after her child has taken her first steps, God is rejoicing as you commit to taking those first few steps to get order in your life—by balancing and properly managing your blessings.

Believe me when I tell you there will be times when you will want to give up: to set this book aside, quit your marriage, quit your job, or give up on your dreams. Times when it may seem difficult to trust God for your healing, a wayward child, or for a transformed life. You are not alone. Life is full of tests, trials, and challenges designed to refine us, develop our character, and teach us how to love, serve, and obey—and in some cases to get us to refocus on what really matters.

Ultimately, what matters and what I want you to keep in mind as you journey through this book is that you are blessed, loved, and forgiven by God. He is the author and the finisher of your faith (Hebrews 12:2). He owns the vision for your future and knows what is in the chapters of your biography!

So what does it mean to be blessed, loved, and forgiven by God, and why is His presence so important in your transformation process? That's what this chapter will attempt to uncover for you.

You Are Blessed!

Mary, the mother of Jesus was blessed, and because she was obedient to God, she was highly favored. Through this favor, blessings rushed in. When she should have been stoned, she was celebrating her marriage to Joseph. When there was no place to give birth, God provided a manger. When Herod tried to kill her firstborn, she was led out of the country, and her child's life was spared. Through all that she endured, God was an "ever-present help" in her time of need. As the angel Gabriel said to Mary in Luke 1:28, I will begin this section by saying to you, "Rejoice, highly favored one, the Lord is with you; blessed are you among women!"

If you have the option to work, go to school, or stay home, you are blessed. If you have a job, home, or transportation, you are blessed. If you have children or no children, husband or no husband, you are blessed. If you can move, serve, give, or love, you are blessed. If you are a child of the almighty King of kings, Lord of lords, you are blessed!

It is not my intention to minimize anything you are going through or have been through. There are women who have been delivered from extraordinary circumstances and still others who will never know what God saved them from. God can use your bad experiences, hurts, and pains to bring about peace, order, and His goodness and mold you into a vessel for honor, "… sanctified and useful for the Master, prepared for every good work" (2 Timothy 2:21).

Knowing that you are blessed is a significant but small part of the journey you are about to embark on. What happens to many women when their lives take an unfamiliar route is that they begin to veer off the road they are traveling on. Some of them are able to get back on the road fairly quickly depending on their level of determination and their ability to adjust promptly to change. For others, it may take a little longer to pick

Introduction: Don't Step without God

themselves up. The rest of them are still trying to find their way out of the ravine after being tossed butt-first in the mud, waste, and muck.

Even though God has put in their midst resources and possessions (in the form of wisdom, strength, people, time, money, experience, endurance, etc.) to help them get back on the road, they are still stuck in the ravine. Why? Because with the blessings came changes and responsibilities that were difficult to handle without God as their guide. This resulted in them being depressed, overwhelmed, frustrated, and at times fearful. They were not careful, and the things that were meant to bless them, distracted them from their God-given purpose, and put them out of order with God.

Our obedience to God is not something we can pick up today and set down tomorrow; it is a continual process of daily seeking hard after God. Jesus said:

> *If anyone desires to come after Me, let him deny himself, and take up his cross daily, and follow Me. For whoever desires to save his life will lose it, but whoever loses his life for My sake will save it (Luke 9:23-24).*

If you are stuck in the ravine, it's time to get out and realize that you are blessed. The fact is that things get done better and more naturally when you align yourself with God. He provides the balance, the creativity, the flow, the joy, the order, the vision, the love, and the grace. Having these things is not only a blessing from above but a by-product of obedience to God.

I briefly mentioned resources and possessions above, two terms widely used in this book, so allow me the opportunity to clarify their meanings as they relate to this book.

Resources are anything ready for use, or that can be drawn upon to get us from point A to point B (or to help us get balance and order). *Possessions* are anything we own or have. We may possess wisdom and use time as a resource to obtain more wisdom by reading and studying the Word of God. We may own a car, sell it, and use the proceeds as a resource to donate to a local food bank.

Resources and possessions are closely related in that—at any given time—a resource can also be a possession. We may possess money, and we may use some of that money as a resource to launch a new business.

Whether God has blessed you with a lot of time, talent, money, wisdom, children, opportunities, or material possessions, the goal for each of us is not to allow our blessings to become a stumbling block, causing us to turn away from a God-focused life

You Are Loved!

I am baffled by the sheer number of women who want to define God's love for them as if there is something they can do to make God love them more or less. The truth is whether you have been obedient or disobedient, God loves you unconditionally. You are God's craftsmanship, the work of his fingers (see Ephesians 2:10); "… fearfully and wonderfully made" (Psalm 139:14).

Of the millions of people that exist on the face of the earth, God knows you by name, and you are not hidden from Him. No aspect of your life goes unnoticed before God, including your sins. You can grieve the Holy Spirit by the choices you make, but it does not change how much God loves you.

To get a biblical perspective on love, let us take a brief look at how author Richard L. Strauss defines the three dimensions of love often expressed in the Bible:

> *Eros* is totally human love. It often refers to sexual love, as the English word "erotic" implies. The basic

idea in eros is getting something for yourself. While it may involve a genuine feeling for someone else, that feeling is kindled by the attractiveness of that person and by the excitement, pleasure, and satisfaction which we believe that person will afford us....

Philia, the next higher level of love, relates to the soul rather than to the body. It touches the human personality—the intellect, the emotions, and the will. It involves a mutual sharing. The closest word in English would probably be "friendship."...

Agape keeps on loving even when its object is unresponsive, unkind, unlovable, or completely unworthy. It desires only the good of the one loved. It lives to make the loved one happy, whatever the personal cost or sacrifice.[1]

As defined above, God's love or agape is the highest form of love. It is the sacrificial love that God expressed toward us when He sent His only son to die on the cross for our sins—giving us eternal life (1 John 4:9-10) and life more abundantly (John 10:10).

You Are Forgiven!

Through God's sacrificial love comes forgiveness. God knows that sin destroys our fellowship with Him. The overwhelming guilt and condemnation we may feel when we've succumbed to our own selfish desires or acted in a manner that's offensive to God; this can often cause us to retreat from Him. As a result, many of us stop praying, reading the Word, and fellowshipping with other believers.

We are not perfect; if we were, Jesus Christ would not have had to die for us—God's grace understands that. As children of God, when we sin, God greatly desires that we immediately do two things—to help us stay in close fellowship with Him. First, we are to confess our sins before God in prayer. "If we confess our sins, He is faithful and just to forgive us our sins and to cleanse us from all unrighteousness" (1 John 1:9). Second, we are to repent of our sins. This is more than just being sorry; it's having a godly sorrow for having sinned against and hurt someone we love dearly. "For godly sorrow produces repentance [the desire to turn away from our sins] leading to salvation, not to be regretted; but the sorrow of the world produces death" (2 Corinthians 7:10, emphasis added).

There is freedom for you in repentance—freedom from shame, guilt, condemnation, hopelessness, and bitterness—which paves the way for a deeper, more intimate relationship with God. The longer you put off repenting, the harder your heart gets toward the things of God.

In like manner, the longer you put off accepting Jesus Christ as your Lord and Savior, the longer you choose to remain in the company of sin. Psalm 1:1 describes it as sitting in the seat of the scornful because once you get comfortable with your sin, it becomes much more difficult to release it and a lot easier to embrace it and take on its ways—to the point of rejecting God.

If you have picked up this book and have not dedicated your life to the Lord and have a yearning in your heart to do so, speak these words out loud:

> Jesus, I acknowledge that I need a Savior, and I want to make you Lord over my life. I repent of my sins and turn from sin to you. I believe with all my heart and soul that you died on the cross for my sins and rose again to give me everlasting life. This day, I confess you as my Lord and Savior, and according to

> Your Word, in Romans 10:9-10, I am saved. I thank You, Lord, for saving me. In Jesus' name I pray. Amen.

If you have prayed this prayer, congratulations; you are now a part of the family of Jesus Christ. With the Holy Spirit, you will embark on one of the greatest journeys of your life: loving, leaning, and learning what pleases our Lord and Savior.

Cherish your salvation as you would any prized possession. Share your decision with a friend, preferably someone who can help you find and get you connected to a local church.

Most importantly, let me remind you that if you are God's child, nothing can separate you from the love of God; not your sins, not your feelings.... Paul, the apostle, put it this way:

For I am persuaded that neither death nor life, nor angels nor principalities nor powers, nor things present nor things to come, nor height nor depth, nor any other created thing, shall be able to separate us from the love of God which is in Christ Jesus our Lord (Romans 8:38-39).

You have a challenging journey before you, one that can bring about incredible results in every area of your life. From personal experience, I can tell you that my efforts to get balance and order in my life proved futile; with God, my efforts proved faithful and fruitful (and birthed the book you are now reading).

Yes, the scope of this book is broad, I admit, but the purpose, balancing blessings and obtaining order provides reason for this. You will need the wisdom of an all-knowing and gracious God to help you be open and honest with yourself. In addition, you will find it comforting to be able to draw strength from God and to be able to confide in and seek advice from someone who will always have the inside scoop, and who will never consider you to be a bother—no matter what time of day.

Create Your Reading Plan

☑	Priority	Description of each step/chapter...
☑	**Intro**	**Introduction: Don't Step without God.** Gain an understanding of how blessed you are and how important God is to getting balance and order in your daily life.
☑	**1**	**S1: Getting Geared Up.** Become the person you truly desire to be and the woman God has called you to be by choosing to seek the heart of God in all that you do.
☐		**S2: Establishing Proper Priorities.** Find fulfillment and more hours in your day by learning how to focus on what matters most. Look at who or what is controlling your time and how to take back your time, so you have more time to invest in the things of God.
☐		**S3: Prayerfully Planning Ahead.** Achieve a sense of purpose in everything you do by including God in the process of planning your day. Learn techniques to organize tasks, and discover ways to increase your overall productivity by praying about your day and planning your day wisely.
☐		**S4: Exercising and Eating Healthy.** Recognize how important your health is to your ministry. Improve your countenance, self-worth, energy level, and quality of life by caring for the temple God has blessed you with.
☐		**S5: Conquering Your Clutter.** Handle paper, email, photos, clothes, toys, and collectibles more effectively by understanding whether your clutter is a resource problem or a possession problem; then, take steps to eliminate the chaos causing your clutter.

☑	Priority	Description of each step/chapter...
☐	📝	**S6: Evolving through Productive Pursuits.** Understand the benefits of gaining wisdom, knowledge, and understanding as you pursue your passion(s). Turn your weaknesses into strength as you learn to cultivate godly character.
☐	📝	**S7: Reviving Your Relationships.** Become a more loving daughter, wife, mom, or friend by following Jesus' guidelines for improving your relationships.
☐	📝	**S8: Making Your Ministry Matter.** Recognize how valuable your ministry is to the body of Christ and how your spiritual gifts can make a difference in the lives of others.
☐	📝	**S9: Getting Financially Focused.** Learn to harness your emotional spending by examining where your desire to spend originated. Achieve financial independence by making wise financial decisions—based on biblical wisdom while tapping into one of the greatest resources you possess as a giver: the ability to be a blessing to others.
☐	📝	**S10: Being Divine by Design.** Grasp how truly beautiful you are in the eyes of God and how God's grace, self-worth, and walking in modesty can make you even more beautiful.
☐	📝	**S11: Caring for your Castle.** Impact the members of your household by applying your skills and calling to help them achieve personal success. Learn how to handle unreasonable and excessive demands to effectively care for yourself, your home, and others.

Step 1

Getting Geared Up

*And you will seek Me and find Me,
when you search for Me with all your heart.*
—Jeremiah 29:13

Oh, the stories you and I could probably share about the frustrations and woes of being what I call "out of order with God." When things that should flow effortlessly seem to always get clogged up, preventing us from focusing on the essential and overwhelming us with the unimportant—thus our efforts to accomplish anything become futile.

When I am out of kilter, simple things that should take a moment or two usually take an hour or two. Some things that should give me pleasure, annoy me, and everything just seems hard. Still, time after time, I pressed on in my own strength, hoping that the Lord would bless my efforts anyway—that is, until I come to the end of myself.

The purpose of this step is to help you focus on making a conscientious choice to seek the heart of God in getting and maintaining balance and order in your daily life. For many women, this simple act of surrender is difficult to do on a daily basis until they, like me, reach the end of themselves.

One of those times for me was at my goddaughter's seventh birthday party. To celebrate this special occasion our close-net-couples' group decided to meet at a Japanese restaurant very close to our house. Although it was my first time eating there, I could see why it was my goddaughter's favorite restaurant. There, in the midst of our table was a large grill used by our Hibachi chef to prepare all our entrées in front of us; and to entertain us in the process. Between chopping vegetables, manipulating his knives, twirling raw eggs in mid-air, and dousing the grill with alcohol to create flames, there were plenty of jokes. We were captivated by the performance, and based on the laughter from our table, others in the restaurant would surmise that we had gotten the house's funniest and most skilled chef.

A few days later, a good friend who had been at the birthday gathering called on the phone and asked: "What happened to you?" and "Where was the beautiful, vibrant person I used to know?" Those questions were followed by more unsettling comments, including: "You looked worn out at the party!" I responded by saying, "What do you mean?" Knowing full well, in my heart and soul, what she meant.

I was drained, and there was no hiding it. I was also at the end of myself, and there was no hiding that from God. Like the desperate and humble prayers of Jabez and Hannah thousands of years ago, I can remember falling on my knees begging the Lord to bless me with a husband, then bless me with a child, then bless me with a house, … bless me with more time, bless me with more energy, … bless me, Lord, bless me. I am sure you get the picture—you have probably been there too! The Lord, being faithful and just, blessed me. The Lord sent me a husband in my early thirties and blessed me with a child when the doctors said, "impossible." He opened doors of opportunities that only God, in His infinite wisdom and power, could do.

My dilemma became trying to balance my relationship with the Lord, my relationship with my husband, being a mom—who had to endure late nights with a cranky or sick child, my career which included constantly upgrading my technical skills, and last but not least, trying to keep a decent and orderly home. Simple things that I needed to do—to maintain my emotional, physical, and spiritual well-being—became those things I would do when and if time permitted. Within three years I felt like I had aged six to seven years. For me to walk up the stairs of our two-story home was breathtaking (literally). During those years I prayed for God to bring balance into my life and struggled to get it. Staying home was not an option; my husband and I had financial obligations we were committed to. My prayer became a personal version of 2 Chronicles 20:12, "I do not know what to do Lord, but my eyes are upon You."

> Are you experiencing those same feelings of being exhausted, overwhelmed, and frustrated with the blessings God has bestowed upon you? If so, how?

Although innately a very organized person, God helped me realize that in the midst of my blessings was an imbalance that sent me on a course of being out of order with His will for my life. The things He sent to bless me and give me joy made me feel frazzled, bewildered, unfulfilled, and out of sync! I had stopped enjoying church ministries, my family duties, and my job, and began feeling as if my life was spinning out of control. Yes, I wanted the blessings, but I struggled with allowing God (the Blesser) to have control over my day-to-day responsibilities, my possessions, and my life. The result was massive chaos in every facet of my life.

⌕ What areas of your life have you failed to surrender complete control to God (focus on the areas in your life where you are not producing fruit, despite all your efforts, or where you're producing fruit, yet not satisfied)?

There is something magnificent about coming to the end of yourself. When all your strength has been depleted, when all your skills, creativity, expertise, manipulation, and conniving get you nowhere, and when all your friends leave or are unable to comfort you, God is able to step in. It was at that moment that I realized balance and order in every aspect of my life would not come without reliance upon God.

Matthew 16:26 essentially says, what does it profit a man or woman if they gain the whole world but lose their soul—by failing to surrender their every day to God.

Jim Cymbala, author of *The Life God Blesses*, says regarding our blessings: "How we respond to the Lord's blessings makes all the difference. The blessings can either humble us and draw us closer to God, or they can lift us up and allow our hearts to become full of pride and self-sufficiency."[1]

Living day-by-day independently of God—as I was—is an expression of pride. Sure, I went to church, prayed regularly, read my daily devotions, and fellowshipped with other believers, but I failed to live a surrendered life, thus releasing possessions, resources, and myself to be wholly and completely used to glorify the kingdom of God. Apart from living a surrendered life, we can never truly be content with ourselves and with the people and things God has blessed us with.

Balancing Blessings

Having balance and order is not perfection, but essentially a desire to prepare ourselves so that we are more receptive to the call of God and to the blessings provided by God.

The word *Blessing* is a derivative of the word *Bless* which is defined in the Bible to mean "happy" or "glad" (see Genesis 30:13; Matthew 5:3-12). To bless someone is to bestow a favor or gift upon them, making them "happy." To be blessed is to receive a favor or gift, making us "happy." Therefore, we can surmise that a blessing is a gift from God or man that brings happiness to the heart of the receiver. A blessing can be a spouse, child, job, home, car, ministry, or special skills and abilities.

Balancing Blessings is the process of being able to manage the things and people in our lives, and the various aspects of our lives, in such a manner that we have peace and harmony in knowing that we are doing what is honorable and investing in what matters most.

Obtaining Order

First Corinthians 15:10 reminds us that we are to do things in decency and in order. Order can be defined as: "a state of peace and serenity."[2] It is also commonly defined as "a fixed or definite plan; system; law of arrangement."[3]

To do things in decency and in order is to do things in a manner that is pleasing and brings glory to God; and allows us to walk in the peace and freedom that God provides.

> *When one part of your life is out of order, you will eventually feel the effects in other parts of your life.*

Orderliness is a command from God. When something is done out of order, it becomes offensive, coarse, and unbecoming; the results are chaos, frustration, stress, and confusion. Most of the disorder is felt in our finances, in our careers, in our marriages, with our children, in our homes, in our bodies, or in our spirits or the relationship we have with God.

Obtaining Order is getting and applying godly wisdom in managing and enjoying our blessings. As explained in the introduction, our blessings are those resources and possessions God has so graciously given us. Our responsibility is to use and care for our blessings in such a manner that we bring honor and glory to God.

Balancing blessings and obtaining order embraces the fact that every part of your life is connected. When one part of your life is out of order, you will eventually feel the effects in other parts of your life.

Having clutter in your home or keeping an unkempt home will affect your ability to be used effectively by God. Why? Because God is a God of order, He sees how you handle your blessings and uses that as a basis for determining how useful or effective you will be in other areas of ministry.

The Cost of "No Order"

I enjoy reading the Old Testament; there are chapters in each of the books that would keep me reading for hours—if time permitted. One of the stories I have always found interesting was the story of Moses when the Lord sent him back to Egypt to free the Israelites.

Over and over, Moses stood before Pharaoh, king of Egypt, and spoke the words of God: "Let My people go, that they may serve Me" (Exodus 8:20). Despite the hordes of frogs, lice, swarm of flies, and other plagues; Pharaoh refused to let the people of Israel go and worship their God. Once in a while, however, Pharaoh would confess that he had sinned (lied) and ask Moses to remove the plague and bless him, but once the curse was gone and he saw a bit of sunlight (relief), he fell right back into his sin.

Step 1: Getting Geared Up

Being on the outside looking in, we can say that Pharaoh got what he deserved. If we step inside the situation with humble hearts, we will find that Pharaoh is not much different from you, me, or anyone else. We can be going through a crisis and beg the Lord to save us or release us from the pain, fear, or guilt. Once God delivers us—gets us out of our predicament and allows us to see a bit of sunlight—some of us step right back into the ravine God just pulled us out of.

So you ask, "What does this have to do with balancing blessings and obtaining order?" Please bear with me as I try to explain through the lives of four Christian women: Susan, Jackie, and Rita, and Rita's daughter Joy—who are all at various stages of Christian maturity.

Example 1: Susan

Susan was an ambitious lawyer at a prestigious law firm in a small town. At church, she was a leader over the children's ministry and very active in the single's ministry, where she met Dave, her fiancé.

Her testimony begins with being extremely busy with work, church activities, Dave, and planning a big wedding. Susan was so busy she forgot to pay a couple of bills on time. The cable T.V. had been disconnected for over a month before she noticed. Plagued with fatigue when she got home in the evenings, she stopped checking her personal emails and began to throw her mail into a box in the corner of her kitchen. Without realizing it, she had run up her credit cards and was overdrawn on her bank account, trying to help cover the expenses of an elaborate wedding. Then there was the new car, and the house she and Dave were having built. A nudge in her heart kept saying: "We don't need such extravagant things." Dave convinced her otherwise, "we deserve it," he would say.

When things settled down, the box of mail became boxes and drawers full of receipts, notices, bills, and reminders that needed her attention. Susan tried going through some of the paper clutter, but the task seemed so daunting she decided to get back to it later. When Susan finally did get back to it, she was married to Dave and together they were filing for bankruptcy. Dave had been laid off from his job going on six months. Susan's job-related stress, coupled with endless doctor appointments and physical therapy sessions after a severe car wreck, forced her to resign from her corporate job.

In this example, it's possible that the couple's financial plight could have been avoided had they thought and planned wisely. There were plagues warning Susan that she was getting over her head in debt—overextending herself, assuming that she would always be employed. Like Pharaoh, her heart was hard, and she dismissed those warning signs until she and Dave were forced to face their financial situation.

What is God nudging you to do or not do regarding a situation in your life?

Example 2: Jackie

Jackie, a nominal Christian, attends church as her energy level permits. She is also considered the new young mother. She married, had her first child at age thirty-eight, and had two more at forty and forty-two. With three children under six, she is fortunate to be a stay-at-home wife and mother.

Before three kids Jackie and her husband (John) were very active in their local church—teaching and serving. After their last child was born, John obtained a second job which helped improve their financial situation, but decreased his involvement even more at church and home.

Jackie, feeling depressed and overwhelmed with her duties and responsibilities at home, begins to let herself go spiritually—neglecting her quiet time with the Lord, halting most of her church activities, and avoiding many of her Christian friends.

Besides being spiritually destitute, Jackie has a weight problem and knows she needs to do something about it. There is a history of heart disease and diabetes in her family; still, she has been unable to stop indulging in sweets and snacks and is too overwhelmed and afraid to visit the doctor. She is out of breath most days, just trying to do the basic chores around the house. Over and over, she makes a mental note to take better care of herself and to recommit herself to the Lord, but she hasn't gotten started. ✼

In this example, there are plagues warning Jackie to take care of the body God has blessed her with—get that check-up, eat better, exercise—but like Pharaoh, her heart is hard. In addition, Jackie has hardened her heart to the fact that there is a bigger battle going on, a spiritual war for her heart—drawing her away from God and from spending time in His presence.

✍ What has hardened your heart and kept you from doing those things that will bring God-given order to your life?

Example 3: Rita and Joy

Rita, a so-so Christian, is a young mother of sixteen-year-old Joy. Joy is a blessing, but if the truth be told, she was an unexpected gift. Rita was sixteen when she became pregnant with Joy. As a result, she quit school, got a job, and married her high school heartthrob, Joey—who was forced to do the same.

Joey had been a high-school football star with a promising future; having to give that up brought bitterness and resentment, which he took out on Rita. If he was at home, there was always an altercation; if he wasn't home, he was working or drinking with his buddies. Finally, right after Joy's sixth birthday—he left without a word to either of them.

Rita, although devastated, continued to work hard. She threw herself into her school work—getting her GED, a bachelor's degree, and a master's degree. She rose from being employed as a sales cashier at a major department store to obtaining a management position in Marketing and Sales with the same retail chain.

Her constant need for approval and self-worth drove her to work long, arduous hours for the accolades she would receive—which was medicine to her soul. Especially since most of her family and friends didn't think she would amount to much after dropping out of high school. Now, she had a good job, a beautiful home, and nice things. Her only regret was that Joy was still left to parent herself—like most nights since Joey left.

Feeling a gnawing loneliness, Joy (the daughter) started attending an evening Bible study once a week at a local church she and her mother used to attend regularly. On one particular evening, she decided to accept Jesus Christ as her Lord and Savior. Excited about her decision, she rushed home to share the news with her mother, who was working overtime, as usual.

Step 1: Getting Geared Up

Desiring to tell someone, she picks up the phone and calls her boyfriend. Her mother told her she was too young to have a boyfriend, but in Joy's young mind, all the popular girls in high school had boyfriends. Upon sharing the news with him, he got angry and asked, "Why did you go and do that?" There was silence on the phone as Joy tried to digest his response. Sensing his disappointment, she asked, "Aren't you happy for me?" He responded by saying: "If this means we can never have SEX, then you need to choose me or GOD!"

You may be shocked by the boyfriend's response, but whether you are a mother working hard to support your children or you are fulfilling some other role in life; daily your priorities will be tested. Sometimes the enemy is bold and sometimes he is subtle, but he is real, and his desire is to get you out of the will of God, by any means necessary. Even if it's you, as a parent, passing the same traps that ensnared you onto your children.

> What behavior or addictive habit does your child (or someone you influence) run the risk of adopting from you (e.g., over-eating, over-spending, over-working, multiple marriages, teen pregnancy, promiscuity, drug abuse, job hopping, church hopping, cursing)?

Although I have changed the names and some of the details, the stories I have presented are real. Each of these stories illustrates the gradual progression away from the wisdom of God—ignoring the essential priorities that lead to obtaining balance and order in our everyday lives. In other words, these women have allowed their days and desires to aimlessly control them—pushing them further and further from God and making it increasingly tough to hear and obey the "still, small voice" of God.

Not seeking godly wisdom for our lives makes us an easy target for Satan—opening us up to being deceived and exploited for Satan's own gain. The Book of Peter warns us to, "Be sober, be vigilant; because your adversary the devil walks about like a roaring lion, seeking whom he may devour" (1 Peter 5:8).

The Call to "Order"

No one is perfect. Each of us has a story of how we got to where we are today. Whether God blessed you with millions and you squandered it all, or you've abused your temple with men, drugs, alcohol, or food, or you've been divorced once, twice, or more—it's time to have a life that God can take delight in. The plagues presented to Pharaoh to let God's people go was a commandment for him to obey. Is there something in your life that God is calling you to do differently? Is there sin in your life?

I believe God is sending us warning signs. He is calling us to have balance and order in our daily lives, to prioritize our days, so that our lives bring glory and honor to Him.

Checking Your Barometer

Life is a balancing act, and how effectively we perform—by handling the stresses and demands of every day—is directly related to the level of order we will have in our day-to-day lives. Having order in our daily lives concentrates our efforts on consistently and consciously choosing God's best.

If you do not strive to have and maintain a healthy balance in your life, someone or something will suffer from the neglect.

Let's stop and check your barometer; what is being out of order keeping you from?

- ॐ The covering and protection of Jesus Christ.
- ॐ Peace and serenity in the confines of your home.
- ॐ The assurance of your child's welfare.
- ॐ Joy, purpose, fulfillment, and contentment.
- ॐ Mental, physical, and emotional wellness.
- ॐ Walking in the anointing of our Lord and Savior.

Let's face it: we have all been guilty of neglecting, taking advantage of, or not seeing the benefit or miracle in the blessings that God has bestowed upon us. If you feel discouraged, don't be. Romans 3:23 reminds us that we have all sinned and fallen short of the glory of God. But be of good courage, our all-knowing and gracious God sent His Spirit—the Holy Spirit—to be our guide in walking in His will, in His ways, and in His wisdom.

Change Is Challenging

This book will challenge you to change every aspect of your life in order to live a more balanced, productive, and Christ-centered existence.

During this process, try not to let the fear of change hold you back. Often, fear can make a person revert to the same old habits, people, and places familiar to them. If you are not on guard, any progress you make can easily dissipate and put you right back where you started.

> *Life is a balancing act, and how effectively we perform—by handling the stresses and demands of every day—is directly related to the level of order we will have in our day-to-day lives.*

The yearning and drive to do something different: replace unproductive habits with productive habits, destructive thoughts with constructive thoughts, and a negative attitude with a positive attitude has to come from the Holy Spirit within you. The Holy Spirit will help you to resist Satan and the tools he uses (e.g., fear, laziness, procrastination, criticism, temptation, opposition, unforgiveness, and other obstacles) to keep you stuck, bound, and mute.

Setbacks will occur, but rather than throwing your hands up in despair because you can't live up to your expectations or be like someone else. Strive to be more like Jesus Christ, who sought God in all things. Jesus Christ set the standard we should strive to attain (Ephesians 4:13).

Ready? Set, Go

Now it is time to gather together the same basic essentials that the disciples of Christ took with them on their missionary journey: "…to the lost sheep of the house of Israel" (Matthew 10:6). Two by two, the Lord sent them out. They had nothing but the clothes on their back, a message of salvation and healing from Jesus Christ (see Mark 6:7-13), and I surmise a song in their heart.

As a disciple of Jesus Christ, you should have nothing less than a faithful friend, the Word of God, and a spiritual song as you journey along.

A Faithful Friend

Although the journey steps can be completed successfully alone, more is accomplished when you work with someone else. There will be times when a faithful friend to share your experiences, trials, and triumphs will be much in demand. Likewise, knowing that someone will check on your progress, hold you accountable, and pray with you will make you more inclined to complete the assigned tasks. Jesus recognized the value of companionship, as He selected twelve disciples to follow Him as He fulfilled the will of God here on earth. Solomon also recognized the value of companionship when he made the declaration:

> *Two are better than one, Because they have a good reward for their labor. For if they fall, one will lift up his companion. But woe to him who is alone when he falls, For he has no one to help him up (Ecclesiastes 4:9-10).*

Recruit a Christian woman you can trust with sensitive information and who is committed to change as much as you are. Daily, pray for one another and hold each other accountable for reading each chapter and completing the chapter questions and challenges. In addition, rejoice with one another and beware of the spirit of divisiveness: envy, jealousy, selfishness, and covetousness — there is no room for that on your journey.

The Word of God
I also suggest that you grab a couple of favorite Scriptures. Commit the Scriptures to memory, tape them to your bathroom mirror, frame them and set them on your nightstand, or have them as wallpapers for your smartphone. Put your Scriptures anywhere you can read, reflect, and remember God's promises.

Being surrounded by the Word of God will keep you encouraged and give you the tools to teach, pray, and encourage others. Most importantly, it will direct you to your source of life (Jesus Christ), who will help you to stand firm when difficulties arise. As Romans 10:17 says, "So then faith comes by hearing, and hearing by the word of God."

A Spiritual Song

Within the book of praises, we are encouraged to sing (see Psalm 30:4; 47:6; 100:2). I believe that while the disciples were walking from town to town as Jesus had commanded them—casting out demons, anointing those who were sick with oil and healing them (see Mark 6:13)—that they sang songs that exalted God, and sang hymns to encourage themselves. "Speaking to one another in psalms and hymns and spiritual songs, singing and making melody in [their hearts] to the Lord" (Ephesians 5:19, emphasis added).

Get a theme song for your journey. A spiritual song that stirs your heart, is uplifting, energizing, and propels you forward when you feel like giving up, or that soothes your soul when you feel uptight and distressed.

In closing, let me encourage you to stay focused and believe that what you are doing will make a positive difference in your life and in the lives of others. None of the disciples quit in the middle of their mission in despair. No one came back to Jesus and said, "But Lord …." They believed that what God called them to do, He equipped them with the grace, strength, wisdom, and the Spirit of God to do it. So whether you walk, skip, or run, roll up your sleeves, and let's get going!

Step 1: Your Daily Call to Order

Chapter Comments:

This step briefly discussed the importance of hiding God's Word in our hearts. If you are having problems finding Scriptures for your journey, consider grabbing a couple of these:

Step 1: Getting Geared Up

- "My help comes from the Lord, Who made heaven and earth" (Psalm 121:2).

- "Trust in the Lord with all your heart, And lean not on your own understanding; In all your ways acknowledge Him, And He shall direct your paths."(Proverbs 3:5-6).

- "And we know that all things work together for good to those who love God, to those who are the called according to His purpose" (Romans 8:28).

- "I can do all things through Christ who strengthens me" (Philippians 4:13).

- "Therefore submit to God. Resist the devil and he will flee from you" (James 4:7).

- "Therefore, if anyone is in Christ, he is a new creation; old things have passed away; behold, all things have become new" (2 Corinthians 5:17).

- "Yet in all these things we are more than conquerors through Him who loved us" (Romans 8:37).

- "For God has not given us a spirit of fear, but of power and of love and of a sound mind" (2 Timothy 1:7).

- "And my God shall supply all [my needs] according to His riches in glory by Christ Jesus" (Philippians 4:19, emphasis added).

- "Therefore humble yourselves under the mighty hand of God, that He may exalt you in due time, casting all your care upon Him, for He cares for you" (1 Peter 5:6-7).

Chapter Questions:

Group Discussion

1. What is the difference between *balancing your blessings* and *stewardship*?

2. What does *having order* mean to you? Do you agree that having order will increase your effectiveness for Christ? If so, how?

3. Read Isaiah 1:18; Isaiah 43:25; Micah 7:18-19. What do the passages say about your sin(s) after you have confessed and repented?

4. Read John 3:16; Romans 8:35-39; 1 John 4:11-12. What do the passages say about God's love for us?

5. What does it mean to you to live a surrendered life?

Personal Reflection

6. What areas of your life have you failed to surrender to God?

7. Can you relate to any of the problems experienced by Jackie, Susan, Rita or Joy?

8. What do you want your life to look like after you have completed this book?

9. Do you have any fears or concerns about turning the chaos in your life into order (e.g., you desire change, but fear you may not be able to stay committed and disciplined long enough to obtain change)? What scriptures in the Bible address the fears and concerns that you have?

10. Reflect momentarily on the fact that you are loved, blessed, and forgiven by God. How do you feel?

Chapter Assignments:

❑ **Challenge 1**: Rewrite 1 Corinthians 14:40 and 16:14 so that those verses speak to you personally.

Step 1: Getting Geared Up

- ☐ **Challenge 2**: Think about and list the areas in your life that need overhauling (e.g., finances, priorities, relationships, health, or self-esteem). Pray and make a commitment to work on those areas.
- ☐ **Challenge 3**: Complete the "Create *Your* Reading Plan" on pages 26-27.
- ☐ **Challenge 4**: Join a small group, or find a faithful friend who is willing to work with you and hold you accountable for working through this book, and for making positive changes in the areas you identified in challenge 3.
- ☐ **Challenge 5**: Find yourself at least two motivating Scriptures to encourage you on your journey.
- ☐ **Challenge 6**: Complete the covenant page (located on the next page) in the company of your small group leader, or accountability partner.
- ☐ **Challenge 7**: Respond to end of chapter questions.
- ☐ **Challenge 8**: Find yourself an uplifting theme song for your journey.

My "Balancing Blessings" Covenant

I _____,
Your Printed Name

commit to the process of balancing the blessings God has bestowed upon me, and to the journey of becoming a woman of order—available and fit for the master's use.

_____
Your Signed Name

_____
Your Partner's (or Group Leader's) Signed Name

...but one thing I do, forgetting those things which are behind and reaching forward to those things which are ahead, I press toward the goal for the prize of the upward call of God in Christ Jesus (Philippians 3:13-14).

Step 2

Establishing Proper Priorities

> *Ponder the path of your feet,*
> *And let all your ways be established.*
> *—Proverbs 4:26*

$\mathcal{R}$emember Orpah in the book of Ruth? We know she was Ruth's sister by marriage; like Ruth, she was a Moabite, a descendant of Lot. She had married Chilion—son of Naomi — who died in Moab like his father Elimelech and his brother Mahlon.[1] The Old Testament does not say much more about her, only that she accompanied Naomi partway to Bethlehem before returning to her own people and gods in Moab (see Ruth 1:15).

Wedge between two decisions, I have no doubt that the choice she made to return home was a very difficult decision to make. With pressure from Naomi to go back and the fear of the unknown in her heart, she did what most of us would do: return to the comfort of home, even though our spirit is uneasy with the decision.

Unfortunately, what we see so clearly in Orpah—a woman void of understanding who turned away from the only true God—we refuse at times to recognize in ourselves.

She was at a fork in the road; in one direction was the road leading to truth, light, salvation, and unknown blessings (in Bethlehem); in the other direction was the road leading to sin, idolatry, and eventually spiritual death (in Moab). She chose the latter. With her narrow view of the future and her hopes of someday remarrying, her prospects seemed brighter in Moab than in Bethlehem. Her sister-in-law, Ruth, chose the path she had neglected to take: allowing God to order her steps and trusting in His eternal view of the future. Ruth's choice led to a husband, a child, and her becoming the great-grandmother of King David—an ancestor of Jesus Christ.

There was no telling what God had in store for Orpah in Bethlehem, but we can surmise that—in Moab—amid people who did not know God and who sought only to satisfy their own personal desires with little or no consideration for the things of God; she would succumb and fizzle under the pressure of a corrupt nation.

You, my dear sister in Christ, daily make your way through the tight and narrow places in life; at times, you may feel as if you've been pushed to your limit, squeezed too tightly, or thrust over the edge. Ready to burst into tears questioning the load you've been forced to bear or the decisions you've made to do *all this*, or be a part of *all that*. I heard someone once say, "Just because you're busy, doesn't mean you're busy doing what God wants you to do." Daily, you will venture to the fork in the road where you will have to make those crucial choices that will either take you closer to Bethlehem (to Jesus Christ) or closer to Moab (away from Jesus Christ). The vehicle to getting to either of these places and the focus of step two is your *priorities*.

About Your Priorities

Before you start looking for the nearest escape route—which by the way, there is none. It is essential for you to have clarity about your priorities. Like Orpah, your priorities will dictate the choices you make, either consciously or subconsciously, for yourself and your loved ones. This is undoubtedly one of the most important considerations that has to be evaluated and re-evaluated repeatedly to ensure that you are in alignment with God.

How you handle challenges and the choices you make with your priorities in mind, will ultimately play a significant role in leading you to the destiny you desire and that God desires for you.

What are your priorities? Who is establishing your priorities? Start by examining how much time and energy you are spending on people, activities, things, habits, organizations, and at clubs. Really analyze why. Do they provide you with joy and fulfillment? Are you reaping material and emotional benefits?

Working overtime to impress the boss or accumulate wealth is not worth your health or having your children parent themselves. Is it your friends? Do they have you gossiping for hours on the phone while your child is watching who knows what on the television, and your husband does not get a proper greeting when he gets home from work? To my single readers, is the desire to be married keeping you in a relationship God is calling you out of? Do you stay and allow your priorities to be dictated by someone you are not married to, or engaged to, simply because you have invested too much time, energy, and emotions into the relationship? Are you submitting to an unhealthy relationship because you are being governed by your desire to have a man?

Just as a choice has to be made between alternatives at the fork in the road, a choice has to be made between two masters. Will you incorporate things into your day that serve and honor God, or will you be consumed by your desires to do what pleases you?

Although Jesus was referring to our money in Matthew 6:24, the following verse can also be applied to anything we put before God or choose over God.

> *No one can serve two masters; for either he will hate the one and love the other, or else he will be loyal to the one and despise the other. You cannot serve God and mammon.*

I was in my early thirties when I finally married, but in my twenties—before I grew in maturity as a Christian—I did not practice Christian dating. I had been asked out by a few men and accepted some of the invitations. For the man I chose to spend further time with the process of getting to know him was exciting. I was taken to nice restaurants. I had my chair pulled out, and the door opened for me. I was given gifts, flowers, and cards and was treated like a pearl. I can remember spending hours talking with *my potential husband* on the phone— until the wee hours of the morning— and then waking up too tired to spend time in God's presence and in His Word. While at work or school I would spend more precious time thinking about my new beau. Then, like clockwork, the queen's treatment diminished, and most of these men fell by the wayside because of value differences. The point is, although I was a Christian, my priorities were being dictated by someone other than God. That person had my attention and became my focus—not God. I missed opportunities available to me at that time in my life because my focus had been interrupted. In some cases, I had to wait at least a year later for the same opportunities to emerge.

My error was that I failed to keep things in the right perspective, desiring acceptance, affirmation, conversation, and attention from someone other than God.

You must be aware of who or what is controlling your life. People and things, if you are not wary, will send you on a detour from the path that God has for you. The opportunity to be a blessing and to be blessed by God is in your obedience to His Word and in your ability (with the Holy Spirit) to stay focused on doing His will.

Our desire should be to have more time so that we can invest that time in the things of God. Having priorities will save us time by guiding our choices and keeping us focused on where our resources and possessions are being expended.

First Things First

Establishing godly priorities begins with putting God first. The Bible clearly says: "But seek first the kingdom of God and His righteousness, and all these things shall be added to you" (Matthew 6:33).

I have noticed that when I don't put God first and try to do things in my own strength, I feel like I am running against the wind. When I stop and seek God's will for my day, no matter how strong the wind blows, I know that I am walking with God and He will give me the strength, wisdom, and resolve to get through my day with peace and assurance.

Mary must have felt the same assurance, sitting at the feet of Jesus, unwilling to budge at Martha's promptings for assistance. When Martha complained, Jesus was quick to mention that Mary had discerned what was of utmost importance—putting God first (Luke 10:38-42).

So, how do you establish godly priorities? First, You must gain some insight as to where your current priorities lie. Table 2-1, on the next page, contains a list of common priorities. Use the column labeled "Present" to circle the number that best indicates where you are on the continuum. Rate your priorities from 1 to 7, with 1 being *not very important*, 4 being *important*, and 7 being of *utmost importance*. Do not be alarmed if a few of the priorities listed do not apply to you.

If you have a good relationship with your children and spend quality time with them daily, then your children are important to you and should rate high on the continuum (6 or 7) for "Children." Suppose you spend a sufficient amount of time versus a significant amount of your time helping out at your local church and you are not a paid church employee. In that case, church service is important to you and should be rated high on the continuum (4 or 5) for "Church Ministries."

To help you identify your current priorities, ask yourself:

- What do I spend the majority of my time doing?
- Who do I spend the majority of my time with?
- What or who do I spend most of my time thinking about or focused on?
- What do I value?
- What do I choose to allocate time, energy, or money to do or enjoy, no matter how busy, tired, or broke I am?

When you have finished the first part of the evaluation, take a couple of days and pray about your present priorities. Listen for God to speak to you through prayer, the Bible, promptings from the Holy Spirit, Christian counseling, friends, a sermon, spiritual books, and your circumstances.

Step 2: Establishing Proper Priorities

Priority List	Present	God-Given
God	1 2 3 4 5 6 7	1 2 3 4 5 6 7
Self	1 2 3 4 5 6 7	1 2 3 4 5 6 7
Spouse	1 2 3 4 5 6 7	1 2 3 4 5 6 7
Child(ren)	1 2 3 4 5 6 7	1 2 3 4 5 6 7
Parents	1 2 3 4 5 6 7	1 2 3 4 5 6 7
Friends	1 2 3 4 5 6 7	1 2 3 4 5 6 7
Extended Family	1 2 3 4 5 6 7	1 2 3 4 5 6 7
Career/Job	1 2 3 4 5 6 7	1 2 3 4 5 6 7
Church Ministries	1 2 3 4 5 6 7	1 2 3 4 5 6 7
Diet and Nutrition	1 2 3 4 5 6 7	1 2 3 4 5 6 7
Health and Exercise	1 2 3 4 5 6 7	1 2 3 4 5 6 7
Hobbies	1 2 3 4 5 6 7	1 2 3 4 5 6 7
Vocation/School	1 2 3 4 5 6 7	1 2 3 4 5 6 7
Household Activities	1 2 3 4 5 6 7	1 2 3 4 5 6 7
Recreational Activities	1 2 3 4 5 6 7	1 2 3 4 5 6 7
Social Group Activities	1 2 3 4 5 6 7	1 2 3 4 5 6 7
Volunteer Activities	1 2 3 4 5 6 7	1 2 3 4 5 6 7
Other _____	1 2 3 4 5 6 7	1 2 3 4 5 6 7
Other _____	1 2 3 4 5 6 7	1 2 3 4 5 6 7
Other _____	1 2 3 4 5 6 7	1 2 3 4 5 6 7

Table 2-1: Priority Evaluation.

In addition, take stock of your life and determine what is working and what is not. For example, my job was definitely working. It allowed me the flexibility to work from home if I had to and the time to spend with my family. After taking stock of her life, I have a friend who had to decide to go back to school to further her education or continue to work two jobs for the rest of her life—to scrape by financially. She decided to return to school in hopes of getting a better-paying job. I have another friend who opted to turn off the television to make better use of her time. You may decide after taking stock of your life to change vocations. The decision is yours; you can continue to exist "as is" or take steps to replace what is not working with a reasonable, moral, and consistent alternative or action that will work.

With God, you have all the tools you need to build your life on "godly common sense." This is because the Spirit of God works in the minds of His children, giving us the knowledge and the ability to understand His truths. Paul said, "For who has known the mind of the LORD that he may instruct Him? But we have the mind of Christ" (1 Corinthians 2:16).

> **THERE IS ALWAYS ENOUGH TIME TO DO THE WILL OF GOD. FOR THAT, WE CAN NEVER SAY, "I DON'T HAVE TIME." WHEN WE FIND OURSELVES FRANTIC AND FRUSTRATED, HARRIED AND HARASSED, IT IS A SIGN THAT WE ARE RUNNING ON OUR OWN SCHEDULE, NOT ON GOD'S.**
>
> ELISABETH ELLIOT

Once you have sought God regarding your priorities and you feel confident to continue, return to Table 2-1. Use the column labeled "God-Given" to establish your God-given priorities according to what God has pressed on your heart.

God-given priorities are those people and things that you plan to make the necessary adjustments for —in your time and your other resources—in order to align your will with the will of God. This does not mean you have to stop doing the

Step 2: Establishing Proper Priorities

activities you enjoy, but it does mean that you cut back in areas that are less meaningful and not necessary.

Whereas your present rating under "Children" may be a 3, the Lord may be speaking to you about increasing your involvement with your children—especially in the area of spiritual growth and development. Therefore, your God-given rating for "Children" may be a 6. Is it possible that the Lord is calling you into the ministry or to be a missionary overseas? Is the Lord prompting you to go back to school, volunteer, change professions, or take more time for yourself?

In reassessing your priorities, realize that as a woman of God, some things should consistently rate high on your list of priorities. As I stated earlier, your first priority should be developing and maintaining your personal relationship with God. The quality of your day, your ministry, and your life is directly related to how much time alone you have with God. Each day, God has something special He wants to share with you; therefore, you need to be in the right place spiritually to hear and receive Him.

In Luke 10:25-29, we find a story of a lawyer who tried to test Jesus Christ by asking Him, "What shall I do to inherit eternal life?" Jesus reversed the question back on the lawyer and asked him, "What is written in the law? What is your reading of it?" The lawyer replied: "'You shall love the Lord your God with all your heart, with all your soul, with all your strength, and with all your mind,' and 'your neighbor as yourself.'"

This passage reminds us how important balance is; nothing should take precedence over our personal relationship with God. In the same respect, neglecting our other responsibilities does not honor God.

Secondly, if you are married, you should lovingly respect and honor your husband. If he is not saved, this is a prime opportunity to witness to him—not necessarily with words, but in good deeds. Show respect toward him by being cordial and courteous; surprise him by cooking his favorite meal occasionally; step up your dress and appearance around the house; and schedule date nights. Even though your time may be limited, find little ways to bless your husband.

Lastly, if you have children or work with children, you are responsible for influencing them for Christ. This involves helping them grow in the knowledge of and in service to God by lovingly teaching, modeling, disciplining, and encouraging them according to godly principles—in hopes that they will someday dedicate their lives to Jesus Christ and influence others to do the same.

The Priorities of the Proverbs 31 Woman

Let's be honest: at the end of a hard day, we want to have lived it well and productively. We want to have done our best to honor God, serve others, and fulfill with eagerness our basic obligations so that we might be encouraged daily by the words describing the Proverbs 31 woman:

> *Many daughters have done well, But you excel them all.... Give her of the fruit of her hands, And let her own works praise her in the gates (Proverbs 31: 29, 31).*

Having priorities assists us in preparing for the days ahead. The priorities a Proverbs 31 woman sets regarding her household allow her to walk in confidence that her family's basic needs have been met. "She is not afraid of snow for her household" (v. 21), and I assume the challenges that accompany winter weather. She is skilled at using her hands or bartering what her hands have produced to meet her family's basic cloth-

Step 2: Establishing Proper Priorities

ing needs (v. 19). This verse ends with the statement, "For all her household is clothed with scarlet" (v. 21).

May I remind you that this godly woman is not a figment of someone's imagination? She is any woman of strength whose priorities allow her to yield herself wholly to the will of God. This woman could be you or someone you know and admire. Therefore, I will speak of her often and as if she exists in our modern-day culture; in reality, she transcends culture and time to teach generations of women how to be virtuous, loving, and gracious.

Making Adjustments

Return to Table 2-1, and find your highest-rated priorities in the "God-Given" column. These should be the priorities rated a 6 or 7, but could also be a 4 or 5. List those priorities below, from highest to lowest (list 7's, then 6's and so on).

1. _____

2. _____

3. _____

4. _____

5. _____

6. _____

7. _____

Once you've listed your top seven God-given priorities, use Table 2-2 on the next page to write at least two tasks the Lord is calling you to do or work on in that area of your priority. For example, if "Spouse" was a God-given top priority for you, the beginning of your list may look something like this:

Spouse: Samuel Smith
- *Establish and go on a date one night a week.*
- *Greet husband with a smile and pleasant conversation daily when he gets home from work.*

If the Lord has given you a desire to start your own business, your list may include the following:

Career/Job: Start My Own Business
- *Research the market (supply and demand) for my product.*
- *Take a business startup course.*

After completing Table 2-2, be sure to add each God-given task to your Master To-Do List and calendar (we will discuss both items in step three, "Prayerfully Planning Ahead").

In addition, keep your priorities in mind when making decisions. If what you've been asked to do is outside your sphere of responsibilities or purpose in life, don't feel you have to say *yes*. Also, remember that your priorities can and will change based on your season in life. You may be single today, married tomorrow, without a child today, with a child tomorrow, or a follower today, a leader tomorrow. Quarterly re-examine your priorities, making the necessary adjustments as God leads you to do so.

Step 2: Establishing Proper Priorities

1. _____
   - _____
   - _____
2. _____
   - _____
   - _____
3. _____
   - _____
   - _____
4. _____
   - _____
   - _____
5. _____
   - _____
   - _____
6. _____
   - _____
   - _____
7. _____
   - _____
   - _____

Table 2-2: Focus List.

The Sweet Taste of Priorities

Balance and order can only be achieved with godly priorities, which characterizes a woman with focus and sets her apart from other women.

I found a wonderful description of a "Focused Woman" by Elizabeth George in her book, *Loving God with All Your Mind*. Here is what she says characterizes a focused woman…

> First, a focused woman knows where she is going. She has a sense of God's call on her life, and that call gives her direction each step of the way and makes it easier for her to make decisions. With her sights set on these God-given goals, she is able to say no to the trivial. She chooses from among her options that which moves her toward her life goals.
>
> This focus for her life also gives her greater energy for reaching that goal. She doesn't waste energy wondering what to do or wandering aimlessly from option to option. Knowing exactly what she wants to do and needs to do, she pours her energy into those things. Her knowing what to do and her knowing that God will enable her to serve Him where He has placed her gives her confidence as well as energy. She knows where she is headed and why, and she makes all that she does count for her Lord.[2]

༽ Are you making all that you do count for the Lord?

Step 2: Your Daily Call to Order

Chapter Comments:

Whether we realize it or not, our priorities pave the way for spiritual victory. John Maxwell provides an interesting formula for spiritual success that emphasizes the need to focus on God and His priorities for us:

If you want to be distressed—look within.
If you want to be defeated—look back.
If you want to be distracted—look around.
If you want to be dismayed—look ahead.
If you want to be delivered—look up![3]

Chapter Questions:

Group Discussion

1. Read Judges 17:6; 1 Kings 3:9; Proverbs 19:21; Matthew 6:33. Why is it important to establish godly priorities?
2. What blessings would we lose by not establishing priorities and failing to recognize God's authority in our lives?
3. Read Luke 10:38-42. What happens when we neglect to put God first?
4. What keeps us from putting God first?

Personal Reflection

5. Who or what have you allowed to dominate your daily schedule outside of your priorities?
6. What significance does Jesus' death on the cross have on your daily priorities?
7. How can you rearrange your schedule to focus more on your God-given priorities?

Chapter Assignments:
- **Challenge 1**: Use Table 2-1 to evaluate your present priorities.
- **Challenge 2**: Pray over your present priorities.
- **Challenge 3**: Take stock of your life and determine what is working and what needs to change.
- **Challenge 4**: Respond to end of chapter questions.
- **Challenge 5**: Use Table 2-1 to identify and write down your God-given priorities.
- **Challenge 6**: Use Table 2-2 to identify two things under your top seven God-given priorities that your are prepared to start working on immediately.

Step 3

Prayerfully Planning Ahead

A man's heart plans his way, But the Lord directs his steps.
—Proverbs 16:9

$\mathcal{T}$ime has been allocated to each one of us equally. We each have twenty-four hours a day, seven days a week. Jesus, in His brief time here on earth was able to accomplish God's will by helping to bring His work of salvation, to fruition.[1] Yet many of us have trouble accomplishing a few items on our daily to-do list.

Proper use of our time honors God. Not seeking God's direction for our day is like running a race our way. We are moving; we can hear the pounding of our feet meeting the pavement; we can feel the air breaking by the quickness of our motion, taste the dryness forming in our mouths, and even smell the aroma of whatever is being consumed by the air. Since we are running aimlessly, we might each add a whimsical hop or a skip to our run—depending on our own unique style and personality and how excited we are that we are in motion (doing something). We know energy is being consumed as sweat pours down our faces, backs, and chests. We are determined to be a success, to win, to make millions, to show them, or to be first. The only problem is we chose to run eagerly ahead of God. By leaving God in the dust, *we* were blinded from seeing that *we* were headed in the wrong direction and that the presence of God was no longer guiding us. In our own attempt to run the race our way, to fulfill our own agenda, God retreated. That's what happens when we leave God out of our day, out of our week, out of our month, out of our year, out of our life. James told those who considered their days totally in their own hands:

> *Come now, you who say, "Today or tomorrow we will go to such and such a city, spend a year there, buy and sell, and make a profit"; whereas you do not know what will happen tomorrow. For what is your life? It is even a vapor that appears for a little time and then vanishes away. Instead you ought to say, "If the Lord wills, we shall live and do this or that" (James 4:13-15).*

Let's mull over a portion of the last sentence. The condition here is: "If the Lord wills," any alternative condition is your will—if you refuse to recognize the presence of God and acknowledge that He is in control of every aspect of your life. That is the focus of this step: helping you recognize God's authority in your life by including God in your life choices and planning your days wisely.

The Heart of Planning

The book of Proverbs is about planning and acting wisely, two life skills a prudent man or woman should constantly develop.

Step 3: Prayerfully Planning Ahead

The problem many of us have is leaving God out of our plans. Consider how many times you have made major life decisions based on your feelings, needs, or desires. Consider also the number of times you have acted impulsively and how things turned out.

We are finite beings, limited in our abilities. We have no idea what a day holds. Once something happens, we cannot reverse the effects. Our only security rests in consulting with an all-knowing and all-powerful God and acting upon the promptings of the Holy Spirit.

The heart of planning, for Christians, requires us to plan our day with regard to God. It is essentially stewardship—focusing our day to care for the things of God in light of His coming. This does not mean we stop engaging in normal activities and the necessary things in life. It does, however, incorporate three important resources God has made available to each of us: heeding, watching, and praying, as expressed in Mark chapter thirteen:

> *Take heed, watch and pray; for you do not know when the time is. It is like a man going to a far country, who left his house and gave authority to his servants, and to each his work, and commanded the doorkeeper to watch. Watch therefore, for you do not know when the master of the house is coming—in the evening, at midnight, at the crowing of the rooster, or in the morning—lest, coming suddenly, he find you sleeping. And what I say to you, I say to all: Watch! (Mark 13:33-37).*

Heeding is giving attention or directing our attention to the fact that our time here on earth is a precious gift from God to do His will—heeding how we spend our time and with whom.

Taking heed focuses our efforts in an attempt to make the wisest decision in order to bring about a peaceful resolution. A resolution we can live with and God is pleased with. Whether the decision is simple or complex, when attention to what matters most is combined with a day-to-day dependence on the Lord, the wisdom that is produced can be an indispensable guide in helping us balance our blessings.

Watching means to take caution, to pay attention, to consider every step before it is taken. It is implemented when we act vigilantly in planning our day-to-day activities—being mindful of anything that may get us too far off our God-given course. The Bible says, "See then that you walk circumspectly, not as fools but as wise, redeeming the time, because the days are evil" (Ephesians 5:15-16).

Praying reminds us that God is in control. He owns everything and created everyone on earth (Psalm 24:1). Praying over our day helps us align our to-do list with God's to-do list for us. When we align ourselves with God, we obtain balance. With balance, we are less tempted to try to be "everything to everyone, which is an impossible task for anyone," nor will the convicting Spirit of God allow us to be idle and unfruitful.

Apply this message to your daily life by taking heed, watching, and praying for your marriage, children, ministry, job, and things happening in and around you. As you pray, the divine wisdom of the Holy Spirit within you will keep you mindful of your work, responsibilities, and anything that may hinder your relationship with God.

> *See then that you walk circumspectly, not as fools but as wise, redeeming the time, because the days are evil.*
>
> —Ephesians 5:15-16

Preparing a Place to Plan

As queen of your castle, manager of your domain, and or CEO of God's "Fortune 500" family, it's important that you have a base of operation. A place where you can plan and manage your household responsibilities and family activities—in a manner that increases your efficiency, your family's overall efficiency, and glorifies God.

📖 Where do you manage your household affairs?

Personal Workstation

Whether your personal workstation is a desk with everything you need on it, or a box (or bag) with everything you need in it, you need a private workstation to manage your household. Your workstation should contain the same basic supplies you would need if you worked in an office: accordion, calendar, devotional book, laptop or tablet, envelopes, highlighters, hole puncher, letter opener, paper, paper clips, pencils, pencil sharpener, pens, postage stamps, ruler, scissors, stapler, stapler remover, staples, stationery, sticky notes, and tape.

Use your desk, or if you have a box, take the box to the kitchen or dining room table. Use this area to sort mail, pay bills, check emails, plan meals, update your calendar or task list, or handle other household organizational activities.

Keep your desk or box as organized as possible. Make sure to have a trash can and shredder nearby to keep the paper clutter to a minimum.

In addition, use this space to devote time and attention to your devotional reading—daily remembering and renewing your commitment to God. Proverbs 16:20 says, "Whoever gives heed to instruction [the Word of God] prospers, and blessed is he [or she] who trusts in the Lord" (emphasis added).

Time with God builds your trust in Him and provides the discernment you need to manage your household and plan your days wisely.

Family Workstation

Manage your family time with a family event calendar to track after-school activities, school programs, church events, family outings, work schedules, business trips, and meetings.

If it's just you and your husband, and you both have very busy schedules, use the calendar to coordinate activities and events and to keep one another informed.

If using a paper-based calendar, the calendar should be kept in a centralized location—like the kitchen. Hang the calendar anywhere you know it will be seen and used regularly. Then, consider giving everyone in your family their own color marker to post activities and events that pertain specifically to them.

Enforce the use of the calendar by establishing consequences for your children for not using it. Make sure, however, that they understand the implications and the impact on the family schedule.

> *Time with God builds your trust in Him and provides the discernment you need to manage your household and plan your days wisely.*

If everyone in your household has access to a smartphone or web-enabled tablet, your scheduling system could include a digital or online calendar. The benefits are: not having to reenter recurring events, and changes to the family calendar are immediately available to each family member. In addition, you have the option to set up push notifications that will send text and email reminders before an event occurs.

Step 3: Prayerfully Planning Ahead

Tips for Planning Your Day

Now that you have a place to work with all your needed supplies, let's look at how you can begin to organize your day.

In planning your day, I suggest you use lists. Using lists is almost unavoidable unless you have a superb memory. Put it down on paper or in your smartphone so your mind does not get bogged down with a lot of things to do. Inexpensive planners can be found at most discount stores and should contain the following basic items: calendar, daily to-do list, contact list, expense list, and lined note paper.

If you decide to make your planner, a three-ring binder with those items will serve the same purpose. Many of the items can be downloaded for free on the internet.

In addition, there are a variety of applications or apps that can be used on your computer, smartphone, or tablet device. These apps can assist you with tracking your expenses, managing your contacts, organizing your tasks, and scheduling events. The key is finding the right productivity apps. Look for apps that are aesthetically pleasing and easy to navigate. With any productivity app, you should have the ability to:

- change the list's appearance and create custom list views that fit your scheduling process;

- filter and sort listed items;

- sync with multiple online platforms, so you have flexibility in when, where, and how you get your information.

Whether paper-based or digital, your planner should allow you to see your entire month at a glance. Each entry on your calendar should contain, at most, a description (three words or less), the time, and a contact number.

Consider using the same planner for scheduling personal and work-related tasks and events. I use a color coding system to separate work from personal. Color coding can also be used to symbolize activities in your calendar for each member of your family.

Once you have your planner, set aside time daily and weekly to plan. Every Sunday morning, before preparing for church, I plan my week; during the rest of the week, I use the time before bed to review and refine my schedule for the next day. Decide now on a consistent time, daily and weekly, in which you will pray, plan, and prepare for the days ahead. Write your decision in the space provided below:

- My Daily Prep Time: _____
- My Weekly Prep Time: _____

Tasks vs. Projects

Before we start planning our day, it is vital that you know the difference between a task and a project. A task is a job that requires a single step to complete; for example, picking clothes up from the cleaners. If multiple steps are required to perform a task, then the task would be considered a project. A good example would be planning a party, which requires multiple tasks. These tasks would be listed individually on your Master To-Do List (discussed next). A suggestion is to list the event and under the event, the tasks required to prepare for that event; for example:

Dinner Party
- decide on date
- decide on a party theme
- decide on a location
- prepare guest list

Step 3: Prayerfully Planning Ahead

- ☙ prepare invitations
- ☙ select catering service
- ☙ book entertainment
- ☙ mail invitations
- ☙ select decorations

The Combination To-Do List

Using the concept of tasks and projects, the most efficient way I have found to get things done and to have a constant reminder of what needs to be done and when, is to use a combined Master To-Do List and Weekly Task Tracker (see Table 3-1).

In the following paragraphs, I will explain how to create and use the combined list and then discuss how you can automate the process using a task-management app.

First, grab a sheet of lined paper from your organizer and fold it in half lengthwise. Write the words "Master To-Do List" at the top of the page on the left-hand side. Under this title, add everything you need to do within the next few days or weeks—in no certain order. This will be your Master To-Do List that will be used to populate your Daily To-Do List. Your Master To-Do List should be updated whenever you think of something you need to do.

Label the other side of your lined paper "Weekly Task Tracker." Under here, establish subtitles for each day of the week (Monday through Friday). Use the subtitle "Weekend" for Saturday and Sunday. Allow approximately four to five lines between subtitles to add daily-to-do items. For lined paper smaller than 8½" x 11", use the front and back of the paper for more room. Each day, you will select three to five tasks from your Master To-Do List that you feel compelled to do, need to do, and want to do. Example: mail bills, pick up clothes from the cleaners, work on résumé, or go grocery shopping.

When planning what to do each day, select items from your Master To-Do List that you feel you can accomplish in a given day. If you are unable to complete a task on a particular day, move the task to the next day's to-do list.

When you have finished a task, cross it off your Master To-Do List and your Weekly Task Tracker. Each week, start the process over using a new Combination To-Do List. If you need to schedule your day in hourly increments, a Today Page divided into hours may be more appropriate. Use this instead of the Weekly Task Tracker. Transfer appointments and events from your calendar, and tasks from your Master To-Do List, to your Today Page, based on the time you plan to perform that activity.

Master To-Do List	Weekly Task Tracker
~~Prepare monthly bills~~	**Monday**
~~Reschedule doctor's appointment~~	Pick up clothes from cleaners
Drop box off at Good-Will	~~Reschedule doctor's appointment~~
~~Mail bills~~	~~Prepare monthly bills~~
Cancel cable T.V.	**Tuesday**
~~Pick up clothes from cleaners~~	~~Pick up clothes from cleaners~~
Work on résumé	~~Mail bills~~
Go grocery shopping	Work on résumé
Schedule car maintenance	**Wednesday**
	Work on résumé

Table 3-1: Combination To-Do List

Be creative in developing your planner to fit your lifestyle. You can digitalize the Combination To-Do List process by entering everything you need to do within the next few days or weeks—in no certain order—into your chosen task-management app. Each day, choose three to five tasks from

Step 3: Prayerfully Planning Ahead

your task list that you plan to complete. Tag those items. Depending on the app you are using, you can: tag those items by adding them to your favorites; flag those items as *Follow Up, Today*; or tag those items by clicking on an icon adjacent to each task. There are also apps that allow you to drag and drop tasks onto your calendar—into the day slot you plan to complete a task. Once the tasks are tagged, you should be able to filter your view to see only those tasks that have been tagged. Once you've completed a task, mark it as completed. Uncompleted tasks should be moved to the next day or remain tagged.

Whether you use the Combination To-Do List, a digital list, or some other list, without a defined list of what needs to be done and a focus on one or a few tasks, your day will likely be spent going from one non-essential task to another. By prayerfully planning the tasks you want to accomplish in a given day, you will be more set on completing those tasks.

The Notebook

One of the disciplines I have learned from reading Anne Ortlund's book, *Disciplines of the Beautiful Woman*, which has helped me tremendously and has been an enormous source of blessings in bringing order to my life, is to carry a notebook everywhere I go. I still have a planner, but my notebook is more like a companion.

While writing this book, I carried a spiral notebook everywhere I went to jot down my book ideas and anything related to developing this book. In addition, I carried a notebook to house my personal mission statement, my prayer lists, and my business and ministry ideas. I also use it to capture the names of people, things, and places I need to remember for future reference. Items on my capture list might include: details of an upcoming women's conference; a new contact's name, phone number, and address; household needs; and a list of non-essential things I'll do when and if time permits.

Weekly, I comb through my capture list to ensure that upcoming events get transferred to my calendar; names, phone numbers, and addresses are added to my electronic contact list; and errands or tasks that have to be completed within the next few days are added to my Master To-Do List.

Anne Ortlund's philosophy is, "If you keep your notebook with you, to write everything and then read everything, you'll never forget anything again!"[2]

Wherever you are, your notebook will give you the ability to immediately write down what you want to do and need to do. Your mind will be less cluttered, and you will have the ability to regulate how your time is being spent.

Make your notebook as personal and as unique as you are. Decorate the inside cover with favorite Scriptures, memorable quotes, or thoughts and poems that inspire you. Divide your notebook into sections or use the page-by-page method. When one page fills up, use the next available blank page to transfer everything you need from the old page to the new page (note: this is only necessary for lists like your capture and prayer lists). By using this method, your lists will get intermingled, but the use of *Page Tabs* will quickly take you to your most current lists.

Establishing a Routine

It's common knowledge that what you do in the morning sets the tone for the rest of your day, and what you do in the evenings can help make your mornings a lot less hectic.

If we examine Proverbs 31, we get a quick glimpse into the morning and evening routine of a woman most Christian women long to be like. The Bible tells us she rises early to feed her family and maidservants (v. 15). We can rest assured that this is followed by a very productive day with little to no time

Step 3: Prayerfully Planning Ahead

for idleness (v. 27). The evenings are no different for this woman of God, who exudes the fruit of the Spirit, and works until her goals for the day are accomplished (v. 18).

Rising early provides you with a prime opportunity to accomplish many things in the solitude of the morning—while others are still asleep. One of those things is spending time with God.

By giving God the first fruit of your day, you are able to enjoy the company of God as you pray and read His Word—before planning and attending to the rest of your day.

David said of seeking God in the morning: "In the morning, O'LORD, you hear my voice; in the morning I lay my requests before you and wait in expectation" (Psalm 5:3, NIV).

Author Elizabeth George talks about valuing our alone time with God when she says, "You and I endanger our health, our service to others, and our relationship with God when we don't take time to be alone with Him."[3] Before that she says of Jesus, "In His quiet time alone with God before the sun arose, Jesus acquired His focus for the day and He let it shape His plans."[4]

> *Rising early provides you with a prime opportunity to accomplish many things in the solitude of the morning—while others are still asleep.*

In addition to scheduling quiet time with God, your routine should incorporate other things that are done frequently. In your routine, schedule time for yourself—especially in the evenings. You should take at least thirty to forty minutes to do something that relaxes and de-stresses you. Read a book, polish your nails, meditate, soak in the tub, listen to calming music, or work on a hobby.

Within your evening routine, I want to also encourage you to prepare for the next day. Decide what tasks need to be accomplished or where you need to be the following day, then set out the clothes (including accessories) you plan to wear. These basic steps added to your evening routine can help you to relax and sleep better.

I am not a morning person; waking up before 8:00 a.m. poses a challenge for me every single day of my life. I know this about myself, so instead of getting frustrated—within my evening routine—I allocate time to ensure that my lunch and workbag are packed, my clothes are laid out, and I've showered the night before. That way, my morning procrastination does not hinder me from getting to work on time; and never hindered me from getting my son to school on time.

If you are more focused in the morning, schedule your most difficult tasks then. If lack of energy is a problem, stop being hard on yourself—schedule a cat nap. I've known people to go to a safe place during lunch for a twenty-minute nap. If you need it and it will make you feel better, then by all means, get that nap!

Whether you work inside or outside the home, commit to taking at least a twenty-minute lunch break, preferably away from your desk, to provide your body with the nourishments it needs. Refuse to answer any business calls during this time; then find a nice window spot in your house, at your desk, or in the privacy of your car, and take in the sights and sounds God has created for your good pleasure.

Regularly skipping or working through lunch will quickly lead to burnout, and the things you started out enjoying can become mundane and physically draining.

If you have a small home-based business, consider establishing a business routine. Decide the days of the week

Step 3: Prayerfully Planning Ahead

you want to work, then decide how many hours you want to invest. Your work hours might be defined something like this:

Work Days: Monday through Thursday	
7:00 a.m. to 7:30 a.m.	Check and respond to emails.
7:30 a.m. to 8:00 a.m.	Log customer order requests.
8:00 a.m. to 9:00 a.m.	Prepare customer orders for shipping or local delivery.
9:00 a.m. to 10:30 a.m.	Mail or deliver packages.
10:30 a.m. to 12:30 p.m.	Build up inventory (order products or make it yourself) or contact customers.
12:30 p.m. to 1:00 p.m.	Break for lunch.
1:00 p.m. to 3:00 p.m.	Develop new business strategies.
3:00 p.m. to 4:30 p.m.	Open mail, read business correspondence, and file office paperwork.
4:30 p.m.	Workday ends.

If you are a stay-at-home mom with young children, have a daily routine for your kids. If you are a stay-at-home mom with a home-based business, consider hiring part-time help to watch the kids. If that's not financially feasible, schedule your daily routine so you accomplish your most demanding tasks while the kids are sleeping or involved in other activities.

I would also suggest that you dedicate time to have uninterrupted breakfast or lunch with your child(ren); and have a defined start and end time for your business—so it does not spill over into your family life.

When establishing daily, nightly, and business routines, realize that the unexpected may occur. In addition, cut yourself some slack; if you are a person who needs variety, understand that it's healthy from time to time to break up the monotony by doing something out of the ordinary. We are not to get so caught up in our routine (doing the same thing at the same time every day) that we lack the flexibility to be used by God to encourage, support, serve, or comfort someone in their time of need. Besides, being rigidly bound to a routine can dull our sense of adventure and curiosity.

> *Having a routine should better prepare you to faithfully minister when called upon.*

Having a routine better prepares you to faithfully minister when called upon. Why? Because it allows you to quickly survey and assess what needs to be done in a given day. As a result, you are better prepared to react to changes in your schedule. You'll spend less time wasting time and have more time to invest in those things that matter to God.

Lastly, take establishing routines a step further by establishing weekly, biweekly, and monthly routines. These are routines for the things you do less frequently, such as "Date Night" with the spouse, getting your hair and nails done, or preparing bills. Make sure to add these items to your calendar—since they are appointments!

Time Is Ticking

I would be remiss if I did not follow "Establishing a Routine" with a discussion on discipline. Whereas a routine is a resource that helps us build consistency in our daily lives. Consistency is the heart and soul of discipline; whether it's sticking to a diet, budgeting, getting to work on time, or doing chores around the house. Discipline is consistency over a period of time that brings maturity, focus, and results in a particular area of our lives.

If you peruse through any book on the subject of discipline, you are bound to run smack into a section or chapter on:

"Why We Don't Do, What We Need to Do"
"Ways to Put off Procrastinating"
"How to Stop Saying: 'I Will Get to It Later'"
"Getting Unstuck."

The title might be different, but the message pertains to excuses we make that immobilize us and keep us from experiencing God's best.

Let us return once again to the Proverbs 31 woman. Here is a woman who exhibits a great deal of discipline, which can be summed up in the statement, "She watches over the ways of her household, And does not eat the bread of idleness" (v. 27).

While reflecting on that verse, I began to ponder over what keeps us idle and hinders us from being disciplined. The first thing that comes to mind is that there are just some things we have no control over. Of those things we do have control over, I believe, first and foremost, that there is a *failure to trust God*. Second, there is a *fear of failing*. Lastly, there is a *fear of disappointing others*. Below is my expanded list of why we are pulled away from having consistency in our service or from following through on a goal, passion, or project. Each item listed below falls into one of the three broader categories I just touched on.

> the unexpected,
> lack of direction,

- lack of commitment,
- wrong motivation,
- laziness,
- perfectionism,
- procrastination, or
- people-pleasing.

Failure to Trust God

There is absolutely nothing we can do about the unexpected, but expect it. Lack of direction, lack of commitment, and wrong motivation are surface excuses rooted in the spirit of distrust. Failing to trust God to give us divine direction, to order our steps toward His heavenly plan for our lives, then giving us the fortitude and resilience to stay committed to the course. Whether it be in our marriages, ministries, or as minuscule (for some) as keeping a decent and orderly home — there are just some obligations we should remain faithful to. Ask God to give you the fortitude, motivation, and direction to fulfill your obligations so you're not all over the place, but able to stay focused on, and committed to what God has given you the responsibility, talent, and desire to do.

Like me, I am sure you've been roped into participating in something you did not want to do, making it difficult to stay committed. My advice to you is to learn to say no with tact. There is nothing wrong with helping out in the interim when and where there's a need. However, you must decide who you will allow to control your days.

Discern who you're trying to please. In addition, look at what brings you joy. Why devote time and energy doing something God has not required or pressed on your heart to do? Why join the church choir if you can't "catch a note" and God has placed within you the skills and the talent to teach or evangelize? If the choir needs you, that's one thing, but if you joined because the choir travels, or they have a handsome organist (that's single), or you want to be noticed, then you need to check your motivation. The wrong motivation will never keep you committed to anything, because as soon as the motivation leaves, you'll be right behind it. Remember, anything we do for God must be done with God in mind.

If you enjoy being involved in a lot of different activities, put a quota on the number of activities you will allow yourself to participate in. Base that quota on what you believe God is calling you to do, what you can remain committed to, and for how long.

Fear of Failing

Fear has its place in the life of every believer. Nevertheless, for faithful women of God to put the fear of success, change, failure, or criticism over the fear of God, puts us out of order with God. Our faith should *quiet our fears*, giving us the boldness to move forth in faith.

The fear of missing God's best for some Christians is enough motivation to get them moving. They might stagnate for a minute or two with getting started—feeling ill-equipped for the task or as if their resources don't match what is being required of them—but their focus and goal is to glorify God in all things. Those things which are pleasant and those things which are not so pleasant, because ultimately they will have to give an account to God.

> *The wrong motivation will never keep you committed to anything, because as soon as the motivation leaves, you'll be right behind it.*

When we don't move forward by faith, it is usually laziness, perfectionism, or procrastination hindering us—all of which are offensive to God. Why? Because we were designed to do good works—works that bring glory to God.

Laziness

God tells us in His word that we are not to sleep excessively, which is a sign of laziness—if there's nothing physically wrong with us. Yes, we need rest; God designed our bodies to need rest. However, excessive sleeping breeds poverty and want. Proverbs 6:6-11 contains a sobering warning about our sluggish and lackadaisical behavior, it says…

> *Go to the ant, you sluggard!*
> *Consider her ways and be wise,*
> *Which, having no captain, Overseer or ruler,*
> *Provides her supplies in the summer,*
> *And gathers her food in the harvest.*
> *How long will you slumber, O sluggard?*
> *When will you rise from your sleep?*
> *A little sleep, a little slumber,*
> *A little folding of the hands to sleep—*
> *So shall your poverty come on you like a prowler, And your need like an armed man.*

📖 Does your life in any way resemble that of the sluggard's vineyard? Are there weeds resulting from neglect of your God, husband, child(ren), body, home, etc.?

We are told that our virtuous example "…willingly works with her hands" (Proverbs 31:13). The Bible says of diligent hands, "But the hand of the diligent makes rich" (Proverbs 10:4). In other words, the Proverbs 31 Woman is disciplined and willingly accepts the hard work it takes to get from here to

Step 3: Prayerfully Planning Ahead

there in ministry, education, career, or whatever else she sets out to accomplish.

If laziness is a problem for you, get yourself on a daily schedule and commit to using the Combination To-Do List to help you focus on accomplishing one or two essential tasks each day. Do this until you begin to feel a sense of accomplishment in your spirit and laziness no longer has you bound.

Perfectionism

Perfectionism is another form of fear that can hinder our effectiveness. Perfectionism is a great word when referring to God or being complete in Him. In our context, it's a desire to do something to perfection, and because we don't have the time to allocate to the task or we fear not being able to do a job well, we never get started—thus doing nothing. Perfectionism can also be spending an extreme amount of time on one task at the expense of other more important or equally important tasks. It's honorable that you take pride in a job well done. However, if you do not strive to have balance, other tasks will get neglected.

Deal with perfectionism by determining if you are appropriately using or abusing the resource of time God has blessed you with. Begin by setting realistic time limits for yourself (to complete a task or project) and commit to staying within your set limits. Ask yourself often...

- Am I using the time God has blessed me with wisely?

- Is the disproportionate amount of time I spend on a task, project, or doing nothing helping me reach an essential goal?

- Is the time I spend working on a task, project, or doing nothing causing me to neglect my family or other equally important responsibilities?

- If I continue on this course, what blessings might I miss? What consequences might I face?

Procrastination

Procrastination can stem from perfectionism, but procrastination often occurs when we feel fearful or overwhelmed with a task or assignment.

I confess, for most of my young adult life, I had been a major procrastinator, and I still struggle with procrastination. What helps me deal with my procrastination is to ask myself often: "Where would I be if God put off sacrificing His son, because He really didn't want to? Where would I be spiritually if Paul put off writing to the Body of Christ at: Ephesus, Philippi, Colosse, and to Timothy (a young church leader), until he was released from prison?" If God procrastinated, we would probably still be waiting for a savior; if Paul waited, a large chunk of the New Testament would probably be missing—deeply affecting our spiritual growth. Eventually, I realized that God saw my procrastination as putting off a task or responsibility until it was convenient or comfortable for me, not considering the impact it might have on others.

Deal with procrastination by breaking complex tasks into smaller, more manageable tasks. Then, find inexpensive and positive ways to reward yourself as you accomplish each major task or reach a significant milestone.

As a wonderful woman of God, understand and realize that if you do not seek order in the areas just discussed, you are depriving God of the opportunity to use you as a vessel through which He can bless and minister to others.

As Paul said to the Church in Galatia, I will say unto you, "And let us not grow weary while doing good [fulfilling your God-given obligations], for in due season we shall reap if we do not lose heart" (Galatians 6:9, emphasis added).

Fear of Disappointing Others

Lastly, people can also put undue stress and excessive demands on us that prevent us from consistently being able to fulfill our basic obligations. A mother who lives vicariously through her teenage daughter might want her daughter to fulfill her own dreams of winning beauty pageants. So she pushes her daughter to enter numerous pageants and forces her to prepare and practice her talent for hours every day, which could lead to poor grades, poor nutrition, or no close friendships.

If you feel someone is putting excessive demands on you, don't be afraid to confront them. Find out what is truly important to them and what takes up your time. Often, that person is unaware that unreasonable demands are being placed on you. It's up to you to find and maintain a healthy balance for yourself.

If you are a godly wife, I believe you want to lovingly serve your husband, but it's essential to have balance and order in your service. Find out what is important to your husband and what he needs from you, and release some of the unimportant or trivial stuff.

If you are an employee, talk to your employer about teleworking, flex-time, and compressed workweeks to help you balance work and family.

Having balance and order focuses our efforts on what God wants us to be and do to serve Him and others. It's also about being disciplined in our service.

Stewardship Involves Trust

Planning wisely involves trusting God more than you trust yourself, and acknowledging God in everything. Proverbs 3:5-6 says:

> *Trust in the LORD with all your heart, And lean not on your own understanding; In all your ways acknowledge Him, And He shall direct your paths.*

Time with God builds your trust in Him. The three days Esther spent in the presence of God gave her the courage to confront her husband about a decree he approved to destroy her people. God also gave her a plan, and as a result, when she should have been killed for entering the inner court without being summoned, she was welcomed by the king with open arms (Esther 5:2). When her people should have been annihilated, the enemy was eradicated. That's the type of power that comes from trusting God.

We are to trust God, who is omniscient. He knows the circumstances, trials, battles, stresses, and tests coming our way. In light of that, why wouldn't we want to take time to consult with God about our day and our lives? Time with God saves us time; trusting God's guidance enables us to focus on what needs to be done, and the most feasible way of doing it. To think that we have the resources to act without regard for God is unbecoming of us as Christians; daily, we are called to: "walk by faith not by sight" (2 Corinthians 5:7).

Step 3: *Your Daily Call to Order*

Chapter Comments:

In this step, we looked at ways a wise woman of God can attain and apply the power of prayer in planning her day. Next, let us get a glimpse of what a woman who prayerfully plans her day looks like—in our own modern-day Proverbs 31 woman:

She awakens at the designated time, having made sure she got the rest she needed the night before. She kneels down to pray, realizing that it was God who woke her up and is worthy to be praised. She assures that her family is well and considers how she might be of service to them as she goes about her day. She occupies herself with her daily responsibilities, tackling what she needs to do first and what she wants to do later.

Interruptions are welcomed because she is mindful of her God-given priorities. Wisdom is not far from her as she realizes the importance of prayerfully selecting her words and giving a reason for the hope that lives within her. She takes care of herself because she knows her family's health and well-being thrive off her own. She is aware of the presence of God, enabling her to sow peace with her enemies and serve those in need. Procrastination and idleness are her foes, and she realizes gossiping, complaining, and murmuring is only a ploy of the enemy to keep her unfaithful, unfruitful, and unfocused. She makes a habit of talking to God—praying without ceasing—as she goes about her day. Every day is different, and she welcomes the challenge of being better in wisdom and in love than yesterday.

If you want to improve the quality of your day, you have to assume responsibility for how your day is being spent. Pray about your day and plan your day wisely.

Chapter Questions:
Group Discussion
1. Read Psalm 90:12; Proverbs 14:15; 21:5; Ephesians 5:16. What do those passages say about planning wisely?
2. Read Genesis 41:45-57; Nehemiah 2:11-20; 6:15-16. How did planning wisely benefit Joseph and Nehemiah?
3. What method or tool do you use to schedule your day? How well does it work for you?
4. Do you agree that writing things down is a good practice rather than trying to remember everything? What has hindered you from applying this discipline in the past?
5. Read Psalm 119:11, 98, 104. What are the benefits of scheduling time to read, meditate, and study God's Word?
6. What time and energy-saving ideas can you share?

Personal Reflection
7. What recharges and refuels you when you feel drained, disappointed, discouraged, unmotivated, etc.?
8. What additional activities will rising early allow you to incorporate into your day?
9. What can you do to make it easier to wake up in the morning (e.g., wake up to a favorite song, sermon, or radio station)?
10. What tasks or activities can you delegate or eliminate to help you better manage your days?
11. If your time on earth was limited, what would you do with the time you had left?

Chapter Assignments:
- ❑ **Challenge 1**: Respond to end of chapter questions.
- ❑ **Challenge 2**: Buy an inexpensive spiral notebook.

Step 3: Prayerfully Planning Ahead 91

- **Challenge 3**: Make your own or purchase a planner. If using a computer, smartphone, or tablet device, decide what apps you will use.
- **Challenge 4**: Decide on the sections you want your spiral notebook to contain (e.g., goal lists, combination-to-do lists, expense lists, prayer lists, project lists).
- **Challenge 5**: Set up your spiral notebook.
- **Challenge 6:** Build your Combination To-Do List. If using a computer, smartphone, or tablet device, get familiar with the apps you will use.
- **Challenge 7**: Populate your Master To-Do List or your digital task list.
- **Challenge 8**: Start scheduling your day using your calendar and lists.
- **Challenge 9**: Establish written daily and nightly routines.
- **Extreme Challenge**: If needed, schedule a one or two day personal retreat away from friends and family members to pray, review your priorities, set goals, rest, and organize your planner.

Step 4

Exercising and Eating Healthy

> *Beloved, I pray that you may prosper in all things and be in health, just as your soul prospers.*
> —3 John 2

Each of us could probably confess to having neglected our own body or taken the body God blessed us with for granted. Our bodies were made by God, in His *own* image, so that He might be exalted in us. Our bodies were not made to seek and satisfy our own selfish pleasures, although certain pleasures are allowed by God as a means of blessing us; neither were our bodies created to be abused or neglected.

In step four, we will look at two aspects of a healthy lifestyle: exercising and eating healthy. However, the journey through this step must start with committing your temple to God. Why? Because no matter how strong or courageous you may be, most of us are powerless and lack the self-discipline to present our own body as a living sacrifice—daily laying aside gratifications and temptations to glorify God.

To glorify God with your body means you give God the first fruit of your worship and the best of your service. The only way to effectively do that is to take care of the body He has blessed you with—so that you are mentally and spiritually well enough and physically able to carry out His will here on earth.

If you are ready to make a healthy lifestyle commitment, pray this prayer with me:

> Lord, help me to present my body to you as a living sacrifice, holy and acceptable, which is the least I can do (Romans 12:1, paraphrased). Please help me commit to the process of making healthy food choices for myself and my family, to incorporating exercise into my day, and to replacing unhealthy habits with healthy habits. In addition, keep me committed to getting my yearly checkups and seeing my healthcare provider as needed. Remind me often that my body is the temple of the Holy Spirit because I have accepted You as my Lord and Savior. Thank you, Jesus. Amen.

The Temple of the Holy Spirit

When I was pregnant with my son, unsure if doctors would induce labor at five-and-a-half months, I begged the Lord to help us. I would have rather been pounding the pavement or going door-to-door in the hot sun, giving out salvation tracts, than sitting in a hospital bed in pain. I promised the Lord that if He got me out of this situation, I would jump at the opportunity to serve Him.

Step 4: Exercising and Eating Healthy

Our son was born three months later, happy and healthy, but it was not until I was physically incapable that I began to appreciate my body, which is God's temple.

Do you know how valuable your temple is to God? In 1 Corinthians 6:19-20, Paul declares:

Or do you not know that your body is the temple of the Holy Spirit who is in you, whom you have from God, and you are not your own? For you were bought at a price; therefore glorify God in your body and in your spirit, which are God's.

In this passage, Paul uses the term *temple* to refer to the body of a Christian. As you know, a *temple* is a place where the glory of the Lord is always welcomed (see 2 Chronicles 5:14; 7:1-2). Bible commentators have simply defined it as "a place set apart for worshiping God."

In the Old Testament, temples were built to give God or gods a permanent dwelling place among His or their people. The temple created by King Solomon, for example, was constructed from the finest materials from all around the world; and although there were scores of laborers, there were only a few master craftsmen who were asked to create very distinct designs to adorn the inner and outer precincts of the temple—for the unique privilege of creating a dwelling place worthy of God's presence.

With a number of intricate and fragile parts beneath your epidermal covering, the human body is by far the most complex structure ever made. It is also constructed from the finest materials, but by only one master craftsman—who was greater than all the craftsmen who participated in the building of the temple by Solomon.

As far back as we can tell in history, no temple was as unique in structure and design as the temple Solomon built for the Lord; from the materials and supplies collected to build it, to the people hired to work on it, no temple could ever be built the same.

In the same respect, to have made you after His own image brought great pleasure and joy to your master craftsman (God), and as far as anyone can tell, there has never been anyone, and there will never be anyone as unique in structure and design as you—no one else has your DNA or your fingerprints. You were custom designed for God's unique purpose and plan.

In the Old Testament, only the consecrated priests could enter the inner precincts of the temple for a designated purpose. In like manner, only the Holy Spirit, when invited, can enter the inner precincts of a human body (to be a light to understanding the Word of God and the ways of God).

With the Holy Spirit residing within you, your worth to God is far greater than the temple built by Solomon, and what you are capable of doing with your life here on earth will have greater impact on people than a building.

Sometimes, it takes a jolt for us to realize what a blessing it is that "in Him we live and move and have our being" (Acts 17:28). You were bought with a price, a price so high that no amount of silver or gold could redeem you. Redemption could only come through the blood of Christ.

Your Body, God's Temple

If you are responsible for the well-being of someone besides yourself, you know that getting sick is not an option. Even if you get sick, sleeping it off is not always an option. So much depends on your wellness: your livelihood, your family, your home, your mental and emotional stability, and let's not forget, your ministry. In Romans 12:1, Paul pleads with Christians in Rome and believers everywhere to "present [their bodies] a

Step 4: Exercising and Eating Healthy

living sacrifice, holy, acceptable to God, which is [their] reasonable service" (emphasis added).

However, there are people who take better care of their Bible—by not writing in it, keeping it stored in its original box, or dusting it off every week—than they do of the body God has blessed them with.

Having a healthy temple is an integral part of your service. A true axiom says: "If you take care of your body now, it will take care of you later." This *does not* mean you need to strive to be model thin; the goal should be to find a healthy balance for the size and frame God created you to reside in. This *does* means you should quit smoking, drinking, or indulging in sinful behavior that can negatively impact your body and your relationship with God.

> *So much depends on your wellness: your livelihood, your family, your home, your mental and emotional stability, and let's not forget, your ministry.*

If I may speak freely for a second, I believe that most conveniences that were meant to make our lives easier have actually made some of us lazier. We use our cars to take us places we can easily walk to; television and digital devices have been instrumental in decreasing or replacing family activities and outings—allowing us to be sedentary for more extended periods since most of our entertainment is *at our fingertips*.

In addition, the number of women facing infertility is concerning, and I am convinced the number is rising. I believe many of these cases result from not caring for one's temple. We are pulled in many different directions and do not always take the time to see the doctor, eat healthy, and get adequate sleep each night.

If you are facing infertility, know that there is nothing too hard for God. Whether you are a mother desiring to have more or still waiting on your first, we as women have an opportunity to look after the well-being of any child the Lord has laid on our hearts. Your desire to be a mother does not have to start or stop with your biological child or children.

A Vision Is Vital

Getting back to weightier matters. If you are overweight, then losing weight and getting healthy should be a goal for you. If you are not overweight, then getting fit and being healthy should be a desire for you. However, most goals and desires do not come to fruition without a vision.

George Washington Carver said, "Where there is no vision, there is no hope." The Bible says, "Where there is no revelation, the people cast off restraint" (Proverbs 29:18). In other words, they lose the self-discipline and faith necessary to reach their goal.

Visualization is the process of picturing in your mind what you desire to achieve—giving life to your thoughts and focusing your efforts toward reaching specific goals.

To start, grab your personal journal and write down a healthy lifestyle vision for yourself.

Your vision should be very detailed, expressing how you want to look and feel, what activities you want to pursue, or what outfit you want to fit into.

> I HAVE LEARNED OVER THE YEARS THAT WHEN ONE'S MIND IS MADE UP, THIS DIMINISHES FEAR, KNOWING WHAT MUST BE DONE DOES AWAY WITH FEAR.
>
> ROSA PARKS

Step 4: Exercising and Eating Healthy

I asked Lisa, a longtime friend who has struggled with her weight for twenty years, if I could share her vision with you. Here is what she wrote:

> My healthy lifestyle objective is to lose 119 pounds, tone up my muscles, and develop healthy eating habits. By the end of the year, I visualize myself being able to walk without the weight of bricks on my knees and the undue pressure on my back. I want to look in the mirror and see a healthy, vibrant person. I want to feel younger and live longer without the threat of family diseases like diabetes and heart disease hanging over me.

More people fail or give up from being unable to see progress than any other reason—especially when it comes to losing weight. Counter this by ensuring your vision is firmly planted in your heart and mind. As a result of Lisa's vision and hard work, she lost fifty-nine pounds in six months. She says, "Now when I look in the mirror, I see a healthy and vibrant person who has so much more to give and achieve."

What is your healthy lifestyle vision?

Following through on Your Vision

Next, establish a fitness objective. Are you trying to lose weight, get into shape, tone up, or run a marathon?

Based on your objective, decide what aspect of getting fit you want to focus on or improve: cardiovascular, muscle strengthening, or flexibility. If your objective is to lose weight, you may decide to focus on aerobic activities and stretching, and later incorporate weight lifting. If you want to tone up, your focus might be on weight training, moderate stretching, and moderate cardiovascular exercises.

Cardiovascular activities strengthen your heart and lungs, whereas muscle strengthening and stretching increase flexibility and improve circulation. Lifting weights or using strength training machines prevents the weakening of the bones as you get older, and of course, stretching helps to reduce joint and muscle stiffness.

❧ What is your fitness objective?

Once you have your objective and know what aspect of fitness you want to focus on, decide what you will do to improve your fitness. Some ideas are: aerobics, biking, cross-country skiing, dancing, hiking, lifting barbells, running, swimming, stair climbing, tennis, walking, or yoga.

When deciding on an activity, consider what you enjoy doing; then, decide when and how often you plan to engage in those physical activities. If you enjoy dancing, you may decide to take a class three nights a week, for one hour, at a local community center.

Furthermore, I encourage you to learn exercises and techniques that will aid you in protecting yourself against predators. Persuade your church leaders to sponsor a women's self-defense class. The local police department should be happy to send representatives to support your efforts. If not, most congregations have one or two trained black belts who may be looking for a ministry opportunity.

To tie this all together for you, let's look at Lisa's profile, whose vision was defined above.

Fitness objective:	Shed 119 pounds and get into a size 18 within a year
Focus areas (prioritized):	1. Body Control 2. Cardiovascular 3. Stretching 4. Weight Lifting
Enjoyable activities:	Hapkido (a Korean martial art), TaeAerobics, swimming, and tennis.
Fitness goal:	To shed 119 pounds and get into a size 18 by attending Hapkido & TaeAerobics classes twice a week; TaeKwonDo class once a week; and stretching daily.
Fitness commitment:	I commit to my fitness goal to: [*insert fitness goal*].

Who Has Time to Exercise?

Finding time to exercise can be very challenging; however, it's an important step to improve your overall quality of life. The exciting part for you is finding creative ways to incorporate exercise into your day without taking away from everything else you need to do.

Let me encourage you to exercise by reminding you that you have a holy God inside you. He has a purpose and a plan for you that requires your energy and vitality. If that revelation does not motivate you, just think of exercising as regularly doing activities that will improve your overall health, quality of life, and maybe save your life.

I am convinced that we are capable of finding time for anything we really want to do. Most studies reveal that exercising twenty to thirty minutes, three to five times a week, is enough exercise with proper dieting to help you eventually meet any reasonable fitness objective—including losing weight.

In addition, most health experts agree that if you do not work out and have excessive fat around your waist, you could be at risk for future health problems like diabetes, high blood pressure, high cholesterol, heart disease, or stroke. According to Dr. Oz and Dr. Roizen, your waist should not be greater than thirty-five inches if you are a woman and not greater than forty inches if you are a man.[1]

Getting Started with Your Program

In this section, I will give you some quick but essential steps to help you get started on a successful exercise program. Be wise in heeding my advice; it is for your safety and well-being.

❑ **Step 1**—I highly recommend consulting a doctor or physical therapist before you start working out, especially if you have a physical condition, are over fifty, or have not worked out in a while. Make sure you declare to your doctor your intention—to start working out as soon as she (or he) gives you the green light.

Whatever instructions your doctor gives you, please follow them. You may also want to ask your doctor what exercises she recommends you start with. In addition, have your cholesterol, blood pressure, weight, and Body Mass Index (BMI) checked by your doctor before starting your exercise program. Your BMI uses your height along with your weight to calculate the percentage of body fat you have.

❑ **Step 2**—Must haves for your workout are good running shoes if you plan on walking or jogging; even if you are going for a moderate walk, tennis shoes with cushioning will protect your ankles and knees from undue stress and pressure.

Walkers, joggers, or runners may also consider investing in a pedometer. A pedometer is a great motivational tool next to having a partner. It simply counts your steps and then displays the number of steps or the distance you have traveled during a given time frame. The recommended number of steps per day is at least 5000. If you want to lose weight, try doubling that number. Pedometers can be found in fitness trackers or smart watches—which have the added benefit of monitoring your heart rate and tracking calories burned.

A journal to house your fitness vision, objective, and to chart your progress is also necessary, along with comfortable workout clothing.

❑ **Step 3**—Once again, I emphasize the need for a partner. You'll need someone to pray with; it is also the best way to stay focused, motivated, and inspired. Most importantly, you'll have to give an account to someone of your progress.

In finding a workout partner, make sure you both are headed in the same direction, or have similar fitness objectives. I recommend you find someone you are compatible with. I am not just talking about someone who shares your values; that is important. However, so is fitness compatibility. It's not fair to leave your partner in the dust while you continue at a pace that's difficult for him or her to keep up.

If you have allowed your health to get extremely out of control, and if you can afford to, hire a fitness trainer to help you get started. Your fitness trainer will familiarize you with exercises you can do to meet your fitness objective and show you how to use various exercise machines (if working out in a gym).

❑ **Step 4**—Your partner or your fitness trainer will need to help you take your body measurements (arms, waist, hips, and thighs) with a cloth tape measure—do this monthly to analyze your progress. If you're trying to lose weight, understand that losing weight is a painfully slow process—it will take some time for the needle on the scale to start inching down. Your challenge is to stay focused on your vision and your fitness objective.

❑ **Step 5**—Begin each workout session by warming up your muscles with a moderate walk or jogging in place, then proceed with some light stretching. If you have been exercising for a while, focus on increasing the length of time you workout, how much you lift, or how long you walk. The goal is to challenge yourself by adding a little more to your weekly workout. If you walked for fifteen minutes last week, try walking for twenty minutes or picking up your pace a bit.

Let me conclude this section by encouraging you to look for ways to add a bit of variety and fun to your fitness program. Go bike riding with your children or ballroom dancing with your husband. Also, consider engaging in a light workout while watching your favorite television show, dancing while cleaning your house, or walking to the corner store (if it's safe) instead of driving.

You Are What You Eat

As Gentiles saved by God's grace, there are no dietary restrictions upon us in the New Testament, like there were for the Israelites under the Mosaic Law in the Old Testament. However, even though the Bible does not explicitly address everything we should or should not eat, we are told: "For every creature of God is good, and nothing is to be refused if it is received with thanksgiving" (1 Timothy 4:4).

Eating healthy and caring for the temple God has blessed you with provides you with fuel and energy to serve God and others more effectively. It enables your body to function properly (especially the heart); you are able to think more clearly; you look younger and healthier; you remember more; and you become less anxious. But wait, there are also other benefits. In addition to building up your immune system, it may also impact your genes!

As I was writing this book, I found a wonderful article in the *Parade*—a magazine insert that comes with my local newspaper—that addresses the question "Can Food Change Your Genes?" by Dr. Mark Hyman, co-author of the book, *Ultra-prevention*.

The general idea behind the article was that if we alter our diets and lifestyles early enough, we can prevent certain diseases and disabilities from occurring. We are essentially reacquainting our bodies with the diet to which our bodies are best adapted biologically.[2]

"All of us are susceptible to certain illnesses because of our family histories…" says Dr. Hyman. "But the field of nutrigenomics is demonstrating that, if we alter our diets and lifestyles early enough, our genes do not have to be our destiny."[3]

Suggestions were to eat more unprocessed foods—fruits, beans, nuts, seeds, and whole grains—and to "include in your diet wild fish such as small salmon, sardines and herring."[4] Other great fish choices are tilapia, flounder, and whitefish which are believed by experts to have none or less of the toxic chemicals—mercury and polychlorinated biphenyl (PCBs)—that other fish may carry.

Of course, Mama was right when she said, "Eat your vegetables." Leafy green vegetables are a great source of folic acid, which is believed to reduce your risk of getting cancer and heart disease.

Of all the areas I have covered in this book, this section was the hardest for me to implement. Before I considered my body the temple of the Holy Spirit, I lived off of convenient foods and processed foods, which are high in sodium and contain saturated and hydrogenated (trans) fats. Trans fats can also be found in margarine, shortening, fried foods, and most prepackaged foods. The essential fats we should be getting more of are the healthy fats like the Omega-3 fats found in some fish, nuts, avocados, and flaxseed; and Omega-6 fats found in low-fat dairy and lean proteins.[5]

In addition, let us remember, fiber which is important to the health of our digestive tract. It can be found in vegetables (artichokes, lima beans, soybeans, etc.). It can also be found in fruits (grapefruit, blackberries, and raspberries).

I want to encourage you, for the health of your family and yourself, to become familiar with reading food labels—assuming you are not. Your first brief lesson is to avoid foods high in cholesterol and sodium and highly processed foods, particularly those containing corn syrup, white sugar, and saturated and trans fats.

Step 4: Exercising and Eating Healthy

Just as the day will come when you will have to face the consequences of missed opportunities, the day will also come when you will have to live with the consequences of neglecting your body. Instead of looking back with regret, why not rather live with the consequences of having taken care of your temple? Even if you're fighting sickness in your body now, eating healthy is bound to bring positive results: more energy, a stronger immune system, or longer days.

What Are You Eating Daily?

Here is a recommended list of what your body should be getting daily. This list is not conclusive, but *food for thought* recommended by most doctors and nutritionists to get you on the pathway to a healthier you.

- Drink eight glasses of water a day, that's 64 ounces. Start by drinking at least one glass when you wake up in the morning and another before you go to bed at night. In addition, consider drinking a glass before and after every meal.

- Eat a balanced breakfast, lunch, and dinner. If trying to lose weight: eat smaller portions; reduce calorie intake; always make time for breakfast; and never eat a big meal at least a couple of hours before bedtime.

- Take one multivitamin with one of your glasses of water. Make sure your vitamin contains folate or folic acid. "About 800 mcg (micrograms) a day of folic acid is sufficient for most people. Vitamins B_6 and B_{12} also are recommended to keep homocysteine at an ideal balance."[6] In other words, to prevent folate deficiency. Foliate deficiency occurs when your body is deprived of the needed vitamin B to function properly.[7]

- Consume between five and six servings of fruits and vegetables. Consider having a fruit with your breakfast, a salad for lunch, vegetables with your dinner, and fruit snacks between meals.

- Get your vitamin D by drinking nonfat milk and orange juice. Also, don't forget to enjoy some fun in the sun, providing you with vitamin D.

⚑ Can you think of anything else you should eat or do to improve your overall health?

The Health Kick Commitment

Having a healthy attitude toward food takes little effort. The effort is in deciding to consistently choose an adequate portion of those foods that will help you live healthier.

My "Health Kick Commitment" aims to help you stop eating what is harmful and start eating what is healthy. The negative aspect of not pursuing a healthy lifestyle puts you out of order with God and at risk for a wide variety of health problems—the older you get. Balance and order in this area of your life will come when you commit to your health and well-being today, not tomorrow.

Here is my challenge to you, which is designed to help you get a better handle on the types of foods you consume daily. Select foods that you have a habit of eating or drinking regularly that you know are not healthy for you, and replace them with healthier food choices. Use the "Health Kick Commitment" worksheet (located at the end of this chapter) to help you remember your new food choices. Be as specific as you can in deciding what food exchanges you will make. Below are some suggestions to help you get started:

Step 4: Exercising and Eating Healthy

- Choose more lean poultry and fish; and less of the other types of meat.

- Broil or bake your meats instead of frying.

- Choose whole-grain and whole-wheat bread, rice, flour, cereals, pasta, and tortillas.

- Buy skim or one percent milk instead of whole milk.

- Eat fruits and vegetables versus chips, cookies, candy, or cake.

- Drink water instead of sodas or juices, or sparkling water instead of sodas.

- Choose unsalted versus other alternatives (e.g., select unsalted crackers over salted crackers).

- Choose low-fat, low-butter, or nonfat versus other alternatives (e.g., select nonfat sour cream over regular sour cream).

- Consider fruit smoothies instead of milkshakes.

- Cut back on refined sugars (corn syrup, white sugar, high fructose syrup, artificial sweeteners, etc.); choose natural sugars (maple syrup, molasses, or unfiltered honey).

I drank two cups of hot chocolate in the morning while at work for years. I decided to replace my hot chocolate with a cup of steel-cut oatmeal or green tea with lemon—both help control cholesterol. On the weekends, I enjoyed a bowl of the most sugar-packed cereal on the market; I swapped that for sugar-free, whole-grain cereal with fruit.

Don't worry; after a while, your taste buds and body will become accustomed to your new dietary changes. Using the

"Health Kick Commitment" Worksheet, you decide the dietary changes you will make. My desire is to help you stay committed to the course of building a healthier lifestyle, not to turn an upside-down diet right side up in a day or a week.

Stick to your commitment for thirty days or until it has become a fixed habit with you. After you've served your time well, build a new list, but still remain faithful to the first.

If you remain faithful to your convictions to exercise and make healthier food choices, within a few months, you will have increased your energy level, self-esteem, and maybe even transformed your life.

ଔଓ

Step 4: Your Daily Call to Order

Chapter Comments:

This step dealt with two aspects of a healthy lifestyle: exercising and eating healthy. I talked very little about the emotions that may be hindering you from living a healthy life.

It is no secret that eating excessively may be an emotional response to something that has happened in your past; therefore, don't be ashamed to seek counseling. Balancing blessings and obtaining order means you make a conscious effort to get to the core of this self-destructive behavior. A friend once told me that briefly journaling her thoughts and emotions before she ate anything gave her insight into what was driving her compulsion to overeat. At times, it was boredom, fatigue, or stress; other times, it was depression over a matter; and occasionally, it was simply hunger.

What is driving your compulsion to overeat? Are you prone to over-eating when you feel anxious? What time of day are you inclined to eat more than you should? These are the types of questions you have to ask yourself if over-eating is a problem.

Chapter Questions:

Group Discussion

1. Read Romans 12:1; 1 Corinthians 6:19-20; 9:27. What does the Bible say about our bodies?
2. What comparisons can we draw between our bodies and the Old Testament tabernacle?
3. Share ways we, as women, can incorporate exercise into our day without burdening our schedule.

Personal Reflection

4. How do you feel about your present health?
5. How are you abusing or neglecting your temple (e.g., not eating healthy, not exercising, over-extending yourself, or abusing a substance)?
6. What actions are you committed to taking now to help you live healthier later? Share your decision with your accountability partner or small group for accountability.
7. If you desperately needed God's healing for yourself or a loved one, how would you approach the throne of God?

Chapter Assignments:

- **Challenge 1**: Respond to end of chapter questions.
- **Challenge 2**: Make an appointment for a checkup and consult your doctor about starting an exercise program.
- **Challenge 3**: Complete the "Fitness Vision Profile" in Appendix A.
- **Challenge 4**: Take your body measurements; record your measurements in your fitness journal or app.

- **Challenge 5**: Plan a week's worth of healthy breakfast meals, and commit to only eating from those options for thirty days or until eating a healthy breakfast becomes a habit.

- **Challenge 6**: Plan a week's worth of healthy lunch meals to include one healthy snack for each meal. Make a thirty-day commitment to only eat from those options.

- **Challenge 7**: Decide on an activity you can do with others or your workout partner, or find ways to incorporate your family into your workout program.

- **Challenge 8**: Complete the "Health Kick Commitment" worksheet; make two copies and tape one to the front of your fitness journal and another to your refrigerator.

- **Challenge 9**: Learn how to make smoothies. Smoothies are a great way to add nutritional value to your diet. Experiment with fruits, yogurts, and low-fat milk or soy milk, then add protein powder, flaxseed, or other powder supplements for even more nutritional value.

- **Extreme Challenge**: Get in the habit of preparing healthy dishes for your family or friends by committing to prepare two or more healthy sit-down dinners per week.

- **Group Challenge**: Approach your church leaders about hosting a self-defense class for women in your church and the surrounding community.

My 'Health Kick' Commitment

I_____,
Your Printed Name

commit to eating healthy by making healthier food choices. I will refuse to buy or house the following food items that I love and enjoy but are not good for me; I will replace them with other food items that are better for me and move me toward a healthier lifestyle.

Give Up	Replace With
1	1
2	2
3	3
4	4
5	5
6	6
7	7

_____
Your Signed Name

_____
Accountability Partner's Signed Name

Step 5

Conquering Your Clutter

*For one's life does not consist in the
abundance of the things he possesses.*
—Luke 12:15

We begin this part of our journey at the foot of our own self-made mountain—probably looking up as if we have an impossible journey ahead—by examining the physical clutter in our homes and then conquering the chaos that hinders mobility and productivity in every aspect of life.

There is no doubt in my mind that our physical surroundings are a reflection of us. I find it very difficult to pursue peace amidst an array of clutter. When my house is cluttered and out of order, other aspects of my life usually reflect that.

Likewise, no matter how much time a person spends in prayer and worship, reading the Word of God, fellowshipping with the Body of Christ, and serving others; clutter always has a way of thwarting one's inner spirit. You could have just finished praying, and while feeling great about the time you spent with the Lord, the phone rings. You answer it only to hear a recorded message on the other end of the phone from your credit card company, notifying you that your bill was consecutively thirty days past due. As a result, you've incurred late fees and a punitive increase in your interest rate. Imagine how you would feel after a message like that—deflated, discouraged, disheartened, or angry with yourself. You know your bill was late twice because it had been hidden under a pile of unsorted mail. You could have just as easily stubbed your toe or tripped on something that you've been meaning to put away for weeks. Whatever the circumstances, if it brings discomfort, interferes with your walk, or upsets the Spirit of God within you, it needs to be addressed—that includes your mountains of physical clutter. But be of good cheer, with God, "Every valley shall be filled And every mountain and hill brought low; The crooked places shall be made straight And the rough ways smooth" (Luke 3:5).

Are You Caught Up in the Clutter?

Working around clutter takes energy that can be used more efficiently elsewhere. Clutter is defined as "a number of things scattered in disorder."[1] There is mental clutter, spiritual clutter, emotional clutter, and the physical clutter our possessions create. In this step, we will address our physical clutter.

So, how can you gauge whether you have a clutter problem? Most organizational experts will agree you have a problem if any of the following apply to you:

- ❑ You regularly need help finding things.

- ❑ You feel frustrated and overwhelmed when you walk into your home or certain parts of your home.

Step 5: Conquering Your Clutter

❏ You are losing money by paying late charges, punitive fees, or re-buying what you cannot find.

❏ You have unorganized piles of paper, clothes, toys, books, and other stuff lying around the house. In addition, your drawers, closets, and chests are stuffed to capacity.

❏ You are uncomfortable inviting people to your home because it's rarely presentable.

❏ You have no more space to put or store things.

❏ You have yet to allocate a home for all your possessions.

❏ You are tripping over things lying around the floor.

❏ Your spouse or roommate is annoyed with how disorganized things are around the house and has often expressed their feelings in a cutting and hurtful manner.

❏ You are regularly late for meetings, appointments, events, or activities because you're wrestling with your clutter.

❏ You have stuff you have not used or seen in years.

❏ You have a hard time releasing things you do not need.

If you have answered *yes* to three or more of these questions, whether minor or major, you could have a clutter problem.

Dealing with clutter can be an intimidating and overwhelming task. However, it is an essential step on your journey—over your self-made mountain of clutter—you do not want to dismiss.

God's Mandate for Order

How befitting for us to travel to the book of Numbers—where the nation of Israel was camped at the foot of a real mountain, Mount Sinai—to understand how important order is to God.

It would be at Mount Sinai where a generation of Israelites would prepare to enter the promise land. The preparation process involved receiving customs they were to practice and the laws they were to abide by. In addition, they were sanctified, and a census was taken. All this was done to keep and maintain order in the lives of the Israelites.

> *NOW the LORD spoke to Moses in the Wilderness of Sinai,... after they had come out of the land of Egypt, saying: "Take a census of all the congregation of the children of Israel, by their families, by their fathers' houses, according to the number of names, every male individually, from twenty years old and above—all who are able to go to war in Israel. You and Aaron shall number them by their armies. And with you there shall be a man from every tribe, each one the head of his father's house (Numbers 1:1-4).*

God had told Abraham hundreds of years earlier, "I will multiply your descendants as the stars of the heaven and as the sand which is on the seashore" (Genesis 22:17). Can you imagine counting sand? Moses, Aaron, and their assistants had this long and arduous task. Yes, I'm sure there were periods of frustration, but they were being obedient to God's command—to count the descendants of Abraham, including all the men able to fight in battle.

Imagine what it would have been like for the Israelites to go into battle not knowing their military strength. In addition, the tribes had to be accounted for to proportionately divide up

Step 5: Conquering Your Clutter

the Promise Land. Without this pertinent statistical information, occupying and organizing their new home would probably have been done aimlessly and illogically.

Laws were given and customs established so the Israelites would have order in their relationships, order in their service, and order in their conduct. God was so meticulous about having order in the camp that His people were organized and arranged around the tabernacle by their family, clan, and tribe.[2] In addition, multiple books in the Old Testament give specific details on the preparation and offering of sacrifices, the construction and the care of the tabernacle, and the roles of the Levites.

In the first book of the Old Testament, we are told that God created the heavens and the earth, then all that is in it. God then created man in His image. *Order* was actively involved in the creation of the world and, might I add, the salvation of the world.

> *How insignificant our clutter may seem to us versus preaching God's Word and ministering to the masses, but if we are to obey God, should we not obey God in all things?*

How insignificant our clutter may seem to us versus preaching God's Word and ministering to the masses, but if we are to obey God, should we not obey God in all things? Remember the command given to us by the apostle Paul? It simply states: "Let all things be done decently and in order" (1 Corinthians 14:40).

In reality our minds, hearts, and souls yearn for order. A desire put there by our creator. This is evident in the fact that our effectiveness for God increases when there is order in our homes. If you think I am comparing things to people or apples to oranges, let us look at what resources our clutter consumes:

- **Time**—Precious time is abused as we lag in doing those important and necessary things God has called us to do. Instead, we're looking for something we've misplaced or tangled up in the urgent versus focusing on the important.
- **Money**—financial resources are absorbed as double purchases are often made when a particular item cannot be found. In addition, cash flow dwindles when late charges are assessed, when bills are not paid on time, and when funds are consistently being allocated to pay for non-essential and unplanned conveniences designed to simplify life—for the moment.
- **Peace**—harmony is swallowed up as frustration develops when we begin to feel overwhelmed and consumed by our material possessions, the daily responsibility of maintaining our possessions, and the debt we assumed to possess our possessions.
- **Space**—less usable space can cause discontentment, often having us believe we need more room or a bigger house. Why? To accommodate more things!
- **You**—the availability of God's people dwindles. The clutter becomes like fetters on the ankles of a prisoner, limiting your ability to smoothly transition from one place to another and slowing you down on the course God has for you.

The Rich Young Ruler

Now that we understand how important order is to God let us fast forward from the Old Testament to the New Testament, where we are introduced by Matthew to the rich young ruler—in chapter nineteen—who had everything and was obedient to the Ten Commandments from his youth. Yet, this young ruler still felt the need to go before our Lord, Jesus Christ, and say: "Good Teacher, what good thing shall I do that I may have eternal life?" (v. 16).

I have come to the conclusion that the convicting power of the Spirit of God refused to allow this young man to be content and at peace with his good works. So, he sought Jesus for assurance of his salvation. With a discerning eye, Jesus quickly revealed the source of this young man's deficiency: the love of things.

Jesus said to him, "If you want to be perfect, go, sell what you have and give to the poor, and you will have treasure in heaven; and come, follow Me" (v. 21).

Before him was one of the most incredible opportunities a Christian could ever ask for: the opportunity to attend the University of Jesus Christ. To be taught by one of the greatest teachers the world has ever known. Who not only taught Biblical precepts but lived by them. Imagine having a loving, gracious, all-knowing instructor teaching every single one of your classes. With the right motive, the only way you could not succeed is to do what the rich young ruler did, which was to not show up or walk away. Matthew concludes this story by saying: "But when the young man heard that saying, he went away sorrowful, for he had great possessions" (v. 22).

Here is a prime example of someone whose heart is in the right place, but he is weighed down by his personal possessions, diminishing his effectiveness for Christ.

This rich young ruler had formed an attachment to his possessions, which in his mind, had a greater value to him than God. Of course he—nor would we—ever confess to such a thing, but his life was a product of what he valued most.

There is nothing wrong with having things; Abraham, David, and Solomon had many possessions. The concern is valuing our things above God and the accumulation of things we don't need. Is a luxury home or car payment keeping you from serving God full-time? Paul reminds us not to be brought under the power of anything (see 1 Corinthians 6:12). As Christians, we must guard ourselves against overindulgence in material things—that nothing comes between us and our relationship with God.

> *A life devoted to things is a dead life, a stump; a God-shaped life is a flourishing tree.*
>
> *—Proverbs 11:28*

Anything we value above God becomes an idol in our life, our personal graven image, putting us out of order with God and in direct violation of His First Commandment: "'You shall love the LORD your God with all your heart, with all your soul, and with all your mind'" (Matthew 22:37).

With balance and order comes discipline and restraint; we don't always need what we want, nor do we always need what we have. The resources and possessions that God gives to bless us are not intended to replace Him or distract us from seeking hard after Him. They were meant for our benefit, and to provide us with a visual reminder of the goodness of God.

We honor God when we surrender to Him those things we've allowed to become an idol in our lives. We are told in God's Word: "A life devoted to things is a dead life, a stump; a God-shaped life is a flourishing tree" (Proverbs 11:28).

> Are you willing to give up your most cherished material possessions if God asks you to, so that you may be complete in Jesus Christ?

Getting a Grip on the Clutter

While writing this book, I ran across a beautiful testimony by a woman who understood the blessing in "Simply Living."

When her husband went back to school for a career change, their family of six had no alternative but to downsize. In the process of simplifying her family's life, she began to question the need for accumulating stuff. Here is what she says getting a grip on the chaos did for her:

> It was pure bliss walking through our house once the clutter had been packed away.... Cutting down on the clutter carried over into other areas of my life. I experienced a spiritual purging as well. Changing my focus helped me be more available to do God's bidding, reach out to others and teach my family the importance of being thankful every day.[3]

Once you've accepted that you have a clutter problem in your home and you're motivated to do something about it, grab a sheet of paper and something to write with. Walk outside your front door, wait a minute or two, then walk back inside. Begin taking notes on any clutter eyesores you see throughout your home. This includes any clutter in a space or room that hinders you from considering that area a pleasant place to be. It could be paper piled high on the kitchen table, toys all over the family room floor, boxes stacked to the ceiling in the dining room, books all over the floor next to your bed, clothes covering the floor in your laundry room, or closets stuffed to the point that its contents threaten to take over the room it resides in. Please note if you physically cannot enter a room or closet, that entire space is condemned as an eyesore.

You will use your list with the following suggestions to conquer your major clutter eyesores in your home.

The Decluttering Process

Most professional organizers will agree that the first step toward getting organized requires you to analyze the situation before you dive in. Here's my "triple A" principle for dealing with clutter. Principle #1: **Analyze** why the problem exists. Ask yourself . . .

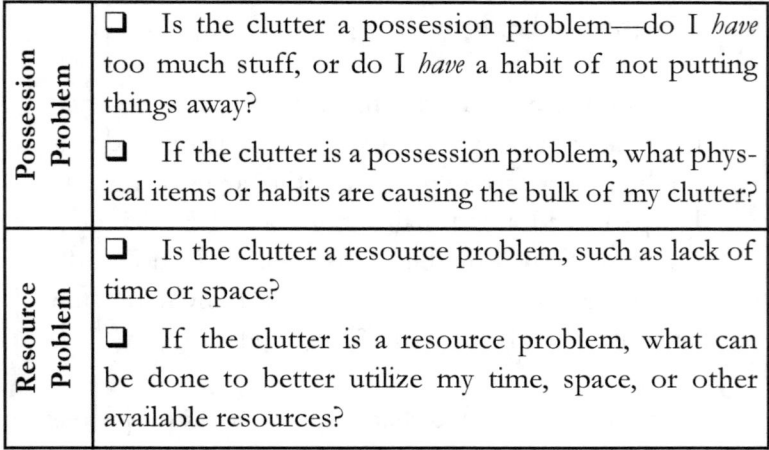

Possession Problem	❑ Is the clutter a possession problem—do I *have* too much stuff, or do I *have* a habit of not putting things away? ❑ If the clutter is a possession problem, what physical items or habits are causing the bulk of my clutter?
Resource Problem	❑ Is the clutter a resource problem, such as lack of time or space? ❑ If the clutter is a resource problem, what can be done to better utilize my time, space, or other available resources?

Principle #2: **Attack** the clutter by taking action to eliminate it. Have either boxes, durable trash bags, or plastic containers for this task. It is common to label them: DONATE, SELL, STORE AWAY, KEEP, and TRASH. For closet clutter, if you have clothes that are frequently dry cleaned use two KEEP bags and label them: KEEP(MACHINE WASH) and KEEP(DRY CLEAN). Two keep bags prevent you from sorting through and separating your clothes again later.

Principle #3: **Aim** to minimize future clutter and maintain the look of order. This may involve getting rid of some things, using tools designed to optimize the usage of your space, changing your daily or nightly routine to include tidying up, or changing bad habits—such as not putting things away—into good habits.

I suggest dedicating a weekend or a week to conquering a major clutter culprit (clothes, papers, books, toys, etc.). If your weekends are full, take a week and allocate twenty to thirty minutes each day to eliminate your clutter. This is a simple process of first deciding what clutter pile you want to confront. If the cluttered area is too much to complete in the time allotted, divide it into smaller sections and tackle a section a day. Don't forget to set your timer and clear as much away as possible. By the end of the week, you'll be amazed at how much you've accomplished.

Last but not least, do not be afraid to enlist the help of others. The Proverbs 31 woman had maids! You'll be pleasantly surprised by how many people will jump at the opportunity to help you get order in your life. In return, you can help them do the same. If you have to hire someone and money is scarce, consider a teenager in your neighborhood or from your local church.

Clothing Clutter

To help you understand my "triple A" process, let's first tackle the bedroom closets and those piles of clothes lying around the house. Applying principle #1, begin by taking a long, hard stare at one of your closets. Attempt to truthfully analyze what is causing your clutter problem. Is it a possession problem, a resource problem, or both? Write your thoughts below:

_____
_____
_____

Whenever I got home from work, I had a tendency to undress in my bedroom and just set whatever I was wearing on the bed, chair, stationary bike, or anything nearby. To change this habit, I put a basket on the floor in my closet to toss dry-clean clothes and made a simple commitment to hang up my other clothes or toss them into the hamper.

Moving on to principle #2:

❑ If items are on the floor, start by picking them up off the floor. Store them in one of these places: the trash bag, the donate box, the sell box, the storage box, the keep box, or hang the item up immediately. If it is shoes you want to keep, find a place to line them up. If it's hats or accessories, find a place to stack or store them neatly.

❑ Once the clothes and other stuff are off the floor, pull all your empty hangers out from the rest of your clothes. Hang all empty hangers at the end of your closet. If you have too many hangers, throw the wire hangers out—they are known for stretching clothing—and donate plastic or wood hangers.

❑ One by one, physically pick up each clothing item now hanging in your closet and decide whether to keep it or let it go. Do the same with shoes and any accessories.

- If you have not worn the item in over a year or over three years for formal attire, let it go!
- If the item no longer fits or no longer fits your style, let it go!
- If the item turns off or terrorizes your husband or would terrorize any prospects, let it go!

One keep exception is if the clothing item is of historical significance, such as a military uniform or something you want to pass down to your children or grandchildren someday.

Applying principle #3, take aim to minimize future clutter and bring order to your closet.

Consider categorizing your clothing items by color, type (skirts, pants, shirts, or suits), or purpose (casual, work, or formal). Do the same for your shoes and other accessories.

Decide from your previous analysis what tools can be used or purchased to help maintain order in your closet. Consider using a second hanging bar to expand hanging space; an inexpensive plastic dresser to keep lingerie and other accessories; shoe bags for storing shoes off the floor; shelf dividers for separating sweaters and other foldable items; or clear containers to store accessories and out of season items.

Visit your local hardware store for other closet organizational ideas. If you're considering installing a closet organizer, shop for one that meets your current needs and is flexible enough to meet your changing needs. Lastly, remember to schedule time monthly or quarterly to keep your closet maintained.

Those Clothing Piles

Now, for those clothing piles around the house, take your boxes or bags and move them to the other areas of your home in which you have non-closet clothing clutter. This may be in your bathroom or laundry room. Start with principle #1: Analyze why the problem exists. Next, principle #2: Attack the clutter by sorting and putting your clothes in the appropriate bags. Lastly, principle #3: Aim to minimize future clutter. If it's a possession problem, consider scaling down towels, sheets, and other linen. If it's a resource problem, develop a washing routine specifying when washing will be done, by whom, and what type of clothes will be washed on any given day. It may also be helpful to make sure each person in your home owns a hamper—to store dirty clothes.

The Laundry Basket

Unfortunately, just as we had piles of clothes that needed to be hung up, dry cleaned, or laundered, there are piles of clean clothes that need to be folded and put away.

If you are only responsible for your laundry, this should be a breeze; if not, you'll need a bag for each family member. Start by sorting through the clothes, separating them by family members, and then putting each member's clothes in their own bag. If you have not done so, teach your children—and maybe your husband—the art of folding their own clothes. Have the older children put their clothes away and help their younger siblings do the same.

Consider folding clothes by priority—prioritizing by person or purpose. If you stay home, your hubby may need his clothes folded for work, which would make folding his clothes of higher importance than your clothes or your children's clothes. If you work or go to school, consider folding and putting away your work or school clothes before your sleep attire or towels.

There is nothing wrong with grabbing a towel out of the laundry basket when needed, as long as you are making progress toward getting your laundry folded and put away. The key to living out of a laundry basket is to search first among your unfolded clothes for what you need before taking from among the folded clothes. With consistency, most of your clothes will be folded and put away before you realize it.

For mismatched socks, throw them in a basket and make a game of finding matches. Give your kids a dime or a quarter for each match they find. If you are single, you could probably borrow your girlfriend's or your neighbor's kids, but your best bet is not investing in a lot of socks. Consider stockings or tights for the colder months.

Paper Clutter

Another major clutter culprit is paper. Getting rid of paper clutter takes long suffering, patience, and a good shredder, but you will be relieved not to have to deal with the heaps of paper scattered around your home.

To eliminate the paper trails, use the list you created at the beginning of this step to find a hub of paper clutter you want to conquer. Start by applying principle #1. Write your thoughts in the space provided below:

_____
_____
_____
_____

To implement principle #2, use an accordion-style file folder or hanging folders that fit comfortably into your filing cabinet to help you organize. If you know you do not need an item, trash it or shred it immediately.

Let's begin by sorting through your paper clutter and separating them into the following suggested categories:

- ❑ unopened mail

- ❑ receipts

- ❑ legal documents (contracts, wills, titles, licenses, and decrees)

- ❑ financial records (pay stubs, bank statements, canceled checks, credit card statements, loans and promissory notes)

- ❑ income taxes (previous returns and all supporting documentation)

- ❑ insurance policies

- ❏ articles (from newspapers, magazines, and catalogs)
- ❏ utility bills
- ❏ investments (annuities, bonds, stocks, and real estate)
- ❏ warranty manuals
- ❏ miscellaneous items[5]

Also, include a personal folder for each family member to store information such as: report cards, certifications, awards, diplomas, medical information, and sentimental items.

It is recommended that you keep receipts from major purchases, appliances, collectibles, art, and antiques for as long as you own the item. In addition, the IRS has up to seven years to audit an individual, so it is a good idea to store income tax returns with all the documents used to complete the return until that audit period is over.

If you need a copy of your tax form, from as far back as four years (or beyond), send form 4506, "Request for Copy of Tax Return" to the IRS. This form can be found at: www.irs.gov/pub/irs-pdf/f4506.pdf

Add more filing categories as you need them, but keep it simple. You may also want to add subcategories for each of the above categories, using vanilla folders that fit nicely within the hanging folders.

While you are going through your paper clutter, do the following:

- ❏ Pull out vital records: birth and death certificates, licenses, Social Security cards, titles, deeds, wills, and passports.

- ❏ Set aside recent insurance policy statements, investment papers, and pertinent military forms.

Step 5: Conquering Your Clutter

❑ Put these items in a small box or container—preferably a fire-proof box—that's easy to grab if a fire or emergency requires you to evacuate your home immediately.

Sorting through your paper clutter also gives you a prime opportunity to create a grab-and-go folder. This folder will temporarily retain anything requiring your immediate attention in the way of: reading, responding, praying, paying, mailing, or delegating. This folder should also be designed to take with you anywhere you know you'll have a long wait—so you can make productive use of your time while waiting.

Minimizing Paper Clutter

Keeping in line with principle #3, consider the following suggestions for minimizing paper clutter:

> **Handling bills**—Organize and minimize the number of bills coming in by arranging to have your bills automatically deducted from your bank account, paying bills online, or by making a bill-paying system. Do the latter by obtaining twelve 6" by 9" envelopes, one for each month of the year. At the top left of each envelope, punch a small hole and place a ring through the holes—binding the envelopes together. Label each envelope with a month of the year beginning with "January." Below the month, create a transaction register by labeling four columns: Date Paid, Description, Amount Paid, and Check Number. Immediately, when you get a bill in the mail, place it into an envelope based on the month you plan to pay the bill. As you pay each bill, instantly record payment information in your column register for that particular month.

☙ **Handling mail**—To reduce the amount of junk mail you receive, allocate a specific location where you place and open mail. This location should have a shredder and recycle bin nearby. Immediately discard or shred junk mail, flyers, catalogs, and non-essential literature. Place bills in your bill organizer, and recycle the outer envelopes. Place mail that requires a written response in your mail inbox or in your grab-and-go folder (discussed earlier).

I also implore you to contact the Direct Marketing Association (DMA) and have your name removed from junk mail and phone solicitation lists produced by companies that subscribe to their mail and telephone preference services. The form is available at the DMA website located at: www.dmachoice.org. There you'll also find an online tool to help you tailor your mail preferences to match your interests. If someone is under your care or if a family member has passed away, the DMA choice site will allow you to register to have mail solicitations stopped for them.

While getting rid of unwanted junk mail, get rid of those pre-approved credit cards or insurance offers by requesting to be removed from appearing on direct marketing lists obtained from the main credit reporting agencies. Visit: www.optoutprescreen.com, or call 888-5OPTOUT (888-567-8688).

☙ **Handling magazines**—If you have a lot of newspapers, magazines, and catalogs, clip out the articles or advertisements that interest you. Keep them organized in a folder or a binder with sheet protectors—sectioned off by dividers representing your different areas of interest. If you can scan the articles or find the same or similar articles online, store those digital articles together in a content-management application like Evernote or OneNote. These applications are simple to use and allow you to save, organize, and retrieve electronic information and files using digital notebooks or meta-tags.

ख **Handling printed photos**—If you have tons of photos, toss photos you really don't like. Store the rest in an organized manner by investing in photo storage boxes. This makes it easier to classify photos by date or by special event. If you have photos you want to share, keep them in photo albums with acid-free pages—designed to protect photographs from rapid deterioration over time. Another way to share and make memories more meaningful is to create photo scrapbooks for yourself and family members. Investing in a digital camera or using a smartphone to take pictures minimizes the number of printed photos that need to be stored. With digital photos you can immediately share photos online, create digital art galleries, or create digital photo books of your family's favorite memories, pictures, or artwork without taking up a lot of space

ख **Handling school work**—At the end of each school year, minimize your child's artwork or school work by selecting the best of the best or that which has more significance to your child. Store the selected items in a self-decorated memory box. Some items, including artwork, can be scanned to preserve the memories and save space; however, I have found that most kids' art projects are too large, too bulky, and too glittery to do anything but display it, box it up, or snap a picture of it (and toss it).

◊ **Handling books**—Maintain control of books by having regular book swaps with friends who enjoy reading or getting a library card. You can also download e-books to a computer, tablet, or digital reader. A digital reader can be purchased for around $100 and pays for itself over time. Digital books on average are cheaper than hard or soft-cover books because there are no printing or delivery costs—making it an eco-friendly alternative to paper-copy books. Nor do you have to worry about making more space in your already over-populated bookshelf; several e-books can be stored on a single device or application.

If you have not cracked or referenced a book in five to seven years, consider letting it go. Donate the books that are in good condition to nursing homes, hospitals, non-profit ministries, or support groups. Another way to maintain control of book clutter is to use other methods for obtaining information, like the Internet.

Digital Clutter

Digital clutter was not as big a deal when I first published this book. Sure we had to deal with some unanswered emails and archived emails in our inboxes and maybe a few documents stored on disks, but that's nothing compared to what we deal with today. Besides emails and documents there are friends, followers, photos, songs, books, movies, apps, and so on.

In keeping with our decluttering process, ask yourself: "Is my digital clutter a possession problem, a resource problem, or both?" If it's a possession problem, examine how much storage space you are consuming and then analyze how much storage space is reasonable to store your needed files and active applications. If it's a resource problem, evaluate how you process and organize digital content. Is there a specific time each day, set aside, for checking and responding to your emails? Are you storing the same file in multiple locations?

To minimize and organize your digital clutter, here are a few basic ideas for conquering digital clutter in four major areas:

> ଊ **Handling email**—Begin by scaling down your email accounts; try to limit them to no more than three. Do this by identifying the purpose of each email account and whether similar accounts can be combined. It's reasonable for an individual to have a personal account, a business account, and a miscellaneous account for subscribing to newsletters and posting to newsgroups or other public places. Then have all your email accounts forwarded to a single email account or configure your email system or smartphone to receive mail from multiple accounts into a centralized destination. .

Although you can use the search tool to find a specific email, creating folders helps to keep your email box organized and your inbox folder clutter-free. The names of your folders can be based on life roles (parent, friend, homemaker, worker, shopper, taxpayer, etc.); or functional areas (Career Management, Financial Management, Family Management, Project Management, etc.); or customized to fit the type of emails you accumulate.

Manage your email inbox by ensuring your junk email or spam filter is turned on. This will send email tagged as spam to your junk or spam folder, so you only have to be concerned with legitimate emails. Living in a mobile society, most of us are able to read and respond to important email immediately throughout the day.

However, it's helpful to designate quiet time (twenty to thirty minutes) each day to respond to emails that require some thought and consideration. You'll also want to set aside time each week or every other week to do some email housekeeping:

- review, then delete emails in your junk email folder;
- manually delete emails in the sent items folder;
- read and respond to overlooked emails;
- make sure event or appointment emails have been posted to your calendar;
- and create templates to quickly respond to emails that are similar in nature.

A final suggestion for managing your email is to automate your email application to send certain types of incoming mail to an email folder that you specify. For example, you can specify that email containing the name of your child's teacher be routed to a parent folder.

ය **Handling Electronic Documents, Files, Folders**— If you have tons of electronic documents and files—paper clutter in electronic form, use the same process for sorting and organizing paper clutter. You'll still need to ask yourself: "Do I need this?" If the answer is no, begin deleting files you no longer need and folders with nothing saved in it. Consider moving files you are not ready to delete into an archive folder so your most used documents are easier to locate and retrieve. Next, develop a folder structure that matches either your paper filing system or the type of information you will be accumulating. Please make sure the folders have descriptive names that represent its contents. Here's a snippet of my folder structure:

📁 *My Archives* folder is for storing old files I may need to reference someday.
📁 *My Working* folder is a temporary place for holding documents, scripts, and image files I am currently working on and need quick and easy access to.
📁 *My Downloads* folder is my default location for files and applications that I've downloaded from the web.
📁 *My Projects* folder contains subfolders for all the long-term projects I've been working on.
📁 *My Documents* folder is the default operating system document folder that contains subfolders that somewhat match my paper filing system.

Two other default folders that I use are *My Pictures* and *My Music*. A rule of thumb that I have regarding organizing electronic documents is never to have subfolders more than three levels deep and to keep the number of folders that I use at each level to around seven, definitely no more than ten.

Protecting Your Identity

With the increased use of social media and computers in general to shop and bank online. It's important to minimize your risk of becoming a victim of identity theft. An obvious first step is not to post personal identifying information (PII), such as your Social Security number or your driver's license number, on social media sites (this includes your phone number and full birth date). Second, ensure that any business, association, or person requiring your full birth date, Social Security number, account numbers, or driver's license number is legitimate. Third, avoid giving out your personal information via phone or email unless you initiate contact.

When submitting PII online, make sure the site is legitimate. Look for an official logo, a listing of credentials, or a statement of site authenticity. Ensure a lock icon appears in the *address* or *status* bar and the website's address starts with *https://* instead of *http://*. The *s* means the page is secure, so your information will be sent over the Internet encrypted.

More rigorous steps to protect your personal information involve shredding old documents containing any portion of your personal information and examining your credit report from each consumer reporting agency—Equifax, Experian, and TransUnion—once every six months. Visit: www.annualcreditreport.com for details on how to obtain a free credit report.

Is Your Kitchen Out of Kilter?

Most people can honestly say that the kitchen is the heart and soul of a home. It gets more usage by more people than any other area of the home. The kitchen—not the living room or family room—is the gathering place for eating, conversing, playing games, doing homework, reading the newspaper, and sorting the mail. It was that way for me growing up and continues to be that way for many households. So it stands to reason that the kitchen can quickly become cluttered.

Hopefully, you have taken steps to eliminate any paper clutter in the kitchen using the guidelines discussed earlier. In this section, we are more concerned with what is lurking or lingering in our refrigerators, cabinets, drawers, and pantries.

Apply principle #1 by taking a long, hard look at your kitchen. Analyze what is causing your kitchen clutter. Is it a possession problem, a resource problem, or both? If it helps, refer to the list of kitchen eyesores you made at the beginning

Step 5: Conquering Your Clutter

of this step; this will aid in identifying what is causing the bulk of your clutter. Write your thoughts in the space provided below.

_____
_____
_____
_____

Get your boxes ready. You will start by visually dividing your kitchen into four working sections. Since most kitchens are square or rectangular, the division would produce four equal squares or rectangles. The working sections will allow you to conquer your kitchen in a more manageable fashion. My suggestion is to take one section at a time, spending about an hour a day decluttering.

Use cardboard boxes to temporarily hold items you want to transfer to a new location, and try to get rid of the things you plan to donate right away—to keep clutter down to a minimum.

Using principle #2, let's attack this section by implementing the following steps to declutter:

❑ Organize cabinets or drawers by pulling everything out of each of them. Clean or wipe down the space being organized, then immediately decide the fate of its contents. Sell or donate things that are not used very often or have not been used in over two years; do the same for those items that you only need one of; and trash broken items or electronic items you've neglected to have repaired.

❑ Organize the refrigerator or pantry items by trashing the obvious (moldy and spoiled food). Next, look for the expiration date on cans, boxes, and jars—trash anything with an expired date. Consider donating unopened canned goods and boxed foods, and if you have multiple packages of the same item opened, consider combining them into one box.

❏ Organize your kitchen space by following an important organizational rule of thumb: *store items in close proximity to where they will be used.* I keep my cooking and baking items close to where I prepare my food. In addition, my utensils are stored in a drawer nearby.

❏ Another organizational rule of thumb is to *group like items together.* I group together the following items: baking items, cooking items, utensils, glassware, Tupperware, seasonal items, and canned goods—which are categorized by type (vegetables, fruits, soups, and sauces).

Applying principle #3, here are some ideas for organizing your kitchen and minimizing future clutter:

- Use containers inside your cabinets to group items together. Containers can be used for storing small envelopes and packets of cereals, soups, mixes, and condiments.

- Need more cabinet or counter space? Consider a ceiling rack to hang pots and pans, or have your microwave installed over the stove.

- Use drawer dividers for utensils, including cooking utensils. Drawer dividers are also great for organizing miscellaneous items like: small tools, rubber bands, pens, and so on.

- Use vertical dividers in your pantry or lower cabinets to separate groups of items—for example, cookie sheets from your pizza and cake pans.

Have fun creating your own or adjusting the ideas given above to generate creative kitchen solutions that work for you and your family.

Another's Clutter

Whether it's your spouse, parent, roommate, or child, at some point in your life, you may be forced to deal with another's clutter. First, begin by dealing with your own clutter. There's nothing more disturbing than trying to point out the speck in someone else's eye, and you have a plank in your own eye (see Luke 6:42).

Second, try talking to the person and explain to them how their clutter makes you feel. If communicating your feelings yields negative or passive results, reframe from nagging. Be creative, offer to help, or to replace the items that you consider an eyesore with something you both can live with. Consider compromising; you give up something, and they give up something in return.

I have a dear friend (who I will call Sharon) who has been dealing with her husband's clutter since the day she married him. She was thankful for having found a wonderful Christian man (who I will call George) and for having the privilege of combining two fully furnished households. However, the clutter was taking a toll on her. She had hoped that she and George could work together to decide what would be kept or given away, but her attempts to get him to relinquish any of his possessions proved unfruitful. George was perfectly content with boxes stacked in the garage or basement and having large pieces of furniture awkwardly sitting in whichever room he could find space. Sharon was used to open space, and while single, she had refused to buy a complete bedroom set because it took up too much space in her one-bedroom apartment. On the other hand, George couldn't walk by a corner of the house without planning to fill it with a corner shelf, an artificial plant, or a decorative chair.

To accommodate George's things and make more space in their new home, Sharon gave away a lot of her own things—thinking her actions would spur George to do the same. To the contrary, she just made more space for him to keep building onto the clutter he already had. George did not understand Sharon's need for order.

When Sharon and I finally got the opportunity to talk about her situation, she had given up and succumbed to the clutter around her. By this time, she had pockets of her own clutter around the house—which George, ironically, began to complain about. As I talked with her, I tried to help her understand that she could not control her husband's clutter habits; she could only control her response to what was happening around her. It was up to her to find a godly solution to their clutter that did not involve changing anyone other than herself, but still give her the peaceful environment she craved.

To my surprise, Sharon talked with her husband, and they defined a space in their new home where she could create her own clutter-free oasis. Unbeknownst to her at the time, George was also spending time in her clutter-free haven and eventually realized the effect his cluttered environment was having on him (not her)!

Although Sharon's solution eventually helped pave the way for a clutter-free home, you might not get the same ending as Sharon. However, I encourage you to seek God's best in whatever environment He has placed you in and with whom he has placed you there with.

Scaling Down Collectibles

First of all, if your collectibles have any value, they are not lying on the floor or stored in boxes around the house.

Collectibles are meant to be displayed, which leads to my second point. Unless you have the space for everything you collect and can give each item a home, limit what you collect. Instead of purchasing everything in a series, make it more meaningful by collecting specific items within that series.

People were really into Beanie Babies in the mid-to-late nineties. I know people who purchased every single beanie baby for a while—thinking they would make a profit off of them. Then, there were people who only purchased the bears, dogs, or rabbits because they did not have a lot of space to house the entire collection, and that particular type of beanie appealed to them. Who do you think has regrets now?

I enjoy collecting Hallmark ornaments; however, to keep my collection to a minimum, I have limited myself to purchasing one Christmas ornament yearly. The ornament usually reflects something special about my year: a challenge I faced and overcame, a major event I supported, a goal I achieved, or an experience that gave me a new perspective on life.

Be selective in what you collect. Unless you are positive it will make you money in the long run or provide you with something in return for the space it's taking up and the resources you're using to maintain it, save your money!

If your collectibles are frustrating and overwhelming you, it might be time to scale down. Calm down; everything doesn't have to go! Select from your collectibles those items that you really like or have meaning to you and let the rest go. Make some money by having a garage sale or selling your collectibles at a flea market or online. Better yet, let someone else sell your collectibles for you by putting them in a thrift shop or a consignment shop.

If you are having trouble letting go of your collectibles, reflect briefly on what God gave up. "He who did not spare His own Son, but delivered Him up for us all, how shall He not with Him also freely give us all things?" (Romans 8:32). God gave up His most prized possession, the most precious gift of all, Jesus Christ, for us.

Toy Clutter

I definitely know what it is like trying to manage toy clutter. There was a time when I thought toys would keep my sons so busy it would give me time to get things done around the house—that tactic failed to work. They still wanted my time, energy, and attention, and I was still the one cleaning up, picking up, and putting the toys away—which left less time to enjoy the kids and less time to get things done. So you can imagine why I initially thought my problem was a resource problem of: lack of time.

However, after analyzing my situation, I realized I had a possession problem of guilt. The guilt of having to work outside the home put me in a place where I bought toys to make up for the lost time with my kids. Not focusing on the fact that toys will not and cannot compensate for me spending quality time with them, nor could it justify me working. I work to help provide the basic necessities for my family; anything more than that is a want.

Like me, you may have initially considered your toy clutter to be a resource problem instead of really looking into the heart of the matter. Maybe you live by a busy intersection and would feel more comfortable if your child played inside, so you buy toys to keep him safe and entertained. Perhaps she's the only child, so you shower her with toys so she won't get bored. Unless we get balance and order in this area, we will produce children who are "now seekers." Children who find it difficult to be patient and wait on God's best—they want, what they want, now!

Step 5: Conquering Your Clutter

You might not see them kicking or screaming or throwing a tantrum—which could be a major warning sign for you. But in years to come, you might see your daughter marry the first man that asks her because she wants to be married, now! Or you might see your son using his first credit card to make a down payment on a car because he doesn't have the patience to wait until he saves enough money.

If you have emotional issues tied to buying toys, it's time to look at the consequences and the effect it might have on your children. It's vital that we, as parents, cultivate the attitude that our children should have toward things.

Let us get back on course by applying principle #1. Take a long, hard stare at the toys around the house. Attempt to truthfully analyze what is causing your toy clutter. Write your thoughts in the space provided below:

_____
_____
_____
_____

If you have your boxes, find a place to start and apply principle #2. Attack the clutter by searching the entire house for those toy hubs. If you have young children, it may be a good idea to declutter while they are asleep or not at home. Older children will have a better understanding of the process and will be able to help.

This is also a prime opportunity to teach your children about giving. Explain to them that other boys and girls will be blessed by their charitable toy donations and that "It is more blessed to give than to receive" (Acts 20:35).

Now, where were we? Back to decluttering; pick up each toy and quickly decide its fate. Toss toys that are broken and games that have missing pieces. Donate toys your child has outgrown or does not like to play with anymore.

Now that you have minimized the toy clutter, take aim by applying principle #3 to further eliminate toy clutter and to bring order to the toys that have survived your ruthless rampage.

Before you begin, realize that tools used to organize your child's room should be easy for them to manipulate and within their physical reach. It is also beneficial to use clear containers and open storage bins so they can see what is in them. Add some fun to organizing by allowing your child to decorate the containers with pictures or words describing its contents.

Establishing Guidelines

Order can be taught, but the prerequisite is: "Everything must have a home." Teach your child how to clean up after herself once she is done playing. Establish rules of conduct in each room your child frequents; this can be as simple as requiring him to clean up one area before playing in another area of the house. Other suggestions for minimizing clutter might be to establish guidelines for buying toys.

Here are ten questions I try to keep in mind when buying toys for the children in my life that I love and want to bless:

- Does the toy fall within my moral guidelines?
- Do I have the space for it?
- Does it provide educational value, or will she learn from it?
- Will it foster his creativity and imagination?
- How long (to what age) will he be able to use this toy?
- Can she share it with other children?

- Will it keep her preoccupied for at least twenty to thirty minutes daily or on a frequent basis?
- Does it provide physical exercise?
- Will the toy be obsolete soon?
- Why am I buying this toy? Has he earned it via chores, grades, or appropriate behavior?

Our heavenly father loves to bless us, but He doesn't give us everything we want. Contentment is cultivated when children have fewer things to play with. Most children will find pleasure in playing with a box, plastic jug, or some other disposable item lying around the house and have a ball! So if you find it difficult to say *no* to your child, ask yourself: what will overindulging my child now, produce years from now?

Step 5: *Your Daily Call to Order*

Chapter Comments:

If you have reached this point in your journey and have taken steps to eliminate some of the clutter in your home, give yourself a pat on the back. The Christian walk takes commitment and dedication, as does shedding yourself of the physical clutter in your home.

Below is a list of simple organization steps worth implementing to keep clutter down. If applied on a regular basis, these suggestions will help you maintain some semblance of balance and order in your home.

- Spend a few minutes daily or nightly tidying up and putting things away.

- Keep a donation bag near the front door. Whenever you encounter things you no longer need or want, stuff them in the bag to be taken to Goodwill monthly or bimonthly.

- Schedule time as needed to file papers; clean out your closets, cabinets, and drawers; and handle other items that tend to create clutter eyesores.

- Establish a home for everything you own. If what does not have a home, consider getting rid of it.

- Frequently analyze what still ends up scattered about the house. It may be necessary to try several different solutions or processes before you discover what works best for you.

Chapter Questions:

Group Discussion

1. How does clutter hinder our effectiveness for God?
2. Read Chronicles 29:11-12. What does the Bible say about our possessions?
3. Read Philippians 4:11-12; 1 Timothy 6:17-19. What challenge does Paul give to those who are consumed by their possessions?
4. Read Deuteronomy 10:14; Psalm 24:1; 1 Corinthians 10:26. What does God say about our possessions?

Personal Reflection

5. How closely does the interior and exterior organization of your home represent the way you feel or view yourself?
6. What are your reasons for wanting to simplify your life?
7. What is your vision for your home?

Step 5: Conquering Your Clutter 149

8. Do you believe you need things to be happy?

Chapter Assignments:
- **Challenge 1**: Make a list of the clutter eyesores in each room in your home.
- **Challenge 2**: Respond to end of chapter questions.
- **Challenge 3**. Prepare for decluttering by gathering together your boxes, containers, trash bags, or a combination of all three.
- **Challenge 4**: Go through your eyesores list and conquer each hub of clutter using the triple "A" principle for decluttering.
- **Challenge 5**: Write the DMA and have your name removed from junk mail and phone lists.
- **Challenge 6**: Organize your file cabinet or accordion-style file folder to store your important papers.
- **Challenge 7**: Create your grab-and-go folder.
- **Challenge 8**: Gather your vital information and store it in a fire-proof box.
- **Challenge 9**: Conquer an area of digital clutter hindering your productivity.
- **Challenge 10**: Reward yourself for simplifying your life.
- **Challenge 11**: Think of some of the possessions God has entrusted to your care. List them and release them to God in prayer.
- **Extreme Challenge**: Go through your collectibles and consider scaling down.

Step 6

Evolving through Productive Pursuits

Therefore I run thus: not with uncertainty.
—1 Corinthians 9:26

*I*magine for a moment you've been transported back into time; of all the places you could have been taken, you've been beamed back to your senior year in high school. Of all the faces you'd like to see, you're sitting face-to-face with your guidance counselor.

While sitting in your guidance counselor's office, you're gazing out the window and squirming in your chair while she searches for your academic folder. When she finds it, she takes her seat and clears her throat, signaling the beginning of a repetitive lecture—one most seniors are familiar with. Then, with fire in her eyes and excitement in her voice—as if that's supposed to motivate you—she begins to bombard you with legitimate questions you are not ready to address:

"What do you want to do with your life?"
"When do you plan to do it?"
"Where do you plan to do it?"
"How do you plan to do it?"

If her words frightened you back then, they shouldn't at this juncture in your life. You are older now, and these questions can no longer be avoided, including the crucial question, "Why?" Your passion or motivation for wanting to do what you have chosen to do. Frequently, you should reflect on these questions to ensure that the intimate pieces that make up who you are, are not out of alignment with God.

At this leg of your journey, there is no picking up, cleaning up, or straightening up. It is time for a physical break as you find a comfortable spot in your home to reflect on the intimate affairs of being you. I am referring to all those things about you that have directly impacted where you are now and where you intend to be (such as your circumstances, talents, attitude, thoughts, words, passions, and character). All those things that should be changing, maturing, or evolving through productive pursuits.

Productive pursuits are lifelong personal pursuits that can be birthed and rebirthed every day. If you think it's too late for you, think about Sarah (Abraham's wife), whose old barren womb was opened to bring forth Isaac (see Genesis 21:1-2)—reminding us that any age can birth miracles. Then think about Paul's words, "…Though outwardly we are wasting away, yet inwardly we are being renewed day by day" (2 Corinthians 4:16, NIV).

There will always be wisdom to glean from deepening our understanding of ourselves and polishing to do to expand our love and service toward one another. Productive pursuits are endless as long as we have breath.

In Pursuit of Brighter Days

Daily, you are presented with the chance to be better and to do better than yesterday. However, no one can control what you decide to do with the challenges you face and the opportunities life presents. God has given you free will. He has set before you life and death, blessings and curses, and desires that you choose life—which is the opportunity to live a life that is pleasing to Him (see Deuteronomy 30:19).

You might have gotten off to a slow start by not being able to attend the best schools. Maybe your physical condition limits what you can or cannot do. Perhaps you were abused physically or verbally as a child, which has tremendously impacted where you are today. If only one person has defied the odds, there is no reason why you cannot be the second or even pave the way for others by being the first.

Joseph's faith sustained him as he endured being rejected and sold by his ten brothers into slavery. In addition, he spent time in prison for a crime he did not commit. However, with the Spirit of God in him and on him, he became highly regarded as governor of Egypt and saved a nation from perishing during a seven-year famine (see Genesis 37-41). I am also reminded of Nelson Mandela, who spent over twenty years behind bars for fighting against apartheid. Roughly five years after his release in 1990 by F.W. de Klerk—whom he shared the 1993 Nobel Peace Prize with—he became the first black President of South Africa.[1]

In his book, *Lincoln On Leadership*, Donald T. Phillips describes Abraham Lincoln as one of the most remembered presidents of the United States. At the age of nine his mother died. In addition, there was an estrangement between him and his father—who never quite understood him.[2] He was teased heavily as a child for being "gangly and gawky-looking."[3] He tried a variety of careers until he found his niche in politics.

After failing numerous times at getting into public office, Lincoln ran again in 1858, this time losing the Senate seat to Stephen A. Douglas. Although depressed and discouraged, had Lincoln succumbed to another failed attempt to hold a public office, he would not have run and won the presidency two years later.[4] Author Napoleon Hill said of Lincoln, "Lincoln had that rare trait of being able to turn on more willpower instead of quitting when the going was hard and success was not in sight."[5]

I am also reminded of Helen Keller and Wilma Rudolf; two women who overcame insurmountable physical handicaps to achieve goals you and I would probably have deemed impossible for them.

The Power of Binding

Whether the example is male or female, the Bible reminds us that "Whatever you bind on earth will be bound in heaven, and whatever you loose on earth will be loosed in heaven" (Matthew 16:19). I believe this was such an important concept Jesus wanted His disciples to grasp and understand, that He repeated it a couple of chapters later in Matthew 18:18.

> *Whatever you bind on earth will be bound in heaven, and whatever you loose on earth will be loosed in heaven.*
>
> *—Matthew 16:19*

To bind something is to prevent it from having the ability to move freely about and to reign over your life. When you loose something, you give it the freedom to move about with surety and security. In other words, you have been given the keys to the Kingdom of Heaven; your future gets brighter when you decide to bind self-defeating attitudes, behaviors, feelings, and thoughts that mock your true nature. This could be the spirit of abuse, insecurity, ignorance, fear, adultery, unforgiveness, loneliness, or whatever else has you bound.

Start by getting the help you may need and deserve. Seek out a counselor or a support group in your local area. If none are available or it's too costly, find out what services your local church offers. In addition, read biographies and testimonies of women and men who have had similar struggles and how God delivered and helped them.

A practice that has helped me deal with difficult and painful situations is journaling my feelings and then releasing God's Word on my circumstances. God's words are riddled throughout the Bible. God's Word says, "Let not your heart be troubled, neither let it be afraid" (John 14:27). His truth reveals that I am the righteousness of God in Jesus Christ (see 2 Corinthians 5:21). His promises remind me that I am never alone (see Matthew 28:20).

I want to encourage you to find ways to positively express yourself—allowing you to release the hurt and pain bottled up inside you. Sing, dance, write poetry, write letters, journalize, draw, paint, compose,... Solomon journaled, David composed, and Paul wrote letters. In their words, you can hear their concerns and understand why they were feeling discouraged, defeated, depressed, and drained at times. However, before completing most of their works, they had found God's peace. They had discovered that through positive venting (expressing themselves in a peaceful manner), they were able to loosen the ropes that had them tightly bound and eventually be set free by focusing on God rather than their feelings or circumstances.

- David bellowed: "You have filled my heart with greater joy than when their grain and new wine abound" (Psalm 4:7, NIV).

- From a prison cell, Paul said: "Rejoice in the Lord always; Again I will say rejoice!" (Philippians 4:4).

- Solomon, one of the wisest men of his time, found peace in the words: "Fear God and keep his commandments, for this is the whole duty of man" (Ecclesiastes 12:13, NIV).

📖 What one thing can you start doing today to improve the quality of your life?

Testimonies of Strength and Courage

In November of 1873 Horatio Gates Spafford's four daughters were drowned in raging water, when the ship they were vacationing on, the S.S. Ville Du Havre, collided with another ship. Over two hundred people died in that fatal crash. His wife Anna survived.

While traveling by the spot where his daughters had drowned, on his way to England to comfort his wife, the peace of God came over him and he was able to write the following lines to the well-known gospel hymn, *It Is Well with My Soul*.[6]

> When peace, like a river, attendeth my way,
> When sorrows like sea billows roll;
> Whatever my lot, Thou hast taught me to say,
> It is well, it is well, with my soul.[7]

We will have difficulties no matter where we are in our Christian walk. The key is not to be bound by our struggles. I asked Christine—a special friend of mine and a mighty woman of God in my eyes—who has been fighting cancer for about

Step 6: Evolving through Productive Pursuits

five years, to share with you and me how she continues to model grace, dignity, and faith in God despite her circumstances.

> *Dear Reader, whatever your circumstances in life, you should always have faith in God. God is always there to lead you in the right direction. He is there for you always, as long as you keep Him in your heart and talk with Him every day. It took me forty years to realize this, but I am so glad I have reached this pinnacle in my life before I have breathed my last breath on this earth.*
>
> *I have been fighting the spread of cancer in my body for the last five years. Of course, I had to stop and wonder: "Why me?" I was thirty-eight when I was diagnosed; my youngest child was one year old, and the entire family was devastated. I asked God, "Why me? What did I do to deserve this?"*
>
> *I was alone when I first got the news and cried as I left the doctor's office. I drove for about a mile before I parked the car, in a grocery store parking lot, to contemplate my future. I asked God to guide me in the right direction and to not leave me at this crucial time in my life.*
>
> *Again, I had to ask, "Why me?" I always felt like my family was cursed. My mom died in 1990 at the age of forty-nine, and my father died in 1998 at the age of fifty-seven. All my brothers and sisters felt that we were destined to die at a young age also. My oldest sister died in a car accident on New Years Day 2005; she was only forty-three years old.*

Still, I wanted to know, "Why me?" Was it because growing up we were not raised in the Church? Was it because my father was an alcoholic who beat his wife and kids? Was it because I had never established a relationship with God? I believe the latter was my answer.... I did not know God. In order for me to see and believe in Him fully, cancer had to start growing inside me. God could have allowed those around me to suffer to test my love for Him, but He knew (like Job) that I needed a stronger fight.

I have been stripped to the core, losing one breast and my hair; in addition, my hands and feet have been discolored.... God saw that I prayed only when necessary, and I didn't speak to Him daily like He wanted me to. To wake me up, He allowed everything that is so cherished by females to be taken away from me.

Now, I fight with a smile on my face because I know that I am not alone. My anchors are the verses: Roman 5:1-2 and Isaiah 60:1-3, reminding me that God's grace will be manifested in me and God's glory will be seen on me.

Every individual is different, so the path to God will not be the same for everyone. You have to continually draw courage from the Word of God to stay focused and prosper as a Christian.

Fighting cancer with chemotherapy and radiation is like battling the devil every day; yet my dosages have God mixed in them, so I believe the medicine in me is full of love.

In my five-year battle with cancer I have rarely thrown up, that is because God is holding

Step 6: Evolving through Productive Pursuits

> *everything down for me.... When you see me, I do not look sick; that is God's grace shining through me—which gets me up and going better than coffee. I hate that I had to suffer to see the light, so I always tell people not to wait to embrace God. Instill His word in your kids at a young age so God will grow with them instead of watching from afar.*
>
> *God stripped me to the core, but now He is in me and blessing me with His Word. That is why I can wear my wig proudly ... and embrace the Lord with a lasting faith for His Word.*
>
> *Your Friend in Christ, Christine Baity*

Life will have its challenges. There will be moments when you will feel utterly deserted, confused about the twists and turns your life has taken to bring you to your present circumstances. Sometimes, your circumstances are to help you experience the fullness and depth of God's love in a different light of understanding. Sometimes, circumstances exist so that you may be the salt and light for others. As Christians, we are not exempt from pain and suffering. Jesus suffered on the cross for our sins, and Hebrews 4:14-16 reminds us that because He suffered and was tempted, He is able to comfort and help us in our moment of need. So, we are not without a God who does not understand our plight.

Whatever has you bound, it is all right to cry out to God. As the psalmist said: "Weeping may endure for a night, but joy comes in the morning" (Psalm 30:5). Believe that God has a supernatural way of fashioning your life and life's circumstances, to provide you with a comforting peace that He is your:

- Jehovah-Jireh (the Lord your provider),
- Jehovah-Ropheka (the Lord your healer),
- Jehovah-Rohi (the Lord your Shepherd).

In Pursuit of Self Knowledge

I read somewhere that: "Self-knowledge is one common goal that will help everyone achieve personal success." Why? Knowing yourself provides you with the information and tools you need to better yourself and, most importantly, better understand yourself.

The first year I got married, daily I tried to beat my husband home from work so that I could sneak a cat nap and be refreshed by the time he got home from the office. I wanted to have the energy for the things he wanted to do. My husband, unlike me, was and still is a sociable and high-energy person. He is always ready to go someplace, visit someone, or do something with little or no notice. On the other hand, I was and still am the opposite—not as energetic nor spontaneous. Going home and rejuvenating after a long day at work was and still is an essential element in maintaining my sanity. My husband didn't and doesn't need that.

I remember trying to step outside my comfort zone to be more like my husband. I took up activities and ministries that—as I look back—were actually more suited for his personality and spiritual gifts, not mine. I assumed since we were married that his ministries would become my ministries. I quickly learned that if you are married, God's design for a husband and wife is to complement and bless one another, as opposed to trying to copy, compete, or change one another. According to popular authors and influential psychologists Dr. Henry Cloud and Dr. John Townsend, "Complementing means bringing different perspectives, talents, abilities, experiences, and other gifts to the relationship and forming a partnership."[8] Similar in the Body of Christ, God has made each of us uniquely different, and from God's Word we know that striving to be anyone other than who God created us to be breeds resentment, envy, jealousy, and covetousness.

Furthermore, it is not God's desire for us to vacillate from one extreme to the other. There will be things that we have to do and need to do to be of service to our Lord, our family, the Church, and our community. Still, there will also be things that we will love to do and will feel compelled to do, because God has placed in our hearts a passion for the cause, a people, a task, an activity, or a ministry.

Assessing Your Strengths and Weaknesses

Let us begin our pursuit of self-knowledge by looking at our strengths and weaknesses.

If you have ever been on a job interview, at some point in the interviewing process, you were probably asked: "What are your strengths? What are your weaknesses?" If you are having trouble responding to these questions, you should take some time to reflect on how unique God made you.

To start, on a sheet of paper folded in half length-wise, list what you feel are your strengths or positive assets. This can vary from skills acquired from formal education or specialized training to personal traits. Your personal traits are attributes that uniquely identify who you are. Examples of personal traits are: amicable, dependable, comical, conscientious, creative, generous, hard-working, intuitive, organized, persistent, responsible, or sociable. In addition, add significant contributions and achievements you have made and obstacles you have overcome. It may be helpful, under each asset, to identify why you believe it is a strength.

On the other half of your sheet of paper, list your not-so-positive traits. We all have them, whether we want to admit it or not. Knowing what they are gives you the opportunity to come up with positive solutions to address and overcome them.

Post your positive traits on your bedroom or bathroom mirror. Every morning—while primping your hair or putting on your make-up—review your list, repeating each positive trait aloud, starting with the words "I am blessed to be…" In the evening, visit the other side of your list and affirm the positive about each weakness. If you are disorganized, affirm that: "With God, I am getting better and better organized every day." If you are impatient, declare: "With God, I am gaining more patience daily." Then, take action to develop a weakness into a strength; act upon it daily to cultivate it.

By affirming the positive, you will begin to think and dwell on those things that reaffirm who you really are in Christ Jesus. In addition, you are feeding your subconscious mind with words that build-up, esteem, and inspire positive change.

I also encourage you to examine your strengths and weaknesses in light of the fruit of the Spirit. "The fruit of the Spirit is love, joy, peace, patience, kindness, goodness, faithfulness, gentleness and self-

> HE WHO LIVES WITH LITTLE PRAYER— HE WHO SELDOM READS THE WORD—HE WHO SELDOM LOOKS UP TO HEAVEN FOR A FRESH INFLUENCE FROM ON HIGH—HE WILL BE THE MAN WHOSE HEART WILL BECOME COLD AND BARREN.
>
> C.H. SPURGEON

control" (Galatians 5:22-23, NIV). Do you show love, patience, kindness, gentleness, and self-control toward others?

In evaluating your strengths and weaknesses in light of the fruit of the Spirit, take note of those qualities you already walk in and those qualities you should be walking in as God's child. Allow yourself to be naked in the spirit before God—transparent and open to receive His Wisdom, regarding improvements you need to make.

You may be strong in areas that others are weak, but the goal for every Christian—with the help of the Holy Spirit—is to be more like Jesus Christ, who walked in strength in each of the following arenas:

> ❧ **Love**—God is Love, and you know God if you have love for others (1 John 4:7-10). Love sacrifices; it chooses to faithfully act in a caring, unselfish, and sacrificial manner so others might see the love of God in you.
>
> ❧ **Joy**—your heart is filled with praise and thanksgiving despite your circumstances, struggles, and trials.
>
> ❧ **Peace**—Isaiah 26:3 says of God, "You will keep him in perfect peace, Whose mind is stayed on You, Because he trusts in You." Peace comes when the heart and mind are focused on God, enabling you to remain calm and secure in your faith—despite what is happening in the world around you.
>
> ❧ **Patience**—able to weather the storm and wait on God with a positive attitude in any given situation.
>
> ❧ **Kindness**—Paul defined it well when he said: "And be kind to one another, tenderhearted, forgiving one another, even as God in Christ forgave you" (Ephesians 4:32).
>
> ❧ **Goodness**—even though no one is morally above reproach, you strive to do what is acceptable in the eyes of the Lord (Ephesians 5:10); sowing generosity.

- **Faithfulness**—God is faithful toward His children. As a Christian saved by grace, you are also called to be faithful (1 Corinthians 1:9). Faithfulness is an unwavering commitment to honor and glorify God.
- **Gentleness**—showing love and affection for others.
- **Self-Control**—able to hold back; or to refrain from reacting. Showing tolerance, discipline, and restraint in response to irritations.

Remember, affirming who you are, whose you are, and knowing where you are going is instrumental in binding the self-defeating attitudes and actions that are contrary to who you are in Christ Jesus.

In Pursuit of Character

While writing this book, I was blessed by a poem sent to me via email from a dear friend. The poem is called, "The Five Watches" by Frank Outlaw. This poem simplified for me the role one's thoughts and words can play in fulfilling one's destiny.

> Watch your thoughts — they become words
> Watch your words — they become actions
> Watch your actions — they become habits
> Watch your habits — they become character
> Watch your character — it becomes your destiny

Watch Your Thoughts

It is truly the information age when you can with the press of a few buttons, download any information you want, from music, to news, to email, or talk with anyone anywhere there's a wireless signal available—which is almost everywhere. If you can't afford the luxury of a gadget, and you live in the inner city, all you have to do is walk a block or two—or, in some cases, step outside your door—and you're barraged with massive billboard advertisements trying to influence your actions or reactions.

Likewise, it is almost impossible to turn on the television, tune into the radio, leaf through a magazine, surf the Internet, or step outside the confines of our homes without being a receptacle to all the influences this world has to offer.

All around us are influences trying to penetrate our thoughts and manipulate our minds, telling us how we should feel, think, act, or react. Why is such emphasis placed on the mind? Even though people tend to act based on feelings, the mind helps us distinguish between right and wrong, a truth or a lie—despite external persuasions. It's the mind that allows a person to make a heartfelt decision to accept Jesus Christ as their Lord and Savior then to present their body as a living sacrifice through which the righteousness of God is revealed (see Romans 12:1). It's the mind that allows us to be transformed, that we "may prove what is that good and acceptable and perfect will of God" (v. 2). It's the thoughts in our minds that fuels new business ventures; sparks ideas to fulfill life-long passions; and provides the means to: explore unknown territories, save and change lives, and revolutionize how things are done.

It's also the thoughts in our minds that have the ability to condemn us, put us down, and make us feel defeated, deflated, and discouraged. These negative thoughts can never be stopped, but they can be controlled. With the Holy Spirit, we have the ability and power to decide what to receive and what not to receive; what we will allow our minds to reflect and dwell on or what we will reject.

At times, the struggle that goes on in one's mind is similar to what Immaculée Ilibagiza experienced while hiding in a closet with five other women, fearing for her life. Her story of surviving the Rwanda holocaust is told in the book *Left To Tell*.

Praying silently for her life—while Hutu extremists raided the house she had sought refuge in—Satan tried to interrupt her prayers by planting negative thoughts in her mind, trying to get her to doubt the provision of God in a desperate time of need. Here is what she said the devil tried to get her to accept and her response:

> Why are you calling on God? Look at all of them out there... hundreds of them looking for you. They are legion, and you are one. You can't possibly survive—you won't survive. They're inside the house, and they're moving through the rooms.... They're going to find you, rape you, cut you, kill you!
>
> My heart was pounding.... I squeezed my eyes shut as tightly as I could to resist the negative thoughts... and silently prayed with all my might: God, in the Bible You said that You can do anything for anybody....[9]

Immaculée's focus on God enabled her to endure her circumstances. She said:

> I realized that my battle to survive this war would have to be fought inside of me. Everything strong and good in me—my faith, hope, and courage—was vulnerable to the dark energy. If I lost my faith, I knew that I wouldn't be able to survive. I could rely only on God to help me fight.[10]

She survived through faith, perseverance, and God's grace while thousands of innocent people were brutally killed.

Our circumstances might not be as trying or threatening physically, but mentally and spiritually, a war still exists. I can personally confess to having taken incidents or comments and blowing them up in my mind. The longer I meditated on the incident, the more worked up and emotional I got until it acted upon me or I acted upon it.

Like Immaculée, we must counter those negative thoughts with the truth of God's Word. In the Bible, Paul admonishes us to bring our thoughts under control by "…bringing every thought into captivity to the obedience of Christ" (2 Corinthians 10:5).

Since it's virtually impossible to hide from Satan's or society's influence, we must guard our minds with all diligence—just as we are told in Proverbs 4:23 to guard our hearts.

Guarding our minds and taking captive of our thoughts requires us to think like a soldier safeguarding his domain from anything that attempts to threaten or destroy part of the sanctuary of God—the mind. This means we are on guard against attempts by the enemy to plant seeds that are contrary to the truth of God's Word. Philippians 4:8 reminds us what to think on…

> *Finally, brethren, whatever things are true, whatever things are noble, whatever things are just, whatever things are pure, whatever things are lovely, whatever things are of good report, if there is any virtue and if there is anything praiseworthy—meditate on these things.*

Heed Your Words

Just as we should guard our minds and watch our thoughts, we should heed our words. John 6:63 says, "The words that I speak to you, are spirit, and they are life." If we think of our words as having life, then our words can strengthen, inspire, revive, and energize us. In addition, our words, once they are spoken have the ability to bring about that which was said, and can be so powerful as to affect the way we think about ourselves, and cause a person to take her life over hurtful words spoken.

If you accept the power of the spoken word, whatever type of words you speak about yourself—negative or positive—those words will try to attach themselves to you.

Can you imagine a reasonably healthy woman repeatedly saying to herself: "I'm so fat?" If her spoken words were visible you would see "fat" attached to her in cursive, in print, stamped, posted, and pasted—allowing others to clearly see what she thinks about herself; and because her words have power, they immediately begin to act as an adversary—dictating how she views and treats herself, and how others view and treat her.

If words—positive or negative—are spoken often enough, those words will penetrate our hearts and souls and cause us to act or behave based on what we believe to be true about ourselves. If you have been told or if you have told yourself repeatedly that you'll never amount to anything, you'll probably subconsciously try to live up to those expectations. A verse in Proverbs reminds us that "death and life are in the power of the tongue" (18:21).

To understand the power of the spoken word, let's visit the eleventh chapter of Mark, verse twenty-three says:

For assuredly, I say to you, whosoever says to this mountain, 'Be removed and be cast into the sea,' and does not doubt in his heart, but believes that those things he says will be done, he will have whatsoever he says.

Our words can move mountains!

So, how do you protect yourself from the spoken word (unconstructive criticism, negativity, and condemnation)?

Understand where the words are coming from. The words people speak have to do with the condition of their hearts and souls. Your words have to do with the state of your heart and soul. Just as you can be wounded by the words people say, people—including yourself—can be wounded by the words that you utter. "For out of the abundance of the heart the mouth speaks" (Matthew 12:34).

As your sister in Christ, I would rather you say nothing than speak curses upon yourself or toward another. There will be enough people in this world talking negatively about you—criticizing, backbiting, gossiping, and slandering—so it's imperative that you counter that with God's truth by speaking blessings to yourself. The Bible tells each of us regarding our spoken words: "For by your words you will be justified, and by your words you will be condemned" (v. 37).

📖 How have people's words affected you?

In Pursuit of Passion

Our thoughts and words are instrumental in building character, but what we *do* is just as essential. I'm not just referring to our habits but our passions that propel us into action or cause us to step up and out of our comfort zone. That inner passion within you that changes destinies—your destiny because you chose to make a difference and the destinies of others because what you chose to do positively impacted or will positively impact lives.

Passion for something energizes us, brings us fulfillment, and motivates us. Outside of our passions, the work may seem like something we have to do. Although as children of God, it is important to have passion for what we want to do and what we need to do. If we are honest, life is motivated by necessity for most of us instead of gratitude and the opportunity to serve. You get up in the morning and go to work because you have bills to pay. You go to school to get an education because you want a good-paying job. On the other hand, passion is motivated by a deep longing to make a difference in an area God has made dear to your heart.

Just as each of us is different from another, our passions are also different from those of our neighbors. In addition, there are positive passions and there are negative passions, and any longing in our heart that goes against the character of God, is not of God.

Jesus' passion here on earth was to see people delivered from demons, illnesses, and diseases, and to seek and save the lost from the tribe of Israel (Luke 19:10). Paul's passion was to preach the Gospel to the Gentiles (Galatians 1:15-16). Mother Teresa's passion was for the poor and needy in Calcutta, India. Martin Luther King Jr. was passionate about the social injustice experienced by Black Americans in the 1960s. God is passionate about having a relationship with us (Exodus 34:14) and seeing us come into the unity of the faith (Ephesians 4:13).

I love the Lord, and I have a heart for women. I also enjoy spending time with my family, organizing stuff, planning activities and events, writing, and learning new things—especially how to use technology to maintain a consistent level of work-life balance. In response to my passion, I have started small women's groups with close friends and neighbors, and created and sent out Christian newsletters via email to whoever would receive them. More and more, God began to press on my heart to write—as a ministry—help guides and materials dedicated to women's mental, physical, spiritual, and emotional growth and well-being. God has also placed a passion in *your* heart.

📖 What is God nudging *you* to do?

Step 6: Evolving through Productive Pursuits

Identifying Your Passion(s)

In identifying your passion(s), you will need an open mind to put aside any restrictions that have hindered you in the past. These restrictions might be money, time, duty, lack of confidence, or fear. Here are some scenarios to get you thinking about your God-given passion(s); be as specific as you can in answering each question.

1. If unlimited funds were given to you to support any cause you so desire, what cause would that be (e.g., fighting for social injustice, world poverty, the rights of the unborn child)? Why?

   _____
   _____
   _____

2. If you had an audience of non-judgmental listeners eager to hear anything you had to say, what topic would you be excited and passionate about sharing (consider your hobbies, skills, past experiences, talents, abilities, interests, focus, or giving your testimony)?

   _____
   _____
   _____

3. If you were to receive, as a gift, more time and energy in your day without any interruptions, what would you spend that extra time doing to positively impact or serve those around you?

   _____
   _____
   _____

4. If the sky was the limit, what specific group of people (men, women, preschoolers, pregnant teens, the homeless, etc.) would you enjoy serving? Why?

_____
_____
_____

5. What are you doing in your local church, at home, at school, or in your community that gives you peace, confidence, and self-assurance that you are making a difference and doing what God has called you to do?

_____
_____
_____

6. What one positive thing would you rather see happen than anything else (in your life, in your school, in your church, in your city, in your country, etc.)?

_____
_____
_____

7. Based on your answers, can you jot down what you believe the Lord is calling you to do? Pay close attention to the action verbs, nouns, and pronouns you used in your responses to the questions above.

_____
_____
_____

If you are having problems determining your passion(s), go to God in prayer and ask Him to reveal to you the passion(s) he has placed in your heart. Christ says in John 15:7, "If you abide in Me, and My words abide in you, you will ask what you desire, and it shall be done for you."

Next, pay attention to the people, causes, and activities that energize and excite you. Who says you can't mix your love of sports or scrapbooking with sharing the Gospel of Christ? Lastly, put yourself out there; find out what needs to be done in your local church or community and start serving. God is bound to honor your service by revealing the passion(s) He has placed within you. The sooner you start doing what God has equipped you to do, the more fulfilled you will feel.

Not Following Your Passion

Not following your passion is like never achieving a goal, which eventually produces regret. Jesus tells the parable of the loaned money in Matthew 25:14-30. He spoke of three men each who had received money from their master to invest according to their ability to handle it—so there was no excuse for feeling overwhelmed. Failure could only come from not putting forth an effort.

If we were to take a modern-day look at this story, talents could represent almost anything: our passions, our possessions, our time, or our skills and abilities. Whereas two of the servants doubled their talents (labored to bring forth an increase based on their gifts, skills, and abilities), the servant with the least amount of talent buried or refused to invest his talent for fear of losing it.

In the servant's defense, he might have been intimidated by the competition (the spiritual gifts, skills, and abilities of the other servants). However, instead of trying to improve upon what he had or even honor God by making the best with what he had, he chose to do nothing. He even took his disobedience a step further by burying his talent in the dirt—inadvertently showing his disregard for his master and his contempt for his talent. What's apparent here is that the servant did not understand that his present life would have eternal consequences. When this servant was confronted by his master, instead of immediately taking responsibility for being lazy, fearful, busy, or disobedient, he chose to shift the blame. He accused his master—the same loving and gracious person who trusted him with one talent—of being difficult. He said to his master, "Lord, I knew you to be a hard man ..." (v. 24). Then, he finally admitted that he was afraid and went and hid his master's talent in the ground (v. 25). But the disrespect did not end there. The same verse ends with the servant saying: "Look, there you have what is yours." As if his master should be satisfied with the fact that he is returning the talent that was given to him.

It's no surprise that the master was furious with his unprofitable servant and dealt harshly with him, calling him "wicked and lazy" and then casting him out into outer darkness (v. 30). What this parable and the following verses clearly illustrate is that God will call us to give an account of our life and how we used our talents ...

> *But why do you judge your brother? Or why do you show contempt for your brother? For we shall all stand before the judgment seat of Christ. For it is written: "As I live, says the LORD, Every knee shall bow to Me, And every tongue shall confess to God." So then each of us shall give account of himself to God (Romans 14:10-12).*

As wise servants, discovering and fulfilling our God-given passions should be an exciting endeavor, allowing us to expand the influence of God here on earth, and produce fruits that honor and glorify God.

In Pursuit of Wisdom

Just as we are to pursue our passions, we should also be in pursuit of wisdom. Wisdom begins with knowing, loving, and fearing the God we serve. Wisdom is applying God-given discretion to our daily lives, and it is the mind of God revealed unto those who diligently seek to please Him.[11]

In the book of Proverbs, wisdom has been compared to getting gold, being better than rubies, more profitable than silver, and obtaining wisdom is to love your soul.

So, who gives wisdom? The Bible says the Lord gives wisdom (Proverbs 2:6), and wisdom and might are His (Daniel 2:20), which cannot be compared to the wisdom of the world—for it was the wisdom of God that established the world (Jeremiah 10:12).

One who has wisdom is blessed; without it, one is subject to making foolish and costly decisions. Consider two women depicted in the book of Proverbs. As early as the second chapter of Proverbs, we are provided with a picture of the immoral woman, "the seductress who flatters with her words" (v. 16) and disdains wisdom and discretion. Then, at the end of the book—saving the best for last—we are introduced to a woman whom most of us uphold as a wise woman of God. The difference between these two women, beyond the obvious, is the fear of God. Proverbs 9:10 says, "The fear of the Lord is the beginning of wisdom, And the knowledge of the Holy One is understanding." The fear of God resulted in one woman responding positively to godly wisdom, whereas having no fear of God resulted in another woman responding negatively to godly wisdom.

The immoral woman, out of the foolishness of her heart (dependency on her own intellect, intuition, and wisdom) forsook the moral guidance and wisdom that was given to her probably by her elders, and with no fear of God, she turned her back on His commands (2:17)—choosing instead to be led astray by her own ungodly desires.

The actions of this foolish woman can only be described as godlessness. Author Max Lucado in his book, *In the Grip of Grace*, describes godlessness as follows:

> A life minus God. Worse than a disdain for God, this is a disregard for God. A disdain at least acknowledges his presence. Godlessness doesn't. Whereas disdain will lead people to act with irreverence, disregard causes them to act as if God were irrelevant, as if he is not a factor in the journey.[12]

To the contrary, walking upright before the Lord was evidence of the wise woman's reverential fear of Him. The actions of our wise woman of God prevented her from wanting to do anything that displeased, dishonored, and disrespected a God she stood in awe of. The Bible says in reverence to her due diligence to the things of God: "...a woman who fears the Lord, she shall be praised" (31:30). Her blessings for walking in wisdom:

- Her children call her blessed (v. 28).
- Her husband praises her (v. 28).
- She exceeds peers in the pursuit of excellence (v. 29).
- She reaps the fruit of what she has sown (v. 31).
- She is praised for her hard work and dedication—done to bring glory and honor to God (v. 31).

Gaining Godly Wisdom

The secret to obtaining godly wisdom is through cultivating a deep reverence for God. Respect for God comes as we frequently seek His face in prayer, strive to obey His commandments, and feed our soul with His Word by heeding

Step 6: Evolving through Productive Pursuits

Wisdom's called to: "Get wisdom! Get understanding!" (Proverbs 4:5).

James, the half-brother of Jesus said, "If any of you lacks wisdom, let him ask of God, who gives to all liberally and without reproach, and it will be given to him" (James 1:5). However, in all our asking, if we continue to ignore the wisdom of God contained in the Word of God, then we are asking in vain. The Bible is how God speaks to us. It is our manual for finding God's purpose and plan, and our significance in life. God's Word is unchanging; however, the richness of its transforming power is life-changing to the faithful reader. Jeremiah proclaimed of God's Word, "Your words were found, and I ate them, And Your word was to me the joy and the rejoicing of my heart" (15:16).

If you are new to the Body of Christ, commit to growing in your understanding of the Bible. If you have problems understanding the Bible, try a modern translation like the New International Version (NIV). Then, begin reading and meditating on a chapter a day in the New Testament—starting with the book of Matthew.

If you are a seasoned Christian, continue to "exercise yourself toward godliness" (1 Timothy 4:7). Just as the Gospel of Luke states that the boy Jesus grew in grace, wisdom, and favor (2:52), you are to also "grow in the grace and knowledge of your Lord and Savior Jesus Christ" (2 Peter 3:18), Here are some ideas to feed your soul with God's Word:

- Read at least one spiritually uplifting book monthly, quarterly, or frequently as time permits.

- Memorize one scripture a week.

- Find a specific topic in the Bible that interests you and do an extensive study in that area. Some ideas are: Women of the Bible, The Writings of Paul, The Book of Revelation, The Holy Spirit, The Fruit of the Spirit, or The Proverbs 31 Woman.

- Read and meditate on one proverb daily—read a chapter in Proverbs that corresponds with the date of the month. Highlight any verse that speaks to your heart, and consider doing a word-by-word study on that particular verse.

- Develop your leadership skills. Consider mentoring someone, leading a prayer group in your home, or teaching a Bible class at your local church.

What will you commit to doing to saturate yourself with the wisdom of God?

Gaining Worldly Wisdom

As believers, we are to walk in the Spirit of God by adopting an intolerance toward engaging in sinful and questionable behaviors or activities. As sinners saved by God's grace, this is a daily struggle. Paul, in his letter to the believers in Rome, reminds us to:

> ...not be conformed to this world, but be transformed by the renewing of [our minds], that [we] may prove what is that good and acceptable and perfect will of God (Romans 12:2, emphasis added).

The challenge for us is enjoying some of the things of the world without giving in to or embracing corrupt, worldly mindsets. Godly wisdom provides balance while safeguarding us from submerging ourselves into the world's ways. However,

Step 6: Evolving through Productive Pursuits

because we are in the world, there is knowledge that we have to obtain to be productive citizens of the world we live in.

We have to know and abide by the laws of our country. We need to know what is going on in the world to know who and what to pray for and about. We should know what is required of us and what to do on our jobs. It's important to know what is expected of us from our spouses, children, communities, and others. We should also strive to know ourselves better: our likes, dislikes, interests, hobbies, strengths, weaknesses, gifts, and talents.

Knowledge is powerful in the sense that knowledge enlightens; it has a way of ripping through the darkness to bring forth understanding when knowledge is used and obtained in a manner that is pleasing to God. Knowledge is so powerful that it has the potential to change a person's lot in life. As they develop themselves their earning potential increases and hopefully, they add value to the kingdom of God.

Gaining knowledge exercises the mind, and just like any muscle or organ of the body, the mind loses its ability to function properly if it is not used. According to A.J. Jacobs, author of *The-Know-It-All*, once you pass the age of twenty you lose on average 50,000 brain cells per day. The only way to prevent a significant loss of brain cells is to exercise your mind daily. Ideas for exercising your mind:

- Increase your vocational skills by returning to school, taking a course, reading books, studying trade journals, joining a professional association, or finding an occupational mentor.

- Develop your avocation by perfecting a hobby, doing volunteer work, or taking an interest in others (preferably those in your household, church, or community).

- Establish an uplifting reading program. Read books to help you reach your goals, attain your passions, and overcome your weaknesses.

- Keep yourself interesting by stretching yourself. Learn more about the things you enjoy or teach them to others!

In your pursuit of wisdom, let me remind you that no call to get wisdom is complete without the all-inspiring, admonishing, life-tuning, and exhorting Word of God.

In Pursuit of Integrity

In all your pursuits, let me encourage you to walk with integrity. As a child of God you are commanded to live a life of virtue, which points to a consistency between what you do in private and what you do in public. It is how you manage your resources and take charge of your blessings in the secret places that God is able to evaluate your character.

Remember the old saying, "Actions speak louder than words." That is why Jesus didn't just preach the Gospel; He lived it and provided a living example for us to follow. We are not called to be perfect but to press forward in Christ Jesus (Philippians 3:14). To *press* is to show evidence of having made progress toward change in our core being.

According to Colossians 1:10, having integrity means:

଼ You live and conduct yourself in a manner that is pleasing to God.
଼ The works that you do are done to glorify God, and they bear fruit.
଼ You are steadily growing and increasing in the knowledge of God and His ways.

Lastly, Titus 2:7 reminds each of us to:

Show your own self... to be a pattern and a model of good deeds and works, teaching what is unadulterated, showing gravity [having the strictest regard for truth and purity of motive], with dignity and seriousness (AMP).

In Pursuit of God's Timing

One of the things that I love most about our Lord and Savior, Jesus Christ, is that we do not have to get cleaned up or get our act together before He will receive us and work in and through us to bring about His glory. He meets us where we are.

Likewise, your heavenly Father knows your coming, going, burdens, and obligations. He knows how much time you have to pursue a passion or a goal or if it will have to wait while you tend to other God-given responsibilities. There is a time and a season for everything under heaven (Ecclesiastes 3:1). However, that should not hinder you from engaging in productive pursuits, expecting God to work on your behalf, and being ready for the opportunity when God presents it.

Consider the fact that everything you do—at home, at work, at school, at church, or in your community—provides you with the opportunity to use your skills, abilities, passions, and talents. If you have a desire to encourage others, write letters, send cards, or make a phone call to uplift someone in need. If you have the skills to teach and you're a stay-at-home mom, teach your children.

My friend Julie has made numerous trips to Jerusalem and its neighboring cities. She is also an avid picture taker. Having obtained hundreds of pictures from her travels, she has bound them together into a photo book worthy of publication.

My dear sister in Christ, you never know if your journal entries will make a book someday. Perhaps that is why we are told: "Whatever you do, do it heartily, as to the Lord and not to men" (Colossians 3:23-24); and "Whatever your hand finds to do, do it with your might..." (Ecclesiastes 9:10).

○○○

Step 6: Your Daily Call to Order

Chapter Comments:

Everything discussed in this step is a part of living a balanced, productive, Christ-centered life; however, each pursuit takes effort and investment on your part. If taken to heart, each pursuit will expand your horizon and open your eye's mind to the various potentials within you.

To help you find your passion, I created the "Identify Your Passion(s)" worksheet (in Appendix A). The worksheet was created to help stimulate your mind and get you thinking about the people, causes, and activities that motivate you.

Chapter Questions:

Group Discussion

1. Read Psalm 139:2; Proverbs 23:7; Matthew 15:19; Romans 12:3; Philippians 4:8. What does the Bible say about our thoughts?

2. Read Jeremiah 29:11. What type of thoughts does God have toward us?

3. Read Matthew 12:36-37; James 3:1-12. What does the Bible say about the tongue and our words?

4. Read Matthew 25:14-30. Why were the actions of the servant given one talent considered wicked? How does this parable relate to the use of our time, talents, and treasures?

Personal Reflection

5. What are some things you need to bind in your life (e.g., low self-esteem, insecurity, loneliness, adultery, covetousness, or jealousy)? Find verses in the Bible that address those areas in your life that you need to bind.

6. What gives you meaning and purpose when you wake up in the morning (your children, your job, your ministry, etc.)?

7. How do you want to serve others with your life?

8. Meditate on Galatians 5:22-23. Which of these "fruits" do you need to work on or develop?

9. What type of job could you obtain or create that would allow you to pursue your God-given passion? What would you have to do or give up, to make this change?

Chapter Assignments:

- **Challenge 1**: Respond to end of chapter questions.
- **Challenge 2**: Identify your strengths and weaknesses.
- **Challenge 3**: Pray and ask God for His Wisdom to help you deal with a challenge you are facing or a decision you need to make.
- **Challenge 4**: Take an initial step to turn a weakness that you have into a strength.
- **Challenge 5**: Evaluate yourself in the light of the Fruit of the Spirit. What areas do you need to improve upon?
- **Challenge 6**: Begin morning and evening affirmations.
- **Challenge 7**: Answer the scenario questions (starting on page 169) designed to help you identify your God-given passion(s).
- **Challenge 8**: Find ways to help and serve others using your passion(s).

- ❏ **Challenge 9**: Make a list of things you want to do (interests and hobbies you wish to pursue) and places you want to visit.
- ❏ **Extreme Challenge**: If you feel comfortable, write down on paper and prepare to share your testimony of how the Lord has worked deliverance and molded and shaped you through a particular circumstance (that has forever altered your life).

Part 2

GOD NEVER SAID THAT THE JOURNEY WOULD
BE EASY, BUT HE DID SAY THAT THE ARRIVAL
WOULD BE WORTHWHILE

MAX LUCADO

Step 7

Reviving Your Relationships

Therefore encourage one another and build each other up,...
  —*1 Thessalonians 5:11 NIV*

Years ago when my husband and I were dating, I signed us up to go white-water rafting with the single's ministry at our church. Why I would want to do such a thing is beyond me. I prayed that morning before we set out on our journey and again before we rolled our raft off the bank and into the river. I was hoping if we were nice to the water by paddling gently through the waves, we could get away with taking a nice stroll down the river—enjoying the breathtaking scenery. Boy, was I delirious. I don't think I cracked a smile during the entire tour down the rapids; my focus was staying in the raft.

There were two other brave souls in our raft that day besides me and my *now* husband—our other two companions were young men from our church.

Of the fifteen to twenty rafts venturing out on the tour, I realized immediately I was in the wrong one. Whereas my goal was to remain in the raft, the team's goal was to pave the way for others and to finish first. Security was not to be found in their company.

As we conquered maneuvering around the smaller rocks, I began to feel a little more comfortable with the journey, but I never stopped praying for the Lord's protection. I was acutely aware of the power and the pull of the water, and I had no desire to be tangled in the churning rapids or be pinned down by the rapid's powerful hydraulics.

As we made our way to the leg of our journey, what I had feared threatened to come to pass; we had been successful in the past (maneuvering the rocks), but I knew that had nothing to do with the here and now.

After we received instructions and safety tips from the river guides on how to make it around this last huge 18-foot-tall rock *(I am guessing on the size)*, we were off. Rocks, holes, standing and breaking waves were all around us, not to mention the massive rock in front of us. We succeeded in rotating the raft ninety degrees to make our turn, but behind us was a wave of water lifting our raft up and against the eighteen-foot rock. Remembering the instructions provided by the river guides, I quickly leaned in toward the rock. I can remember being suspended there for a second or two, long enough to see my future husband and another one of our guys knocked into the water by a huge wave and then swept down the river by the cold, rushing, frothy-white waters—while my comrade and I floated safely through the rest of the rapids and to shore with our raft *half empty* of water.

Once I felt safe on dry land and could *exhale*, I looked up and saw the legs of my future husband dangling over the sides of the river guides' raft and the river guides paddling him to shore. I knew he would be all right. In addition, I quickly realized that self-confidence is all right, but God-confidence is much better. God kept me in the raft and helped me remember the instructions of the river guides—neither did He leave me to paddle my way to shore alone.

To me, trying to revive and cultivate a relationship is similar to maneuvering the white waters. Unless you put the time and effort into learning techniques to help you maneuver through the rapids, you are going to feel uncomfortable in the raft. Unless you put time and effort into building a relationship, you are going to feel uncomfortable being in that person's presence or even asking them for anything.

Like white waters, people are difficult to read. You can look at the river and gauge whether a storm has upset the river. You can look at people and tell whether something is bothering them; but within the river, you still never know what dangers are lurking, and within people, you never know the hurt and the pain deep within them threatening to make you feel as they do, or even worse. An agitated river agitates its travelers, and like the agitated river: *hurting people, hurt people.*

> *An agitated river agitates its travelers and like the agitated river, hurting people, hurt people.*

If you are honest, you would rather face the churning rapids than a back-biting friend, a thoughtless boss, a contentious co-worker, a rebellious child, or an irritable husband. I am here to tell you that when you trust God with your concerns, He will not leave you alone to battle the raging white waters of relationships.

At this step of our journey, we will look at our basic God-given responsibilities in all our relationships, including our relationships with our husbands, our children, and others. Using Jesus Christ as our example, we will quickly explore six principles we can apply to cultivate and develop any relationship.

First, however, we will look at our relationship with God—who sets the foundation for all our relationships. Then, we will look at how our relationship with others affects us.

Your Relationship with God

Let me begin by telling you how good a friend God is. He sent His son to set positive examples for you, as to how you are to live your Christian life. He gave you His 24-hour helpline so that you may call on Him day or night—whenever you are in need. He gave you the Holy Spirit to be your guide after allowing His son to die on the cross for your sins, so that you might have life and have it more abundantly.

I am personally humbled by God's acts of friendship, but if this is elementary to you, let us look at how faithful a friend you are in return—through some common relationship questions:

❏ Do you spend time daily dialoguing with the Lord in prayer?

❏ Do you take time daily to read and reflect on His Word?

❏ Do you have a special time of worship with your Lord and Savior?

❏ Do you share similar interests?

❏ Are you concerned with whether He approves of your attitude, behavior, friends, actions, or activities?

❏ Are you sensitive to His Spirit?

❏ Do you introduce Him and His son to others?

Your relationship with the Lord has everything to do with how you treat Him on a daily basis. You were created by God for His purpose and plan; and through Jesus Christ you have a friendship with God.

It is a privilege to have God as a friend. In the Old Testament, very few men were considered to be friends with God: Abraham was one (see James 2:23), Moses was another (see Exodus 33:11). God talked intimately with them and shared His plans and desires with them, and He wants to do the same with you and me.

"While life on earth offers many choices," says author Rick Warren, "eternity offers only two: heaven or hell. Your relationship to God on earth will determine your relationship to him in eternity."[1]

📖 If you are saved, can others tell that you have a close, personal relationship with the Lord?

Communicating with God

Since the most essential ingredient to any relationship is communication, let us focus on that for a moment.

Communication is a two-way street; it is not merely praying to God, it is also listening to what He has to say. Authors Henry Blackaby and Claude King of the book, *Experiencing God*, reminds us that: "God speaks by the Holy Spirit through the Bible, prayer, circumstances, and the church to reveal Himself, His purposes, and His ways."[2]

God has so much He wants to share with us that He has opened up far more avenues for us to hear from Him than for us to petition Him, because He knows our needs before we even ask (see Matthew 6:8).

Many of us rise up so fast after praying we do not give God a chance to respond by placing a verse in our spirit, giving us an answer to a prayer, putting a song in our heart, or by hearing God say, "I love you," through people and or things around us.

I want to challenge you to commit five to ten minutes each day to be quiet before the Lord—after your prayer time. Then, jot down in a journal anything the Lord has revealed to you.

I have a close friend named Janice, who has experienced firsthand what it is like to be single and alone and married and alone. According to her, neither is better. What made the difference in one of her alone times was the friendship—through communication—that she developed with God.

She was in a dark period in her life after her husband of five years walked out on her. She turned to Christian friends, but amid prayers, sympathy, and encouragement, she could only find temporary relief. It wasn't until she established a friendship with the Lord that she began to experience His abiding peace, His comforting voice, and a love relationship that no man here on earth could provide. Here is what she had to say:

> *Dear Reader, the four-month separation from my husband had left me drained mentally, spiritually, and emotionally. I was struggling terribly trying not to slip into a pit of depression on this particular March morning....*
>
> *On my usual commute to work, I was praying and talking to God when one of my favorite songs popped into my head. The title of the song was "I'm Determined," reminding me that no matter what is going on in my life, I have to be determined to endure the storm with God as my guide—no matter how bad it gets. It was just a passing thought until I turned on the radio and*

heard the local radio station playing that song. In my spirit, I heard God say, "I know your marriage may be rough and your view of love may be distorted right now, but I love you so much I am going to play your favorite song for you."

Later, while walking out the door of my office building to lunch, I noticed a street vendor with the most beautiful roses that brought a smile to my face. That surprised me because for so long, I had associated roses with something someone bought for me when they had made a mistake—not as a token of love. As I walked on, the spirit of depression started to overtake me, and I was beginning to question my value as a wife, a woman, and most of all, as a person.

As I walked by the vendor on my way back from lunch, I was tempted to buy myself some flowers but quickly realized I had no money. That simple thing sent me over the edge, and the tears started to pour down my face. These were not the tears of joy that had me smiling this morning as I listened to my favorite song on the radio, but these were tears of despair that had me believing I was not worth loving.

It took me an hour to pull myself together when a saved sister working across the hall stopped by my office and said, "I was sitting at my desk when a thought of you dropped in my spirit." She pulled a dozen long-stem, red roses from behind her back and handed them to me. Then she said, "I do not know why God told me to do this, but I am being obedient." Tears of joy started to run down my face as I hugged her and told her, "I know why ..." They were the most beautiful roses I had ever laid eyes on. I knew at that moment God was being more than a friend; He was truly romancing me ...

God's Love is forever, Janice Reid

So often, we look for a person to fill the emptiness within us. We engage in sex when we want intimacy, marry when we really want companionship, and have children when we just want to be loved. I'm not saying that is true for everyone. What I really want you to understand is that everything you need and are looking for can be found in a relationship with God.

The Heart of Any Relationship

As you focus on your relationship with others, it is crucial to understand your values, who is influencing you, and who or what is defining you. This is necessary to effectively lead and influence others for Christ.

People were quick to follow Jesus' direction and guidance because they trusted Him. During His short time here on earth, He lived His values every single day of His life. So, it is safe to say His followers had confidence in His ability to lead them in the right direction.

Jesus' values, combined with an understanding of who was trying to influence Him and how people were trying to define Him, magnified His ability to effectively communicate God's will. In addition, this understanding enabled Him to provide His followers with the tools and information they needed to successfully carry out God's purpose and plan for their life. Jesus knew He was a part of something much bigger than Himself. He trusted God to strengthen Him on the inside,

Step 7: Reviving Your Relationships

so He was strong enough on the outside to defeat the negative influences that sought to destroy Him.

There's an old saying I've modified a bit, but it simply says, "Tell me who your friends are and what you value, and I will tell you who you are." As a woman of God, what do you value? Who is influencing you? Who or what is defining you?

What Are Your Values?

Values can be defined as "the social principles, goals or standards held or accepted by an individual, class, society, etc."[3]

As Christians, it is easier to know who we are by first knowing who we are in Jesus Christ. Our true identity is wrapped up in knowing our Lord and Savior, and our values are identified in the Word of God.

To live outside your values is to live a life of confusion, in which you constantly question your purpose, your self-worth, or behave unbecomingly.

Consider Saul, a well-respected Pharisee who killed and persecuted Christians—in his mind—for the God of Israel (see Acts 26:9-10). Did he have values? Yes, he had values—they just were not godly. His values were dictated by "self" (his own beliefs and standards of right or wrong), not by what God had defined in His Word.

Once Saul (renamed Paul) understood who Jesus was and what He did on the cross for him, his name and values changed to redefine himself as a child of the only true God.

Having values validates who you are and what is acceptable and unacceptable as a child of God, regardless of who others want you to be and what they want you to do.

Who is Influencing You?

Just as ignorance of God and what Jesus did on the cross can misdirect our values, wrong influences can do the same.

First Corinthians 15:33 warns us to consider our associations closely; to not be misled, "Bad company corrupts good character." The next verse says, "Come back to your senses...and stop sinning; for there are some who are ignorant of God..." (15:34, NIV).

Our associations have the potential to lead us away from our values and influence us to do things we would never consider doing on our own. From friends we adopt thoughts, attitudes, and elements of our behavior. If we are not careful, our admiration of a friend or a close associate could open us up to either being positively or negatively influenced.

An example of being negatively influenced is a Christian woman acting like her unsaved, club-hopping friends. She embraces their lifestyle as she frequently goes to clubs with them, drinking occasionally only to quench her thirst (so she says). Her attire becomes progressively provocative as her friends encourage her to be more sensuous. She accepts their values as she becomes more and more convinced that the Christian life is depriving her of a good time. She adopts their priorities of "living for the moment" or the next party. Family, friends, or anyone interfering—with her ungodly desires—becomes the target of resentment. Having no rule over her spirit, she becomes like a city broken down, without walls (see Proverbs 25:28), vulnerable to whatever influences her friends expose her to.

In his book, *The Winning Attitude*, John Maxwell says, "The closer our relationship, the more influential the attitudes and philosophies of our friends become to us."[4]

Let me ask you, "Have you ever tried to follow someone in a car?" When they turn, you turn; when they stop, you stop; when they speed up, you speed up; and guess what else? When they are wondering aimlessly about—lost, having no idea where they are headed, you place yourself in the same

Step 7: Reviving Your Relationships

predicament. If you consider the spiritual repercussions, the sobering fact is that you are being lured away from the truth of God and the roadmap He intended for your life.

People you follow who are driving without purpose or direction will lead you nowhere of significance and help you achieve nothing of godly value.

In contrast, being spiritually led or positively influenced by someone means you've allowed someone to be a godly example for you while pursuing the path God has for you.

🕮 Who has the steering wheel in your life?

Who is Defining You?

As I said before, having healthy relationships with others involves knowing what your values are and who is influencing you. It also requires you to gain some understanding of who or what is defining you.

When I defined myself by my job, when I was overlooked for a promotion, I became angry and bitter. When I tried to define myself as a wife, I became dissatisfied and unhappy when my expectations for marriage were not met. When I defined myself by my home, I became frustrated when I could not maintain a spotless house. When I defined myself as a child of God, I was able to recognize my need for God. As a result, God gave me peace in all the roles I walked in daily and in my relationships with others. In other words, I had been looking for people and

> *People you follow who are driving without purpose or direction will lead you no where of significance and help you achieve nothing of godly value.*

things to give me what only God could provide. When I began looking to God, I became more of an interdependent woman.

Author and family therapist, H. Norman Wright, believes that for a person to have a healthy relationship with herself and others, she must be interdependent. He says:

> The person whose identity is found through others often ends up with relationships that are addictive.
>
> *Dependency* in relationships is not a Christian calling except for being dependent upon God, which all men and women are called to be.
>
> An *independent* woman thrives on individuality, few restrictions, and self-gratification. She finds her identity through herself.
>
> But there is a third option called *interdependence*. The interdependent woman has a strong sense of personhood and bases this upon being affirmed by God. She knows she has been given gifts and is willing to use them, but she can also rely upon others. This woman views others as her equal and also values herself.[5]

Our biblical portrait of the Proverbs 31 woman depicts an interdependent woman who knows how to love and be loved, and how to balance her personal pursuits with helping others (see vv. 20, 27). She is perceptive; she understands how to connect with people yet does not automatically succumb to their whims and unreasonable expectations. She is honest and handles her problems with flair, integrity, and maturity (see vv. 11-12). Most importantly, she values herself and others—accepting her own uniqueness and respecting the differences in others (see v. 28). Let me not mislead you: our Proverbs 31 woman is interdependent, but she is totally dependent on God (see vv. 25, 30).

> 🕮 How would you define yourself (e.g., are you a dependent, independent, or interdependent woman)?

Building Intimate Relationships

I am sure you, like me, believe at times that the most uncomplicated relationship to have is with someone who doesn't talk back, disregard, or disagree with what we say or do and who meets all our expectations. Wouldn't that be wonderful? However, God, who has the infinite wisdom and power to do so, doesn't give us what we want at the snap of our fingers, nor does He agree with everything we say or do. So why should people be any different?

A relationship with anyone takes commitment and hard work; running away and isolating yourself does not eliminate the fact that you were designed to have relationships, which is more than just being in the midst of people. It's interacting and connecting with people on a personal level. This includes companionship and fellowship but goes beyond the two to the core of relationships. God's design for any relationship is to glorify Him and reflect His love for His Church.

Just as God has been known to work through pastors and ministers to build up our faith and to strengthen us where we are weak, God uses us to play an essential role in the spiritual development of others. In our close relationships with family members and friends, we should do what Jesus did for His disciples. He passionately prayed for them, modeled how to pursue peace, and actively participated in those activities that were important to them. He also kept His promises, practiced proper protocol, and last but not least, He prepared His heart daily before God so that He might be a living testament example for His disciples. With Jesus as our example, let's look at how we can strive to do the same in our own relationships.

1. Be a Prayer Warrior

People in our homes, churches, communities, and worldwide desperately need our prayers. Jesus Christ, daily sits in the presence of God interceding on our behalf because He knows the purpose and power of prayer. He modeled it for us when He walked on earth. He told Peter, "Satan has asked for you, that he may sift you as wheat, But I have prayed for you, that your faith should not fail; and when you have returned to Me, strengthen your brethren" (Luke 22:31-32).

Through Peter's cockiness, Judas' betrayal, and the disciples' jealousy, envy, and unbelief, He continued to pray for them (see John 17:9-19). He also prayed for us (see John 17:20). If we are to follow in Jesus' footsteps, should we do anything differently? Paul followed Jesus' example by using the power of prayer to intercede on behalf of his brothers and sisters in Christ who were in Rome. He told them: "…without ceasing I make mention of you always in my prayers" (Romans 1:9-10).

The power of faithfully praying brings healing, restoration, salvation, transformation, growth, and inspiration in our lives and the lives of our loved ones. There is no greater tool than prayer to be able to tap into the mercy and grace given by God; to usher in the blessings provided by God, and to receive the strength and hope supplied by God. In our frustration, we may not tap into this power often enough or stop short of our miracle because we are not seeing the results we want as opposed to what God wants. Don't wait for that major crisis to start praying for your loved ones. Start by implementing simple steps today:

> ○ぇ Daily pray for yourself and your inner circle (immediate family members, close friends, and relatives). Ask that *God's will* be done in their lives versus *your will*.

Step 7: Reviving Your Relationships

    ☙ Maintain a prayer list to help you remember the prayer needs of people you happen upon in church, at work, or on the streets.

    ☙ Whenever the Lord places someone or a situation on your heart, be obedient by immediately saying a short prayer for them or that situation. Pray whatever the Holy Spirit leads you to pray; you may never know how your prayers affected another until God calls us all home.

Let your prayers be sincere. You may desire that the Lord change someone, but change may have to start with you. Like a mother who knows her young child, she is able to quickly discern the intentions of his heart (his motives). God is a master at discerning whether you are using prayer to change someone to suit your desire or whether you have decided in your heart to love them regardless if God changes them.

The fact that we have difficulty making adjustments in our own lives indicates how hard change is for others. Only God can place a desire in a person's heart to want change and then motivate them to actively pursue change.

In addition, as you pray for others, not only will you release the power of God's love upon them, but God will reveal things to you about that person that will help you to have more patience, compassion, understanding, and even more love toward them. There may be a reason beyond you why she's withdrawn, why he hordes, why she spends too much money, or why he has pent-up anger. Once you grasp that truth, you'll stop taking things so personally and start praying for that person's deliverance.

A Christian friend told me when her husband is out of order, she calmly and softly says, "I am going to tell Jesus on you." Take your case before God and lay it at His feet—all your pressing issues and concerns regarding that special person in your life.

I have also come to realize that just as important as it is to pray for others, it is also important to pray with them.

2. Be a Peacemaker

Jesus is the Prince of Peace, so it is no wonder He calls us to pursue peace with all men.

Being a peacemaker means we have to lay aside pride for peace. So how do we do that? Matthew 18:15-17 lays out a process for confronting a Christian who has sinned against us. Jesus clarifies that we are to confront this person in private, first, and in a peaceful manner—do your best not to be drawn into a bitter confrontation. If that fails, the second step is to address the issue in the presence of witnesses and then proceed to the Body of Christ (the Church). My advice to you (from personal experience) is to analyze the intentions of your heart before you bring others into your grievances. If gossiping or getting revenge is your intention, or you're very angry or hurt, seek God's guidance in prayer before you proceed.

If you wish to gain a friend, restore a marriage, save your child, or obtain God's peace regarding the situation, find spirit-filled people to assist you—who will gain nothing by helping you settle your grievance but the opportunity to serve.

Taming the Tongue

The hardest part of being a peacemaker for an out-spoken person is holding their tongue. The tongue has the ability to *rob a relationship of peace*. I can be honest about having been in situations where I was quick to speak my peace or eager to spill the beans (gossip) to friends and family members. In addition, if we are honest, some of us are good at rehashing wrongs done to us. We readily await the opportunity to "turn the tables" by pulling out our list of grievances—at the hint of any insult or offense against our character.

Rarely, in the heat of anger, do we just stop for a minute to analyze the ramifications of what we are saying or doing. That's difficult to do when you are hurt or upset. The book of James tells us that our tongue is unruly (3:8); from the same mouth proceeds words that bless and words that curse. Then we are told by James, "These things ought not to be so" (v. 10).

People are unconsciously affected by our words. Think briefly: Are your words helping or hurting, blessing or cursing? Proverbs 16:24 reminds us that, "Pleasant words are like a honeycomb, Sweetness to the soul and health to the bones." And of course, our wise example, "opens her mouth with wisdom, And on her tongue is the law of kindness" (Proverbs 31:26).

Reflect on the kind of words that come out of your mouth when you speak to people (especially your loved ones) . . .

- Do you speak kind and wise words? "… pleasant words promote instruction" (Proverbs 16:21, NIV).

- Do your words express your love and support? "Do not let any unwholesome talk come out of your [mouth], but only what is helpful for building others up according to their needs, that it may benefit those who listen" (Ephesians 4:29, NIV, emphasis added).

- Do you speak to be understood by pausing and thinking about your words before you say them—especially when discussing a sensitive issue—or do you speak to vent? "The heart of the righteous weighs its answers…" (Proverbs 15:28, NIV).

We want to be women people feel comfortable with and can confide in; willing to listen when loved ones want to share their feelings and concerns. I like what John Maxwell and Jim

Dornan say in their book, *Becoming a Person of Influence*: "Nobody cares how much you know, until [they know] how much you care."[6] They go on to say:

> A funny thing happens when you don't make a practice of listening to people. They find others who will. Anytime employees, spouses, colleagues, children, or friends no longer believe they are being listened to, they seek out people who will give them what they want. Sometimes the consequences can be disastrous: the end of a friendship, lack of authority at work, lessened parental influence, or the breakdown of a marriage.[7]

Sometimes, being a peacemaker means we have to *listen more and talk less*—carefully and attentively focusing our minds on what is being said and expressed (verbally and nonverbally).

Keep in mind, "When a man's ways please the LORD, He makes even his enemies to be at peace with him" (Proverbs 16:7). We want our sphere of influence to include our enemies who are compelled to have some level of respect for us because our efforts to pursue peace draws admiration from them—which I believe, gives us the ability to influence a larger number of people here on earth for Christ. We are told in Hebrews 12:14 to "Make every effort to live in peace with all men and to be holy; without holiness no one will see the Lord."

3. Be a Promise Keeper

Have you ever been excited about going somewhere or doing something, and the person you made plans with canceled? Perhaps it was for a legitimate reason, but if you were excited about your plans, you could not help but feel the sting of disappointment. Proverbs 13:12 captures this disappointment

Step 7: Reviving Your Relationships

well, when it says: "Hope deferred makes the heart sick, but a longing fulfilled is a tree of life."

We can not protect our loved ones from every wave of disappointment, but we can do our best to keep our promises to them. In the same respect, if you have committed yourself to a covenant, project, activity, or event, do your best to stay committed. This includes being committed to your marriage, raising your children unto the Lord, and living a godly life.

All through Scripture we can read about the promises of God; one such promise passed on to each of us through the writings of Paul says: "Let your conduct be without covetousness; be content with such things as you have." Then we are told, "... For He Himself has said, 'I will never leave you nor forsake you'" (Hebrews 13:5).

Jesus promised His disciples that He would never leave them nor forsake them. Jesus kept His promise, and He continues to faithfully keep that promise to us today. The Bible says of the Lord our God, He is faithful to all his promises (see Psalm 145:13, NIV) and that He is not a human, that He should lie or change His mind (see Numbers 23:19, NIV).

4. Participate in Their Lives

I heard a pastor say something that has stayed in my heart for years. He was referring to the relationship between a parent and a child, but the same holds true for any committed relationship. The comment that he put into an equation was:

$$\text{Rules - Relationship} = \text{Rebellion}$$

If we bombard people, especially our husbands or children, with our rules—or our expectations—without first attempting to have a healthy relationship with them, then rebellion against our authority or influence is bound to happen.

This does not mean you become your husband's doormat, your friend's pushover, or your child's buddy, but it's vital that you find ways to cultivate a deep, meaningful relationship with each of them.

Someone once told me, "Kids spell love T.I.M.E.." And, of course, I like to remind ladies how they were when they first met their husbands, or if you are single, how you are when you first meet that man you are interested in.

If you are honest with yourself, you went through great lengths to be in his presence and to keep and maintain his attention. You would bombard him with questions about his dreams and goals or take a keen interest in things you really couldn't care less about—before you met him. In short, besides showering him with affection, you gave time and attention to his interests and dreams.

We've often heard that "Christianity is not a religion; it's a relationship." In the same respect that Christianity is not about rules, but a loving relationship with Jesus Christ, participating in the lives of our loved ones involves cultivating the relationship through actively involving ourselves (if physically able to) in some of the things they enjoy. Who knows what success your participation might bring to the lives of your loved ones? I do know from the Word of God that every fishing expedition that Jesus went on with His disciples was successful, not to mention enlightening.

Decide today to engage in those positive activities that God, your husband, your children, and those close to you are interested in. In addition, help each member of your family feel wanted and worthy of your time by allocating special time for each of them regularly. Ensure during this time that they have your undivided attention. Listen attentively to what they have to say. If you are unmarried, enjoy close friendships with other women and family members. If you are engaged, most likely you are doing those things already; the key for you is maintaining balance during marriage and when the children come!

5. Practice Proper Protocol

Practicing proper protocol is recognizing situations in which basic respect and consideration are due. Consider the response of Jesus when asked by his enemies about paying tribute to Caesar in Mark 12:17. He says, "Render therefore to Caesar the things that are Caesar's." Jesus was implying that we are obligated to respect and obey individuals in authority over us and the laws set by our local, state, and federal agencies—as long as it does not go against our faith. He connects this statement with the conjunction "and" plus the words "to God the things that are God's," reminding us that we also have a responsibility to honor and glorify God.

Let's look at how we can practice proper protocol and honor God in the process.

Giving Appreciation

On my way to lunch one afternoon, I heard a woman's voice on the radio giving a commencement speech to a group of college graduates. I wish I knew the school or the person's name, but what she said stayed with me. The voice that resonated from the radio said, "Be thankful, spiritually and worldly." She understood the importance of giving thanks to God, acknowledging and appreciating people, and letting them know it.

Giving appreciation is an expression of love toward another person. It makes sense to believe that if we welcome being appreciated, someone else would also value it.

God shows His love and appreciation for us through every miracle of nature. Showing appreciation can be as simple as responding with a friendly smile, saying "thank you" to a compliment, giving a compliment, or telling someone how much you appreciate their support, kindness, or help. If you have or work with children, teach and often remind them of the importance of expressing gratitude.

If you are having problems appreciating the people in your life, begin to monitor your thoughts and your feelings about them. Thank God daily for your family and friends and those attributes that you love and admire in them. Then, start to consciously think of the difficult people in your life and jot down one kind thing about each of them. As you stop focusing on their failures and shortcomings and begin to see them in a new light, your attitude will change toward them.

God especially deserves our gratitude. You can express appreciation for God and how He has worked out situations in your life by sending up silent praises as you go about your day. If He woke you up this morning in your right mind, say: "I praise You, Lord, for another day to serve you and my loved ones." If He helped you through a difficult meeting, say: "Thank You, Lord, for giving me success on the job and in my endeavors." If He helped you through a trying circumstance, say: "Thank You, Lord, I may have been troubled on every side, yet I am not distressed."

Receiving Appreciation

Wanting to be appreciated is a normal part of being human. It is a desire that God has placed in each of us, and desires it in return. God wants to be worshiped and appreciated for who He is and the blessings He has bestowed upon us. However, if He does not get it, it does not change His feelings or attitude toward us. This is not always true for most of us. When people don't appreciate us, a spirit of bitterness emerges because our expectations for being appreciated were not met.

It took me years to learn that I could not put my expectations on others. If they appreciated me how I wanted them to, their expression of gratitude wouldn't necessarily come from their heart's desire to show thanks.

My father, who used to be a construction engineer, helped the congregation—he was once a member of—build a 3.8 million dollar, 30,000 square-feet church and nursery school. He sketched out the design of the church and managed the construction while working a full-time job—that was thirty-one miles one way (in mostly back-to-back traffic) from his home. And might I point out, that the Church never paid him for his services. When the church was completed, there were no pats on the back or accolades. My father worked to serve the Lord. Although others might not remember his sacrifices for the church building project, God will.

In addition, there are women who are raising children and or caring for an elderly or sick parent. If this is you, know that you are doing someone a service, and it will not go unappreciated in God's eyes. At the same time, do your works unto God, and not for man's rewards, for your labor of good works is not in vain in the Lord (see 1 Corinthians 15:58).

6. Prepare Your Heart

Have you ever noticed your response to people after you have been in the presence of God? I find it wonderfully amazing how God can allow us to have peace when someone is screaming and yelling at us and calling us all sorts of names. Yes, the flesh wants to react the same way and maybe adorn their face with cold icy water from a glass, but God will keep us in His perfect peace when our mind is focused on Him (Isaiah 26:3).

In this world we will have the blessed opportunity to deal with many different types of people—Jesus had to deal with Judas, knowing that he would betray Him. There will be some we admire and enjoy being around, others who are terribly annoying and condescending, and all those in between. Regardless of who it is, we must prepare our hearts to respond in a way that reverences the Lord our God. Yes, we will get angry and upset at times; Jesus got upset. The Bible says:

> *When it was almost time for the Jewish Passover, Jesus went up to Jerusalem. In the temple courts he found men selling cattle, sheep, and doves, and others sitting at tables exchanging money. So he made a whip out of cords, and drove all from the temple area, both sheep and cattle; he scattered the coins of the money changers and overturned their tables. To those who sold doves he said, "Get these out of here! How dare you turn my Father's house into a market! (John 2:13-16, NIV).*

Another time, when Jesus entered the synagogue there was a man there who had a shriveled hand. The Bible says: "So they watched [Jesus] closely, whether He would heal him on the Sabbath, so that they might accuse Him" (Mark 3:2). Discerning their evil intentions, Jesus asked them, "Is it lawful on the Sabbath to do good or to do evil, to save life or to kill?" (v. 4). The Pharisees said nothing. Jesus got angry with them, because of the hardness of their hearts. Then He told the man to stretch out his hand and Jesus restored the man's hand (v. 5).

Jesus got angry, but He did not sin; neither did He use words that He would later regret. The Bible says of the Lord: "The LORD is merciful and gracious, Slow to anger, and abounding in mercy" (Psalm 103:8). Everything that Jesus did was out of love, honor, and respect for His Father, and for our good. With Jesus as your example, commit to preparing your heart before the Lord before dealing with people, especially

Step 7: Reviving Your Relationships

the difficult ones. Pray and ask God to give you the strength, courage, and wisdom you need to respond in love, with patience, and with self-control.

In addition, get so full of the word of God that the Holy Spirit becomes so resident in you that you will automatically respond and react in love.

As Gary Thomas says in his book, *Sacred Marriage*, "That terrifyingly difficult man to love just may be your gateway to learning how to love God."[8] Even though this quote addresses a woman's relationship with her husband, I believe the same can be said of any relationship.

Forgiving

Part of preparing your heart also includes being able to forgive. I will boldly tell you that only God can help us love the unlovable. Only God can help us forgive those who have robbed us, abused us, deceived us, abandoned us, and trespassed against us. I can only share with you what God's Word says about forgiveness and the effects of not forgiving. The choice to forgive is yours. You will either live in bitterness and anger or release God's love, peace, and comfort into your life.

As I write, I have to take a deep breath because I know forgiveness is one of the most precious gifts you could give to yourself and to someone who has wronged you—and who wants and needs your grace and mercy.

The truth is, not forgiving is more damaging to the one unwilling to forgive than to the one who caused the offense. There are situations where our feelings have been hurt by someone who has no idea they have offended us. We dwell on the offense and allow ourselves to get angry over it. Even if it was not a misunderstanding, unforgiveness finds us in an uncomfortable spot. We feel hurt, so we put ourselves in jeopardy of taking our hurt out on someone else—usually those dear to us.

Yes, some things seem so unforgivable and so grievous that harboring feelings of bitterness seems justifiable; however, when Peter went to Jesus and asked Him, "Lord, how often shall my brother sin against me, and I forgive him? Up to seven times?" (Matthew 18:21). Seven times might seem pretty generous to you and me, but to a forgiving and loving God, not even that was enough. Jesus answered, "I do not say to you, up to seven times, but up to seventy times seven" (v. 22). This is hard to hear if you are the one having to forgive. Still to the one in need of forgiveness, it's an opportunity for you to model Christ's love to someone desperately in need of it.

Preparing your heart in this area is first realizing that it takes God to help you love your neighbor as yourself. It takes God to help you bless them that curse you, and it takes God to help you pray for those who despitefully use you. But remember, you do many things that offend God—we all do—but He still loves you, and His arms are open to receive you. Consider Jesus' words on the cross: "Father forgive them, for they do not know what they do" (Luke 23:34).

Striving to have order in every aspect of your life does not come without forgiveness; forgiveness is an order from God. Just as Jesus forgave those who murdered him and has forgiven us of our sins, we are to forgive one another…

- *"Let all bitterness, wrath, anger, clamor, and evil speaking be put away from you, with all malice. And be kind to one another, tenderhearted, forgiving one another, even as God in Christ forgave you" (Ephesians 4:31-32).*

- *"Therefore, as the elect of God, holy and beloved, put on tender mercies, kindness, humility,*

> *meekness, long-suffering; bearing with one another, and forgiving one another, if anyone has a complaint against another; even as Christ forgave you, so you also must do" (Colossians 3:12-13).*

Forgiveness does not mean that you excuse, deny, or justify what was done to you, but it means you no longer allow it to rule and reign in your mortal body, leading you into disobedience.

Each of the principles we have just explored, Jesus used to develop the relationship between He and each of the people He interacted with often (mainly, His disciples). If we examine the fruit of His labor, we will discover that only one out of twelve of His disciples betrayed Him. Though Peter denied Him three times, he realized his error, repented, and returned to the only true God.

Relationships have a way of testing a person's character in the most sensitive areas of their life. Yet, relationships also have the potential to be very fulfilling and rewarding. Jesus's impact on His disciples can still be felt today—every time a lost soul accepts Christ as their Lord and Savior.

📖 What type of impact will you leave on those you love?

Woman to Woman

Now, let us focus our attention on our relationship with other women. This type of relationship is invaluable. There are a lot of women without children and many without a man, but very few women are without a best friend. Even if they have not accepted Jesus Christ as their Savior, they have a sister friend. It could be a friend from school, someone you grew up with, or someone from work or church that you connected with.

It wasn't until I developed and matured in the Lord that I was able to understand how invaluable my friendships with women were. There's a special emotional and spiritual bond that binds mature women of God.

Whereas I threw God's name out flippantly as a carnal Christian saying, "Girl you'll be all right, God will take care of you." As I matured in Christ, I realized the importance of praying for my friends and the responsibility to encourage, sympathize, and support them. Similar to what the spiritually mature women (not necessarily chronologically older) are admonished to do in the book of Titus: to encourage younger women "…to love their husbands and children, to be self-controlled and pure, to be busy at home, to be kind, and to be subject to their husbands, so that no one will malign the word of God" (Titus 2:4-5, NIV).

Wherever you are spiritually, if you look around you'll see multiple opportunities for you to make a difference in the lives of women. It can be as simple as praying with and for them; holding your sister in Christ accountable, teaching, serving, sharing your testimony of struggle and triumph, mentoring a spiritually younger woman, or preparing yourself spiritually to mentor. If time doesn't permit a long involvement in another woman's life, take a spiritually younger woman to lunch and impart your godly wisdom upon her. If you plant and another woman waters, God will surely give the increase (1 Corinthians 3:6). In addition, it's imperative that you get connected to a small group of women for prayer or Bible study. If you are married, connect to godly women committed to their own marriage. If you are single, get connected to women who are committed to celibacy before marriage.

You need a relationship like Elizabeth and Mary, where you can depend on someone for prayer and encouragement in

Step 7: Reviving Your Relationships

a time of need—a sister in Christ willing to travel the distance (literally) to rejoice with you or help bear your burdens.

You need a relationship like Naomi and Ruth in which a seasoned woman of God is planting in your life. You are also inadvertently teaching her a little something about patience, love, and dedication. In addition, you're planting in the life of another woman.

You even need a relationship like Martha and Mary, a sister in Christ who may also be your prayer partner but who is not afraid to step up to the plate and hold you accountable. She may not always be right, but the combination of the Holy Spirit in both your lives will guide you to God's perfect peace regarding the situation.

I can not harp enough on the fact that we, as women, need each other. Whose children can you babysit (for a season) while the mother takes a class or works a second job? What financially strapped divorced mother can you buy groceries for? Is there a woman you can drive to chemotherapy? Is there an elderly woman that you can run errands for?

🞿 How can you lighten a sister's load?

As I mentioned above, another way to make a difference in the lives of other women is to share your testimony. You probably have a testimony that would yank another woman out of the pit of her depression. Twice another's testimony pulled me up out of deep despair, not that I wanted to hear that someone was worse off than I was, but that someone had succeeded (in finding forgiveness, healing, peace, joy, love, and opportunity) despite similar circumstances.

I remember a former pastor of mine talking about a divine opportunity, a particular time and place in which God has set the scene and placed the person or people for you to minister to. I will take this divine opportunity further by applying it to our testimonies. Not everyone needs to know your business, especially if you don't feel comfortable sharing it. If that's how you feel, allow God to set the time, place, and person for you to share your personal testimony with. When that divine time presents itself, your responsibility rests in being sensitive to the moment, cognizant of the promptings of the Holy Spirit, and prepared to share. Be forewarned, this may not be a meeting scribbled down on your calendar; knowledge of this type of meeting only comes when you are attuned to God.

> How in tune are you to God and the promptings of the Holy Spirit to help another woman in need?

Toxic Relationships

Whether you are married or not, if you are in a dangerous relationship that has the potential to be life-threatening, please get to a safe haven right away. There are crisis centers in most major cities, or call the National Domestic Abuse Hotline at 1-800-799-SAFE (7233).

If you are not married, and you are bound together with an unbeliever, your relationship has the potential to be life-threatening with respect to your relationship with God. Paul made it deliberately clear when he said in 2 Corinthians 6:14: "Do not be unequally yoked together with unbelievers. For what fellowship has righteousness with lawlessness? And what communion has light with darkness?"

Most saved sisters (in Christ) do not consider their relationships with unbelieving men to be toxic, but if we as Christian women are not influencing them, then they are influencing us.

I will be the first to confess to missionary dating. Yes, I tried unsuccessfully to get a friend saved to justify dating him.

He was open to attending church with me, although he would have rather been someplace else. We enjoyed many of the same things and even thought the same on most non-Christian subjects. My only problem was getting him connected to Jesus. He was one of many men who did not believe a loving God would send a basically good man to hell. So I spent precious time and energy trying to get one man saved when another man (my future husband), who I knew at the time, needed my prayers of protection and strength.

Since I had been through enough nonsense with men, I did not allow this man to get my focus off of God, and he was so respectful of my relationship with God that he didn't want to lead me astray. That's how considerate he was, but it didn't matter how nice or considerate he was; he was not saved.

While writing this book, I found a humorous quip that shows how desperate some women have gotten and can get while waiting on God to send them their husbands. Adding to the desperation are family and friends frantic to see them walk down that aisle.

> *Do not be unequally yoked together with unbelievers. For what fellowship has righteousness with lawlessness? And what communion has light with darkness?*
>
> —2 Corinthians 6:14

> A young lady came home from a date, looking sad. "Anthony proposed to me an hour ago," she told her mother.
> "Then why are you so sad?"
> "Because he also told me he is an atheist. Mom, he doesn't even believe in hell."
> "Marry him anyway," her mother replied. "Between the two of us, we'll show him how wrong he is."[9]

In their eagerness to get married, I have heard women say, "I would rather marry a non-believer than be single the rest of my life." Blatant disobedience has its consequences, just as obedience has its blessings. During my missionary dating period, I had been celibate for over eight years. Before I got married, people laughed at me and mocked my commitment to celibacy. On one occasion—during a break at work—while trying to encourage someone else to choose the same path, I was told by a male co-worker, eavesdropping on my conversation: "You'll never get married if you do that." His words not only spoiled my opportunity to minister but to a woman in her early thirties, desperately wanting to be married, it sent me into a pit of depression—questioning my commitment to be obedient to the Word of God regarding "no sex" outside of marriage.

What he did not know was that I had many talks with God, and there were many times I had concluded the same thing: "I'll never get married."

My questions to God were…

ଔ What man will stay in a relationship without sex?
ଔ Who am I amid so many beautiful women ready and willing to have sex?
ଔ How can I compete for a man's affection in a sex-driven culture?
ଔ What can I bring to the table to get a man to see beyond the physical and into my heart?

The only answer that God spoke in my spirit was Psalm 46:10, "Be still, and know that I am God." So I held to my convictions, and a year after those words were spoken, God blessed me with one of His sons.

Step 7: Reviving Your Relationships

Sister to sister, I want the best for you, and any man that continues to cause you to sin against God, is not God's best. First Thessalonians 4:3 tells us that for our own "sanctification: [we] should abstain from sexual immorality" (emphasis added).

If you are a single woman looking for a husband, please do not allow the truth to elude you; an unsaved man cannot ask for your hand in marriage. He doesn't qualify to go before your righteous Father to ask Him for anything except for salvation—so he can't possibly ask for your hand in marriage! God is Holy, and anyone who comes before Him has to be covered by the blood of Jesus.

Toxic People

The other side of toxic relationships is dealing with mean-spirited, spiteful, negative, or dishonest people that we cannot avoid for some reason or another. This may be a spouse, child, parent, in-law, co-worker, or boss.

Often our relationship with this type of person results in: physical or mental abuse, negative emotions, destruction or abuse of personal property, fear, or harsh words spoken.

As women, we want to lovingly embrace people, especially those close to us. We also want to be understood, listened to, and supported. The saddest thing about dealing with toxic people is that you can never let your guard down—especially if that person has repeatedly demonstrated that they cannot be trusted.

Whether it's a child who steals from you, a spouse who curses you, a friend who takes advantage of you, or a boss who degrades you, your heart and mind must be on guard against deception. Therefore, you are to love them with your spiritual eyes and ears wide open. This means you understand the intentions of their heart (how they are capable of hurting you) and, of course, what emotions they are capable of bringing out in you. This requires that you stay prayed up and allow the Holy Spirit to give you the ability to love that person despite their actions and see them as someone worthy of being loved. Then, earnestly watch what God can do through you to bring that person into the saving knowledge of Jesus Christ or into a more intimate relationship with Him (and you).

This doesn't mean there won't be people that you will need to release or minimize the space they take up in your life. Our goal is to seek a godly solution to the problem. It may be that Christian counseling is necessary. It may be a family vacation is in order to reconnect with your children. It may be helpful to focus on a common achievable goal to help restore some trust and respect in a marriage. It may also be time for you to stop looking around for someone to blame and to humble yourself so that you can receive God's grace and hear His counsel—which would include Jesus' command to:

> *Love your enemies, bless those who curse you, do good to those who hate you, and pray for those who spitefully use you and persecute you, that you may be [daughters] of your Father in heaven; for He makes His sun rise on the evil and on the good, and sends rain on the just and on the unjust (Matthew 5:44-45, emphasis added).*

Step 7: Your Daily Call to Order

Chapter Comments:
Our happiness in a relationship may be second nature compared to what the Lord wants to teach us and where the Lord wants to take us spiritually.

When you get a chance, I recommend you comb through the book of Proverbs, which provides wonderful advice on choosing a mate and friends. Here are a few verses to reflect on:

> ☙ *"Do not make friends with a hot-tempered man, do not associate with one easily angered, or you may learn his ways and get yourself ensnared"* (Proverbs 22:24-25, NIV).

> ☙ *"The righteous should choose his friends carefully, For the way of the wicked leads them astray"* (Proverbs 12:26).

> ☙ *"A friend loves at all times, And a brother is born for adversity"* (Proverbs 17:17).

> ☙ *"A man who has friends must himself be friendly, But there is a friend who sticks closer than a brother"* (Proverbs 18:24).

> ☙ *"As iron sharpens iron, So a man sharpens the countenance of his friend"* (Proverbs 27:17).

Chapter Questions:

Group Discussion

1. What does Psalm 103:8-13 tell us about the Lord our God?
2. Do you agree with the author that ignorance and negative influences affect our values?
3. Read 1 Thessalonians 4:9-10; Hebrews 13:1-3; 1 Peter 1:22; 2:17-18. What does Scripture say about how we should treat people?

4. What does the Bible say about our relationships with the following:
    - Husband (Proverbs 31:11; 1 Corinthians 7:14-16; Ephesians 5:22-24),
    - Children (Psalm 127:3; Proverbs 22:6; 31:28),
    - Friends (Proverbs 17:17; 18:24; John 15:13-15),
    - Unbelievers (2 Corinthians 6:14)?
5. Read Matthew 18:23-35. After having his massive debt canceled, why didn't the servant forgive the debt of his fellow servant?
6. What vital message do Matthew 6:14 and 18:33 teach us about forgiving?
7. Read Hebrews 10:24. What can we do to encourage ourselves and those around us to be more appreciative toward God and others?

Personal Reflection

8. Think of and write down a difficult time when God befriended you. Be specific in recalling when, where, and how.
9. Read Psalm 42:1-11. How does David's relationship with God encourage your relationship with God?
10. Who or what has influenced or defined you in the past?
11. Read James 3:7-9. What are some things you can do to bridle your tongue in a relationship that needs reviving?
12. What activities do your husband and children enjoy that you can participate in? What other activities can you do together?
13. How do you wish to positively impact and influence the lives of other women?

Step 7: Reviving Your Relationships

Chapter Assignments:

- ☐ **Challenge 1:** Respond to end of chapter questions.
- ☐ **Challenge 2:** Make a list of questions for God and take them to the Lord in prayer. Then, wait expectantly for the Lord's response.
- ☐ **Challenge 3:** List the relationships you cherish and why. List the relationships you are concerned about and why.
- ☐ **Challenge 4:** List steps you plan to take to revive or cultivate a relationship you are concerned about. Begin today to implement one step a week.
- ☐ **Challenge 5** If you are not going through this book within a small group, then consider joining a women's prayer group, Bible study, or Sunday school class.
- ☐ **Challenge 6:** What qualities and characteristics are essential to you in a mentor? List three women in your church or community that match the qualities and characteristics you listed.
- ☐ **Challenge 7:** Ask God to send you a spiritually mature woman with a positive attitude and the qualities you listed above to mentor you. The mentorship can be as short as six months or as long as both of you deem necessary. *Note: Do not be afraid to approach a woman God has laid on your heart about mentoring you.*
- ☐ **Challenge 8:** Start keeping a prayer/gratitude journal. Regularly, write down personal prayer requests and anything the Lord has spoken to your heart. In addition, every day, write two to three things you are thankful for and something positive about each problematic person in your life.
- ☐ **Extreme Challenge:** Consider selecting one to three ladies in your local church or community that you feel compelled

to: (1) mentor for a period of time, (2) encourage over a meal, or (3) spend quality time praying with and for.

❑ **Group Challenge**: If everyone feels comfortable, and if time permits, prepare and share testimonies of forgiveness. Then, thank God for the grace He has given each of you to forgive.

Step 8

Making Your Ministry Matter

Since we live by the Spirit, let us keep in step with the Spirit.
—Galatians 5:25 NIV

With every season there comes change. When the air becomes brisk and leaves begin to alter their color and fall to the ground, we know that autumn has arrived, bringing shorter and colder days—signaling the need to modify our attire and rearrange our schedules.

Like the seasons of the year, there are seasons in every human being's life that can bring about the most beautiful and glorious transformations—similar to the exquisite colors on trees and foliage that autumn ushers in.

As we arrive at the various seasons in life, it becomes evident whether our opportunities, trials, triumphs, and experiences have led to spiritual growth and maturity that radiates from us as God's willing servants or still reveals the residue of rebellious spirits.

We know within the seasons of life, growth will take place. Whether we grow older and wiser or older and more foolish—God be willing, we will still grow old.

This step will focus on determining where you are spiritually, receiving God's restoration, and recognizing your ministry responsibilities by looking at what God has equipped you to do in the body of Christ, and what God has commanded you to "go forth" and do.

Where Are *You* Spiritually?

Before I put a twist on what I envision to be the different seasons of Christian maturity—to help you gauge where you may be spiritually—let me begin by saying: Wherever you are right now spiritually was a matter of choosing to delight yourself in the things of God, or choosing to center your life on yourself (your happiness, your status, your position, your looks, your possessions, your feelings, or your desires).

From our initial acceptance of Jesus Christ as our Lord and Savior until the day the Lord calls us home, we will go through various spiritual stages. We may stay in one stage for years before being allowed entry into the next stage. The rate of growth and progression varies from individual to individual but is still based on commitment and consistency—it is not automatic. In your lifetime, you will slide back and forth, depending on your ability to surrender your life wholly and completely to be used to glorify God.

The Seasons of Christian Maturity

In the *season of spring,* you have recently accepted Jesus Christ as your Lord and Savior. You have concluded that the world has nothing to offer you greater than the saving knowledge and grace of Jesus Christ.

Step 8: Making Your Ministry Matter

In the spring of your Christian life (early years of faith and new beginnings), you may be in desperate need of Christian guidance and encouragement. Still, you are excited about establishing a firm foundation in your Christian faith. You listen with eagerness, study attentively, and read the Word of God with voraciousness. You enthusiastically look for any and every opportunity to plant what little you understand about Jesus into the heart of another. In addition, your values have been redefined as you obediently align yourself with the Spirit of God.

In the *season of summer*, you have grown leaps and bounds. You are still maturing in the Word of God, not necessarily teaching or preaching, but planting the seed of God's Word in the lives of others, bringing them to the saving knowledge of Jesus Christ. You are using your gifts and talents to glorify the kingdom of God and mentoring by sharing what you have gleaned in the Word of God with someone spiritually younger. As a farmer for Christ, you wait expectantly for a heavenly harvest.

In the *season of autumn*, you are filled with God's joy because you are plucking up what you have harvested by seeing those you have taught and mentored plant in the lives of others. In this season, you have become more sensitive to the Holy Spirit. You are still very active in bringing lost souls to the saving knowledge of Jesus Christ. Where others may look back with regret, you rejoice over what you have learned, shared, and taught, realizing that your existence comes with a continual opportunity to keep doing the work of the Lord; "[Being] diligent to present yourself approved to God, a worker who does not need to be ashamed, rightly dividing the word of truth" (2 Timothy 2:15, emphasis added).

You probably assume winter is next; however, so many Christians get to the summer (or even spring) in spiritual maturity and then fall stagnate into the *season of fall*. I know what you're thinking: "Fall *is* autumn." I wish I could concur. Fall here is synonymous with fallen. Having fallen prey to the lies of Satan, you have lost your way—failing to hold on to that which you have learned in the spring and summer seasons. You may find yourself in *fall* by not having set aside the quiet time to tend to the spiritual disciplines of: studying the word, praying, praising, fasting, giving, or journalizing. In addition, you have allowed the cares of this world to steal your joy, consume your days, and hinder you from pursuing godly relationships. You wrestle with obtaining peace, desiring to have it but forgetting who to seek to obtain it. Slowly, you have migrated away from a God-focused life—having ceased involvement in spiritual activities you once found exciting. You may have even stopped going to church regularly, or you church hop in an attempt to circumvent accountability.

Having fallen in the midst of *fall* you have become cold and indifferent to the things of God. Where you were once hot and excited, you are now burned out, lost, or confused. It's possible that your spiritual life, at this point, can now be compared to that of a Pharisee—one who frequently questions God's wisdom, love, and faithfulness.

If you have come to the *season of winter via autumn*, you may not be able to get around like you used to, but you are still allowing God to use you for his purpose and plan. In addition, you take solitude in knowing you have passed the baton once, twice, or more and can reflect on the fact that you have brought up many children for Jesus Christ. You are at peace with your life and are preparing for Jesus to take you home, where you look forward to hearing the words "Well done, my good and faithful servant."

If you have come to the *season of winter via fall*, spiritually and possibly physically, there are years on you, and you have completely forsaken the faith. You may be going through the

Step 8: Making Your Ministry Matter

motions, but there is no spiritual life in you. You're angry and bitter because your life didn't turn out how you wanted it to. You served God for years, and all you can see is what you perceive He did to you or didn't do for you. You're not a babe in Christ, but having grown wary of the things of God, you have relegated Him to last place in your life.

Winter is far colder for you if you have come here via *fall*; the coldness of your relationship with God has set in for a winter freeze. You have fallen, forgotten who you are in Christ Jesus.

> If we were to tune into your Christian frequency, what season would we find you in spiritually?

Our maturity in Christ becomes increasingly evident when we allow the Spirit of God, through the Word of God, to work in us to make us stronger, wiser, and capable of fulfilling our God-given ministries.

Returning to God

I have already talked about obtaining Godly wisdom in step six: "Evolving through Productive Pursuits," and having a more intimate relationship with God in step seven: "Reviving Your Relationships." Hopefully, by now, you have also come to realize where you are spiritually.

The difference between being in *fall* and *winter via fall* and being in the other seasons of life is being receptive to the voice of God to immediately repent of any sin that God makes known to you. Pride, promiscuity, bitterness, unforgiveness, gossiping, and covetousness are just a few sins that will put you out of balance and out of order with God.

If you have fallen into *fall* or been stuck in *winter via fall*, ask yourself, "What has caused me to drift apart from God?"

Most of us are here because our focus in life changed from being Christ-centered to being self-centered—where our needs became greater than obeying the commands given by God. In addition, if we as Christians would regularly examine ourselves, we would conclude that although we are doing many admirable things, many of us are not growing in the ways and Word of God. Spiritual balance and order come when a person humbly confesses and forsakes sin. God says, "Return to Me, and I will return to you" (Malachi 3:7).

Repentance is a crucial step in returning to God. Do not settle for a humdrum Christian existence; quickly confess your sin(s) and ask God to reveal anything that has hindered your Christian walk and put you in the season of *fall* or *winter via fall*.

Your heavenly Father and Friend will meet you wherever you are. He met Rahab in the midst of fornication... He met Ruth in a pagan land... He met Hannah in sheer depression over her barrenness... He met Abigail in a miserable marriage... He will do no less for you. God wants to know about your hurts, pains, desires, and thoughts; His only request is that you remain faithful to Him and remember that His honor is at stake in your Christian walk.

> As God asked Adam and Eve in the Garden of Eden, I will ask you once again: "Where are you (spiritually)?"

Your Ministry Matters

Just as repentance is a crucial step in returning to God, it is also crucial in making your ministry matter.

The freedom repentance offers increases your ministry's effectiveness and God's presence in your life. Put bluntly, a ministry is not a ministry without God. Ministries that matter and make a difference glorify God. If God is not in it, then it is not of God, and just as quickly as it sprang up, it will eventually wither away.

As you strive to get balance and order in your life, your ministry will come more into focus. Like the woman at the well with a notorious reputation for being promiscuous in the eyes of men, she was a lost soul in the eyes of the Lord. Jesus heard the struggle in her heart and purposed to go to Samaria. Consider the words in John 4:4, "But He needed to go through Samaria." Jesus was on His way to Samaria to reveal the bad with the good and the ugly with the beautiful by first gently uncovering this woman's sin, and then offering her His love.

I imagine her heart had been broken many times, and her spirit had been humbled by her circumstances, so she eagerly desired the living water Jesus was offering. Then, the focus of the conversation becomes her sin. Jesus asked her to call her husband, to which she replied, "I have no husband." Jesus says in response to her, "You have well said, 'I have no husband,' for you have had five husbands, and the one whom you now have is not your husband; in that you spoke truly" (John 4:17-18).

Jesus was brutally honest with this woman, which led me to believe that hearing the truth about herself was more liberating than uncomfortable. Before her was a man that loved her in spite of her mistakes, and because He loved her, she was able to love herself enough to receive the truth about herself—without trying to defend her sins, without retreating to the comfort of home, or even running away into the arms of another man. However, we can definitely agree that this was not a topic she wanted to linger on, so she changed the conversation, and Jesus let her. It is possible she offered up a silent confession, allowing Jesus to take her hurt, pain, guilt, and sin; and replace them with His comfort, love, forgiveness, and assurance of salvation. Any way you look at it, the results were astonishing; within minutes He had given the Samaritan woman worth, value, and a ministry that mattered. We are told:

> *The woman then left her waterpot, went her way into the city, and said to the men, "Come, see a Man who told me all things that I ever did. Could this be the Christ?" Then they went out of the city and came to Him (vv. 28-30).*

This woman purposed in her heart to give what had been given to her, leading many to Jesus Christ.

Many of us struggle with our usefulness and effectiveness in the body of Christ. I have heard women say:

- "I'm not that knowledgeable in the Word of God to teach."
- "I'm uncomfortable speaking in public."
- "My checkered past hinders me from stepping out and getting involved."
- "Who am I? What do I have to offer?"
- "I'm afraid to try."

What's your excuse? God stirred up in the woman at the well boldness to go forth. He had lifted her from the depths of her sin. Whereas she was trying to maintain a low profile one minute, the next minute, she was preaching to the masses. She had gone from being a social outcast and the joke of the town to being socially acceptable and a woman with a God-given purpose to share the "good news" of Jesus Christ with others.

Just as Jesus visited the woman at the well, much later, he appeared to His disciples who were also keeping a low profile—right after His death on the cross. However, after the power of the Holy Spirit came upon them, they boldly began to preach

Step 8: Making Your Ministry Matter

the Word of God, and in one sermon, three thousand souls were added to the Church (see Acts 2:41).

Your life and ministry matters to God! The bitter divorce that left you destitute, broke, or depressed, matters. The death of your loved one that caused your world to crumble, matters. The ability to move people with your songstress voice, matters. The skill to sway a person to buy a product you're selling, matters.

Any time you allow God to use you to bless others, you're ministering. Yet apart from the indwelling and empowerment of the Holy Spirit, you could not effectively live a Christian life or walk daily in the ministry God has purposed for you.

Sadly, there is much confusion in the Church today about how the Holy Spirit is released in the life of a believer. What is important is that if you have accepted Jesus Christ as your Lord and Savior, you have the Spirit of God resident in you.

> *God is glorified in a ministry when we share our faith, use our gifts, and walk in love.*

The Holy Spirit is available to guide you daily to help you understand God's Word; to equip you to minister to the masses; and endow you with the ability to use your spiritual gift(s) to honor and glorify God and serve the Church.

Your ministry matters when God is glorified. God is glorified in a ministry when we share our faith, use our gifts, and walk in love. Now that we understand that our ministry matters, let's look specifically at what our ministry encompasses.

We are Required to Share Our Faith

The story "The Starfish Thrower" was initially written by anthropologist and author Loren Eiseley. The story has been told by many different people in various forms over the years;

sometimes the main character is a young boy, other times it's a young girl, but most of the time it's a man. I will use this wonderful illustration of how our efforts to save one life can save many more using a woman as the main character.

The story is about a woman walking along the shore who sees thousands of starfish lying on the beach, washed up by the tide. They are dying in the hot sun. So the woman reaches down with compassion, picks up one of the dying creatures, and throws it back into the sea. She encounters many more during her walk, stopping often to grab another dying starfish and toss it back into the sea. Another woman comes by to question her actions. "What are you doing?"

"I'm saving a starfish," the woman replied. To this response, the other woman asked, "Why?" Implying very cynically: "What difference will it make?" There were thousands of starfish littering the beach. As the conversation continued, the starfish thrower never stopped throwing starfish back into the sea. As she watched a starfish disappear into the sea, she turned to the woman and said, "It made a difference for that one."

Now imagine those starfish are lost souls. What is a lost soul worth to you? Do you have time to:

- lift up (encourage and support),
- build up (provide the resources for growth),
- hold up (endure with another),
- help up (serve those in need), and
- pick up (lend a helping hand)?

Jesus tells his disciples in the Gospel of Matthew, "The harvest is plentiful, but the workers are few. Ask the Lord of the harvest, therefore, to send out workers into his harvest field" (9:37-38, NIV).

Why We Don't Witness

Why are we not reaching the masses? What is hindering you from sharing the Word of God with the unsaved? I will paraphrase a few reasons given by Mark Cahill in his book, *One Thing You Can't Do in Heaven*, as to why we don't witness for Christ:

- we fear being rejected;
- we don't know how to;
- we fear losing a friend or offending someone;
- we assume a person has already heard;
- we are lazy in sharing the Word of God;
- we don't know enough;
- we assume a person won't want to talk about it, or
- we fear not being able to answer their questions.[1]

I know what it is like to get so caught up in the busyness of life—and even doing church work—that you forget that you're on assignment by God to spread the gospel of faith in Jesus Christ. The overwhelming truth is thousands of people will die and go to Hell if we don't step out of our comfort zone and be willing to try.

It is not my intention to make you feel guilty—I struggled for years with stepping out to share my faith. It is my desire to help you understand the urgency of witnessing. We are in the last days. Mark Cahill says, "You can worship God in heaven. You can praise God in heaven. You can sing songs to God in heaven. You can learn God's Word in heaven. But one thing you cannot do in heaven is share your faith with a nonbeliever. Why? Because everyone in heaven is a believer."[2]

This statement by Mark Cahill reminds me of the words of Paul spoken to young Timothy: "Preach the Word; be prepared in season and out of season; correct, rebuke and encourage—with great patience and careful instruction" (2 Timothy 4:2, NIV). As long as we have life here on earth, we have the opportunity to share the Word of God with others.

🕮 With whom have you recently shared the gospel?

Suggestions for Sharing Your Faith

Begin by practicing ways you can share your faith. Most of us would prepare for a job interview by practicing our response to any given number of questions, so consider doing the same for a "life and death" situation. Who knows, you may be the last chance for someone to receive Jesus Christ as their Lord and Savior.

Find an interesting ice breaker, Mark Cahill has adopted the question: "When you die, what do you think is on the other side?" My husband used to carry around a faith cube; he is also great at taking real-life situations and turning them into an opportunity to speak about Christ and eternity. On the other hand, I had to take baby steps in this area, so I started out very informal. Any time I gave a gift, it was an opportunity to minister. I kept short testimonies on the forefront of my mind to pull out whenever the Lord prompted me. I wrote letters, sent out emails, and started newsletters. Through my simple efforts, the Lord has allowed me to plant seeds in the hearts of nonbelievers and the courage to share the good news with people I casually meet while out and about.

> **WE CAN DO NO GREAT THINGS FOR GOD, ONLY SMALL THINGS WITH GREAT LOVE**
>
> MOTHER TERESA

Step 8: Making Your Ministry Matter

You may want to start with your unsaved family members, then branch out to friends, co-workers, and your community, but before you get started, let me ask you a question. "If you were selling a product you believed in, how would you present it to your customer?" You definitely wouldn't present it in a threatening manner, would you? Hopefully, you would be excited and enthusiastic about telling your customers why they must have the merchandise you're selling.

The Proverbs 31 woman "perceives that her merchandise is good" (v. 18); therefore, she has confidence in her product. If you have tasted God's forgiveness, felt His tender mercies, worn His grace, found peace in His presence, and experienced His love, then you have personally partaken of His goodness. Therefore, you should be confident enough to share the wisdom of being God's child with your customers.

The spirit in which you tell someone about Jesus Christ is a major determinant in whether they will receive Him.

Jesus shed His blood for our sins. Salvation is not intimidating or confrontational; it's the greatest gift one could ever receive!

We Are Required to Share Our Gifts

Do you know what your spiritual gifts are? The apostle Paul tells us in First Corinthians, "Now about spiritual gifts, brothers, I do not want you to be ignorant" (12:1, NIV). Yet amazingly, many Christians do not know what they have to offer the Body of Christ.

Our spiritual gifts differ from our talents and passions in that our talents are the natural abilities we were born with that are cultivated. Whereas our passions (discussed in a previous step) are the desires we have to support an effort or help and encourage others within or outside the church. Spiritual gifts can be defined as, "The God-granted empowerment for ministry on the part of believers."[3] Our spiritual gifts were given to us by the Holy Spirit to help the body of Christ to function and grow. Every single believer possesses at least one spiritual gift. Paul mentioned that there are many gifts but only one spirit, the same spirit that exists in all Christians (see 1 Corinthians 12:5). According to Ephesians 4:12-15, our spiritual gifts are for...

- The perfecting of the saints (bringing Christians to maturity).
- The work of the ministry (serving the Church).
- Edifying of the body of Christ (encouraging and uplifting your brothers and sisters in Christ).

In addition, Peter re-affirmed that we are to use our spiritual gifts to serve others. I Peter 4:10-11 says...

Each one should use whatever gift he [or she] has received to serve others, faithfully administering God's grace in its various forms. If anyone speaks, he should do it as one speaking the very words of God. If anyone serves, he should do it with the strength God provides, so that in all things God may be praised through Jesus Christ. To him be the glory and the power for ever and ever (NIV).

Get into the Game!

What is keeping you from identifying what you do best in the body of Christ? Some of us are active in the church because of our desire to please God—that is honorable and necessary at times—but what is more pleasing to God is if you serve where He has equipped and empowered you to function. The body of Christ suffers when you are out of place.

Step 8: Making Your Ministry Matter

Imagine you are on a softball team and the team captain assigns you to play shortstop, but you desire to play a more exciting position, so you station yourself at first base. Now, the team has two first basemen and no shortstop. The second baseman and third baseman working together are able to compensate for the lack of coverage at shortstop—for a while—but the lack of support in that area is definitely being felt by the team. Meanwhile, you and the designated first baseman have been skirmishing for the ball—causing confusion and disharmony in the body of Christ. The assigned first baseman is seeking to serve where he has been called to serve, while you're aiming to show off your skills and abilities in an area you have not been equipped or assigned to function in.

Please get into the game by getting in harmony with the body of Christ. Disobedience (or rejection of God's authority) results in wasted time, energy, confusion, and frustration. As part of the body of Christ, we are part of a team. Unless we listen to our team captain (God) and follow the promptings of the Holy Spirit, others will have to compensate for our absence or disobedience.

On a positive note, when you know where you have been created to function, you are more capable of helping others find their place on the team (in the body of Christ).

I firmly believe that when the spiritual gifts of God's people coordinate in a spirit of harmony within a church unit, the energy that unity creates would ignite a fire in the hearts of God's people and pull lost souls into that church like a magnet.

Study to Show Yourself Approved

If you are unsure what your spiritual gifts are, do a personal study on pertinent passages in the Bible that talk about Spiritual gifts. Below, I have listed the spiritual gifts in each Bible chapter on which you should focus your study.

- 1 Corinthians 12:4-14: word of wisdom; word of knowledge; faith; healings; working of miracles; prophecy; discernment of spirits; speaking in tongues; and interpretation of tongues.

- 1 Corinthians 12:27-30: apostles, prophets, teachers, miracles, healings, helps, administrations, and varieties of tongues.

- Romans 12:6-8: prophecy; ministry; teaching, exhortation, giving, leading, and showing mercy.

- Ephesians 4:11: apostles, prophets, pastors, teachers, and evangelists.

In addition, talk with your pastor or spiritual leader to help you identify an area of ministry within the body of Christ where you can get plugged in, connected, and actively involved—using your gift(s), to glorify God.

I have also listed some books to help you identify and learn more about your ministry in the body of Christ.

- *Discover Your Spiritual Gifts: The Easy-To-Use, Self-Guided Questionnaire That Helps You Identify and Understand Your Various God-Given Spiritual Gifts* by C. Peter Wagner.

- *What You Do Best in the Body of Christ* by Bruce L. Bugbee.

- *Discovering Your Spiritual Gifts: A Personal Inventory Method* by Dr. Kenneth C. Kinghorn.

- *Spiritual Gifts: Their Purpose & Power* by Bryan Carraway.

- *Discover Your God-Given Gifts* by Don and Katie Fortune.

Step 8: Making Your Ministry Matter

We Are Required to Love

Before I conclude this step, let me share with you again what God requires of you and me. We are to…

> "Love the LORD your God with all your heart, with all your soul, and with all your mind.' This is the first and great commandment. And the second is like it: 'You shall love your neighbor as yourself.' On these two commandments hang all the Law and the Prophets" (Matthew 22:37-40).

> "Go therefore and make disciples of all the nations, baptizing them in the name of the Father and of the Son and of the Holy Spirit, teaching them to observe all things that [Jesus has] commanded you; and lo, [Jesus is] with you always, even to the end of the age" (Matthew 28:19-20, emphasis added).

> "…do justly, To love mercy, And to walk humbly with God" (Micah 6:8).

May I also add that you are to use your talents and gifts to bring glory and honor to God, fulfill your God-given responsibilities, and bring into fruition the passions and desires the Lord has placed in your heart.

Everything I have listed above is built on the foundation of love, the greatest gift God has bestowed upon each of us. We love God when we obey Him and use our gifts, talents, and passions to bring glory and honor to Him. We love others when we share the Gospel of Jesus Christ with them because we want to see them in heaven someday. We love ourselves when we live with integrity, purpose, and discipline—taking care of the temple God has blessed us with. We love our surroundings when we enjoy the earth and the fullness thereof—enjoying our God-given possessions without making them idols. Paul put it more eloquently…

> *Though I speak with the tongues of men and of angels, but have not love, I have become sounding brass or a clanging cymbal. And though I have the gift of prophecy, and understand all mysteries and all knowledge, and though I have all faith, so that I could remove mountains, but have not love, I am nothing. And though I bestow all my goods to feed the poor,…but have not love, it profits me nothing (1 Corinthians 13:1-3).*

Step 8: *Your Daily Call to Order*

Chapter Comments:

This step was devoted to helping you understand how important your ministry is to the Body of Christ. To be effective in the ministry that God has for you, you must SOAR for Christ. That is, you must:

S: Share your faith

O: Obey His commandments

A: Actively serve and help others

R: Resist temptation

Chapter Questions:
Group Discussion

1. Read Revelations 3:14-17. What was God's response to the believers in Laodicea that were lukewarm for Him?
2. What steps can a person take to increase their passion for Christ?
3. How does Paul's example of surrendering his life to God, in Philippians 3:1-10, challenge you to do the same so that you can more effectively serve God?
4. How would you explain salvation to someone?
5. Read Galatians 6:6; Ephesians 4:1-3; 2 Peter 1:2-8. What do the following passages teach us about our responsibility for spiritual growth?
6. Read Isaiah 61:1-3. What makes it difficult for a person to believe that their ministry matters to God and that He has a plan for their life?
7. What should our Christian life say to the people (family, friends, co-workers, schoolmates, etc.) around us?

Personal Reflection

8. If you met Jesus at the well, what particular flaw in your character would He address?
9. What concerns do you have regarding your spiritual walk with God? How are you challenged in the area of your concern?
10. Do you know what your spiritual gifts are? How do you feel about your spiritual gifts?
11. How are you using (or how would you like to use) your spiritual gifts to edify the Church?
12. What personal steps can you take to remove the temptation(s) causing you to sin (e.g., take a new route, seek Christian counseling, end a friendship)?.

Chapter Assignments:
- **Challenge 1**: Is there sin in your life that is hindering your relationship with God? Surrender that sin to God in prayer.
- **Challenge 2**: Respond to end of chapter questions.
- **Challenge 3**: Take a spiritual gift evaluation.
- **Challenge 4**: Identify and write down how you can use your gifts, talents, personal assets, and passions to glorify God in your church. It may help you to talk with your pastor or spiritual leader.
- **Challenge 5**: Set spiritual goals to improve or cultivate your relationship with Jesus Christ. Begin today to implement one goal a week.
- **Challenge 6**: If you have never done this, take a bold step and look for the opportunity to share your faith with someone.
- **Extreme Challenge**: If you're comfortable witnessing to people, find or develop a platform (study group, conference, newsletter, class, etc.) to witness and help many more souls.
- **Group Challenge**: Exchange ideas for sharing your faith with people in different environments (e.g., at the park, at school, while carpooling to work, while in a waiting room at the doctor's office). Then, practice sharing your faith with one another.

Step 9

Getting Financially Focused

> *The rich rules over the poor,*
> *And the borrower is servant to the lender...*
> *—Proverbs 22:7*

If you have been reading this book straight through, then you probably feel as if the journey to balancing blessings and obtaining order has taken you through many peaks and valleys. I wish I could say that your journey ends here, but it doesn't.

If I had to equate an activity and a place to describe the financial situation many Americans have found themselves in, it would be roaming aimlessly, smack-dab in the middle of a desert, in midday, trying to find their way out of a dense sand storm. The feeling is frustrating, tiring, and debilitating, not being able to find relief and being vulnerable to all the elements designed to cloud their ability to see and think clearly about their own financial matters.

Besides lack of discipline, the culprit responsible for most of their desolate desert experience is the popular but overused credit card.

The prevalent use of credit cards in the United States has grown dramatically, with 61% of Americans owning at least one credit card and using 23% of their available credit limit, according to 2019 data released by Experian. It also found that more than 511.4 million credit cards have been issued to American consumers, and their dependence on credit cards is increasing.

It's exciting in the beginning to be able to supplement our income or increase our standard of living by paying later, but after a while, the burden of debt becomes our master, and the bondage of debt hinders our ability to be used effectively by God.

If I were to poll a hundred families, the majority of the wives would love to be stay-at-home moms. However, for many families, their debt-to-income ratio makes that desire an unlikely reality. Besides paying off credit card debt, many families struggle to repay student loan debt. According to the U.S. Federal Reserve, student loan debt affects over 40 million Americans.

If your financial situation seems hopeless, allow God to lead you to an oasis in the middle of the desert.

At this step of your journey, the focus will be on getting your finances in order by establishing a clear financial vision and setting goals that coincide with your vision. After that, I will introduce you to practical steps to help you eliminate debt and start saving, then highlight the benefits of investing in yourself and others.

Setting Financial Goals

Getting a handle on your finances requires you to first get a vision of where you want to be financially and then set goals to match that vision. Begin by writing down where you want to be financially five, ten, fifteen, or twenty years from now (e.g.,

Step 9: Getting Financially Focused

retired living in the foothills of Arizona; debt free, prepared for missionary work in South Africa; prepared financially to have children and be a stay-at-home wife and mother).

Next, write down at least three to five financial goals to help you meet your financial vision. Some examples of clearly defined financial goals are:

- Earn in excess of $90,000.00 in five years.
- Build an emergency fund of $5,000.00 before the end of the year.
- Pay off all credit cards within four to five years.
- Contribute $3,000.00 to an IRA annually while eligible until retirement.
- Save $9,000.00 to help fund a planned 6-month missionary trip to South Africa.
- Pay off a $5,000.00 loan on a car within one year.

Keep in mind that your goals should focus on those things that will meet your current and future needs, glorify God, and bring you fulfillment and peace of mind.

If you have a spouse or fiancé, make sure he is part of the goal-setting process. Include your children only if the goals affect them. In addition, consider putting a special note beside each goal stating why that goal is important to you. You'll also want to prioritize your financial goals in order of importance and break up long-term goals into measurable short-term goals.

The more focused and clear your financial goals are, the more likely you are to achieve them. Use your financial vision and goals to motivate you to spend money wisely. Evaluate your progress frequently to determine if you are making satisfactory improvements on a particular goal or if you need to make adjustments.

An important financial goal that should be on everyone's list (excluding those who have met this goal) is to build an emergency fund containing about six to eight months of living expenses. Without this cash reserve, unexpected expenses outside the norm or a job loss can devastate your finances.

Suppose you are single and reading this book. I admonish you to do two things: first, use the suggestions provided in this step to get your own finances in order—assuming they are not in order. Second, if you plan to be married soon, know how your future husband feels about and handles money. Does he view money as a resource to provide food, shelter, clothing, and security for his future family? Does he view money as a resource to build a safety net and to save for future generations? Is he competent about money? What does his current credit situation look like? If he sees money as an object to be acquired then spent, or if he is more interested in talking about what you can bring to the table (how much you make) rather than showing you how he can be the financial leader in the relationship, then take heed. Insist on seeing a copy of his credit report and be prepared to show yours. If he'll hide that from you, he's likely to hide other things from you as well. However, if he is willing to be open and honest with you regarding his financial baggage, be receptive toward him and start working together on a plan of action to best resolve the matter.

About Our Debt

My husband and I were trained as *Crown Financial Ministry* small-group study leaders. Years ago, we taught a class at our local church. One of the concepts that the course tries to get you to understand immediately is that everything belongs to God.

In the class, we go through an exercise of transferring the ownership of all our assets to the Lord. This process acknowledges God's authority over one's life and His ownership over all one's possessions. As 1 Chronicles 29:11-12 declares:

> *Yours, O LORD, is the greatness, The power and the glory, The victory and the majesty; For all that is in heaven and in earth is Yours; Yours is the kingdom, O LORD, And You are exalted as head over all. Both riches and honor come from You, And You reign over all. In Your hand is power and might; In Your hand it is to make great And to give strength to all.*

Besides giving practical tips on eliminating debt, the course provides an understanding of what is acceptable debt and what is not. A home mortgage and a business or vocational loan is considered acceptable debt if it meets the following criteria:

- The item purchased is an asset with the potential to appreciate or to produce an income.
- The value of the item equals or exceeds the amount owed against it.
- The debt is not so large that repayment puts undue strain on the budget.[1]

CNN Money.com describes good debt as "anything you need but can't afford to pay for upfront without wiping out cash reserves or liquidating all your investments. In cases where debt makes sense, only take loans for which you can afford the monthly payments."2

Since it's mostly our wants that get us entangled in debt, let's take a moment to clarify what are needs and what are wants. As you may have guessed, needs are those basic essentials we cannot do without (e.g., food, clothing, and shelter); anything beyond what we need is something we want.

Spending Money Foolishly

Having spent years as a software developer, in my spare time, I like to visit various websites to get ideas, glean how new features and capabilities are being used, and personally critique how sites are set up. One of my favorite sites to visit is Amazon—partially because I'm an avid book reader.

I first discovered the Amazon site in the early 2000s when fellow students in my graduate classes were spreading the word on where to get great bargains on our required textbooks. That was the beginning of my online shopping addiction, which escalated a couple of years after getting married when my seemingly simple life became chaotic.

Online shopping filled the void and emptiness that existed in other areas of my life. It brought temporary pleasure to my day coming home and seeing an Amazon box with the black curved arrow—that Amazon calls a smile—or any package, sitting on my doorstep.

Instead of dealing with the emotions behind my online shopping expeditions, such as when it's triggered. I chose to use time management as my rationale and excuse—not having to go inside a store, saves time. The problem was I was out of order with God. My financial decisions failed to line up with my basic financial responsibilities. During that time my credit score took a plunge as I sacrificed paying bills for the temporary excitement and anticipation of receiving a package in the mail.

Step 9: Getting Financially Focused

It had gotten so bad at one point that I was counting coins to put gas in my car, and avoiding accountability by not sharing and being open with my husband.

When I realized I had a young child watching and mimicking my actions, I decided I had to change. I wanted to be a role model to my son by showing him how to handle money effectively. Randy Alcorn said it well in his book, *Money, Possessions and Eternity*, when he said:

> Everything learned in life, from coping methods to table manners, is learned in families. Families are the heart and soul of society. The home, not the school, is the primary place of learning. In the home, character is built, habits are developed, and destinies are forged.[3]

My personal decision to stop spending money foolishly required me to deal with the emotions that were causing me to overspend. We will talk more about emotional spending and what it can lead to, but ponder on this question for a moment:

> What has happened in and around you that has triggered your compulsion to spend or horde money, and when does it surface? Is it when you're feeling guilty, lonely, depressed, or anxious?

Spending Money Wisely

As women of balance and order, we should exercise wisdom before purchasing anything. Again, the Proverbs 31 woman provides a beautiful example for us to follow:

> *She seeks wool and flax… (v. 13).*
> *She considers a field and buys it… (v. 16).*

Julie, a friend of mine, truly lives out these verses. She, like me struggled for years with a shopping addiction. While I was still dealing with my addiction months after she had her shopping impulses under control, I asked her one day: "What made the difference for you?" In other words, "What are you doing that I need to do?" She responded, "I did what the Lord pressed on my heart to do." She further explained that she took stock of what was working for her and her family's basic needs. She did this by first analyzing the cost of working versus staying home with her daughter. Financially, it was more feasible for her not to work outside the home. Next, she listed the affordable stores that met her family's basic needs and committed to only shop at those stores—only after she made a detailed list of what would be purchased and when.

In addition, she eliminated those spur-of-the-moment shopping trips, purchased many things during the off-season, and only bought needed clothes on sale or at garage sales. Last but not least, she mastered the art of negotiation.

Julie's advice and those two verses in Proverbs 31 reminded me that a woman of balance and order does not act on a whim or illogically. She carefully and closely *considers* her options, seeks God's wisdom and direction, and then makes a rational financial decision based on her well-thought-out choices. Her decision does not only focus on the short term but also the long term as she *considers* the ramifications of her decisions on her and her family's well-being.

We are told in Proverbs 21:5, that "The plans of the diligent lead surely to plenty, But those of everyone who is hasty, surely to poverty."

꾸 Are you spending money foolishly or wisely?

Getting Out of Debt

Besides having a financial vision and setting financial goals, I am convinced that financial success for any child of God begins with prayer. If there is a desire to reverse your financial situation, it should come with a desire to repent or change your actions and thoughts regarding your money and your possessions.

If you are committed to eliminating your debt, ask God to forgive you for letting your financial situation get out of control. Then, ask God to guide you in being a better steward over the financial blessings He has entrusted you with. Ask Him to help you stay committed to paying your tithes from this day forth before you spend any portion of your check. If you will give God the first and best of your income with a cheerful attitude, God will bless your obedience.

I asked my friend Patricia if I could share her testimony of how the Lord blessed her commitment to honor Him. Her goal was to develop a more intimate relationship with the Lord through tithing—despite her circumstances:

> *Dear Reader, in December 1990, I found out I was pregnant with my first child. My family and I were elated because that child would be the first grandchild; however, my excitement fizzled a little when I was laid off in January of the following year—the company I worked for went out of business. Around the same time, my husband—who had a desire to pursue his dream of starting a band—quit his job. He then proceeded to rent a house for his band members while we were being kicked out of our apartment being unable to pay the rent. I was devastated and angry, thinking: "What kind of man would quit his job when he had a pregnant wife,*

provide his band members with a place to live, and leave his wife to fend for herself?"

Although I had intended to be married for a lifetime, looking back, I often wondered if that was my clue that he no longer wanted the marriage.

Deep in debt, homeless, and at an all time low, I had to ask my parents (specifically my stringent father) if I could move back home with them. They agreed, and during that difficult time I recommitted myself to the Lord.

I had been raised in the church, but after I left home I relegated God to the back burner of my life. I rarely went to church, and when my mother would ask me if I had been, I would berate her. But in the midst of my brokenness, things had changed. I told God that I wanted to restore my relationship with Him, so I made a commitment to tithe despite my circumstances. Even though I had no money at the time, I stepped out on faith, believing that God would provide.

Once I got settled in my parent's home, I discovered a state program called "Right from the Start" that helped pregnant, low-income women. This program paid for food stamps, a private obstetrician/gynecologist for me, and a private pediatrician when my baby was born. The blessings continued to pour in as I received unemployment insurance from the state—since I was laid off through no fault of my own. More blessings continued to pour in as I received a part-time bookkeeping position. I was also able

> to continue my schooling at Georgia State University using the GI Bill.
>
> I never fully realized—at the time—what an act of obedience would save me from, but when my daughter was two months old, I had to have emergency surgery to remove my gallbladder. Since I was still under the "Right from the Start" program (which ended when my baby turned three months old), Medicaid paid for the cost of the surgery.
>
> God was truly looking out for me! He knew I could not afford a $27,000 medical bill!

God Blesses the Giver, Patricia Dutchie

God wants us to honor Him with the first tenth of our total income, our tithes. Our tithes and offerings help support the work of the church. Proverbs 3:9 says:

Honor the Lord with your possessions, And with the first fruits of all your increase; So your barns will be filled with plenty, And your vats will overflow with new wine.

Blessings started pouring in when Patricia recommitted herself to the Lord and began paying her tithes. Of course, God gets all the glory, honor, and praises—He is a faithful and just God and looks forward to blessing His children.

If you don't have a penny to your name, honor God by tithing your time. Serve in your local church, in your community, or serve your family with a cheerful, loving, and generous attitude. God desires that we be wise and faithful stewards of the blessings He has entrusted us with—so He can justify trusting us with more.

Steps for Getting out of Bondage

Balancing blessings and obtaining order requires us to break the bondage of debt by dealing with unjustifiable debt, reckless record keeping, poor planning, and overindulgence so that we have more opportunities to invest in those eternal things that truly matter to God.

The following steps are recommended by most financial advisors in getting out of debt. Included is an initial step I took in getting a handle on my own debt.

❑ **Step 1—Fast.** One of the quickest ways to cut back on impulsive spending is to go on a spending fast. Stop spending for thirty days; only buy what you absolutely need. Your efforts here will play a huge role in developing a feasible budget later.

❑ **Step 2—Pull your credit report.** When was the last time you pulled your credit report? Your credit report shows how much debt you have and how committed you are to repaying your debt in a timely manner.

Under the *Fair and Accurate Credit Transactions Act* established in 2003, all consumers are entitled to a free annual copy of their credit report maintained by each of the three major credit bureaus: Experian, Equifax, and TransUnion. Visit www.annualcreditreport.com for more information.

As soon as you obtain a copy of your credit report, review it for signs of identity theft. Ensure your report is accurate and does not contain any strange activities or addresses. If you think you are a victim of identity theft, contact the fraud departments of the three major credit bureaus.

Step 9: Getting Financially Focused

Request that each agency put a "fraud alert" on your credit report. Next, contact all the financial institutions you have accounts with and alert them to your situation. In addition, file a statement with the Federal Trade Commission at 1-877-ID-THEFT (438-4338) or visit: www.identitytheft.gov to help track down and stop identity thieves.

❏ **Step 3—Know your FICO score.** Do you know your FICO score? Knowing it is a sure way to find out what lenders think of you and how deep in the hole you may be. Each credit bureau collects and maintains information on your credit history: how often you pay bills on time, if you've defaulted on a loan, how much consumer debt you have, and so on. All this information is collected into a credit report, which derives your credit score. Your credit score is a quick means of assessing how risky you are to a potential lender. A good score of 750 or above means lenders are confident you'll be willing and able to repay a loan. A high score also increases the likelihood that you'll get their best available rates. If your score is low and you get approved for a consumer loan, your interest rate will likely be higher and your payments larger.

❏ **Step 4—List your debts.** List everything you owe. This will give you an accurate depiction of just how much debt you may be in. On a sheet of paper, list who you owe, how much you owe, and the interest rate. If paying off your debt will require you to deplete your emergency fund, don't do it. Pay as much as you can when you can, and consider paying off your smaller debts with the highest interest rates first. This will afford you a taste of victory in the least amount of time.

❏ **Step 5—List your assets.** List everything you own. Listing your assets will give you an idea of what can be sold to help pay down your current debt. Don't forget those treasures in the attic! In addition, if you are considering bankruptcy, please seek professional advice. It might have taken days or months to get into debt, but getting out of debt will take some time.

❑ **Step 6—Track your spending**. For one month, start tracking your income and expenses. There are a plethora of apps you can choose from to help you track your expenses; make sure your chosen expense app allows you to separate your spending into various customizable expense categories. This basic feature will come in handy when preparing your budget worksheet. To create an income and expense worksheet for those who still prefer to carry notebooks or journals. On a sheet of paper, develop columns for: date, description, amount, and means (whether cash, check, digital currency, or credit card was used to make the purchase). Fill in the columns for every penny spent—even if it's as minute as contributing a quarter to the office coffee fund for a cup of coffee. Tracking your spending will give you a strong sense of where your money is being consumed and where you can cut back to save.

❑ **Step 7—Evaluate your spending**. Divide your expenses into two categories: those that are fixed (paid consistently each month), such as mortgage, car, child care, or credit card payments, and those that are variable, such as eating out, entertainment, clothing, and gifts. Prioritize your expenses and find places where it's possible to cut back. Even if you can afford to splurge, develop a habit of living below your means and ask God how you can responsibly invest the rest of His money.

Step 9: Getting Financially Focused

🕮 How often do you pray about how God wants you to use (invest) His money?

❑ **Step 8—Create a budget.** Examine your spending habits by looking through receipts, your checkbook register, credit card statements, payment apps, and your expense tracking worksheet. Next, complete an initial budget worksheet (available in Appendix A); this worksheet should be updated and revised monthly until you get a better handle on controlling your needs and wants. Bear in mind that a budget is designed to help you reach your financial goals, not hinder you. If you are married, you and your husband should be actively involved in handling the household finances, or if that's your responsibility, it is common courtesy to keep your husband clued up.

❑ **Step 9—Get educated.** Read money magazines and books about investing, visit financial websites, or sign up for a seminar or class on budgeting. With a little effort and education, you can glean enough to make wise decisions that may someday increase your net worth—or at least decrease your chances of being scammed. In addition, if you have money, know what others (your husband, business manager, or accountant) are doing with it. It's not that you don't trust them, but you never know when you will be called to pick up where they left off.

> *Debt consumes huge chunks of our resources that could be used to make significant contributions to our savings.*

Debt consumes vast chunks of our resources that could be used to make significant contributions to our savings. If you have lost hundreds or thousands of dollars in the past because of your debt (paying high-interest rates, fees, and late charges), consider what you would do with that money if it was given back to you. Now, commit to applying those nine essential steps to improve your overall financial situation, which will likely save you hundreds or thousands of dollars in the future.

Some Saving Wisdom

Instead of using our money frivolously, we want our money to be compounding in a savings and investment account.

If you're still not motivated to save, consider that with just a little discipline over time, you can accumulate a substantial amount of money with compound interest.

- If you start at age 25 and simply deposit $10 every week in an account that earns 6% interest. By age 65 you would have roughly 85,000.

- If you start at age 35 and simply deposit $30 every week in an account that earns 6% interest. By age 65 you would have roughly 130,000.

- If you start at age 45 and simply deposit $50 every week in an account that earns 6% interest. By age 65 you would have roughly 100,000.

That's the power of compound interest which produces better results the more you save and the longer you save! All it takes is a commitment to save a small amount of money. Money accumulated consistently over a period of time, even if it is not earning much interest, can help you build your emergency fund or, better yet, help you send your children to college debt-free.

You can also use the "Rule of 72" to remind you of the power of compound interest. It shows you how your savings

Step 9: Getting Financially Focused 261

or investment can grow with compound interest by dividing the interest rate into 72. The result is how long it will take for your money to double without further savings.

For example, you have $15,000, earning 6% interest (after tax). 72 divided by 6 equals 12. In approximately twelve years, your $15,000 will double, so: After 12 years you'll have $30,000; after 12 more years (24 years) you'll have $60,000.

If you are now motivated to save, let me suggest some ideas to help you increase your saving opportunities:

- **Tip 1**. Have a small percentage of your paycheck automatically transferred into a savings account, or begin contributing to your employer-sponsored retirement plan.

- **Tip 2**. Commit to using cash, check, or debit card to pay for purchases or services. If it's necessary to use your credit card, try to pay the debt in full at the end of the month.

- **Tip 3**. Make a list of what you need before you go shopping, and only buy what is on your list. It may be helpful to keep a running list in your organizer or smartphone of your family's needs. My categories are clothing items, household items, and office supplies. In addition, try to review your financial vision and goals before shopping so you'll be less tempted to purchase something on sale but not on your list.

- **Tip 4**. Kick those addictions that are costing you money. If you are a smoker, if you stopped smoking one pack of cigarettes a day at an average cost of $6.50 (varies state by state), you would have saved over $2,300.00 in one year. This money could be used to make an extra payment on your mortgage, car note, or student loan. Other ideas include canceling online subscriptions or club memberships, cooking rather than eating out, or driving less by staying home, walking, or taking the bus.

- **Tip 5**. Talk with your creditors and try to renegotiate the interest rates on your credit cards or transfer the balance to another credit card, preferably with a lower interest rate. Consider canceling and destroying all credit cards except the one(s) to be used for emergencies. If you are considering a consolidation loan, find a reputable agency in your area by checking out the US Justice Department's approved list of consolidation consultants and counselors at: www.justice.gov/ust/list-credit-counseling-agencies-approved-pursuant-11-usc-111

- **Tip 6**. Pay your bills on time. If you can't pay them in full at the end of the month or you're having trouble paying the required amount, pay as much as you can to show your intent to clear your debt. In addition, inform your credit card company of your intention to honor your debt as soon as possible.

Tip #7, Dealing with Emotional Spending

Saving tip number seven—which I've given its own personal space—deals with emotional spending.

Our financial baggage, if not dealt with, will not only affect us but also those close to us. By taming the emotions that have fueled your attitude toward money, you may be able to save money, repair a broken relationship, and become a better steward of the financial resources God has blessed you with.

Step 9: Getting Financially Focused

It is no secret that our emotions have to do with our feelings. It's the same type of feeling we have for people operating in the realm of money, dictating how we use and view money. If money is used as medicine, we make purchases to feel good or to numb the pain. If used as a weapon, money is spent as a means of retaliating against another person to hurt them and make us feel better. An example would be a wife boldly making purchases to get back at her husband for something he said or did that was hurtful, or to boldly proclaim, "You have no control over me." A woman who feels she looks old may spend money on things that make her feel and look younger.

Whereas our *feelings* about money can make us feel energetic, happy, confident, significant, or secure if we have it and lethargic, sad, insecure, insignificant, or undeserving if we don't have it. The *mental* aspect of money concerns our mindset or thoughts about money.

Our thoughts about money can span the gamut and affect our attitude about money, from being nervous about accepting money from another person, including a spouse, to being a control freak about money (accounting for every penny); or just the opposite, having a chronic need to buy something every time money touches the palms of our hands.

In her book, *The 9 Steps to Financial Freedom*, Suze Orman tells the story of a man who did not trust his wife with his money and refused to have a joint account with her. The distrust came from his bad experience at nine years old. His sister had stolen money from him that he had been saving to buy a trampoline. He had harbored those feelings way into his adult life.[4]

📙 Take time right now and try to determine when and where your nature regarding money originated.

Look at what in your past has you feeling the way you do about money.

When I was about nine, my parents allowed me to spend a couple of weeks with relatives, which included and ended with a trip to visit my grandparents in Mississippi.

I was away from my parents—whom I've always felt very secure with—for two whole weeks. Before I left, my mother gave me ten dollars for miscellaneous expenses. She was about to give me twenty dollars, which I was convinced I needed, but she thought that was too much money for a young child to manage.

I was enjoying my time with my relatives and hanging out with my cousins until we took a trip to the mall. The Rubik's Cube was a hot item then, so of course, one of my cousins and I just had to have one (the cheaper key chain version). That took my ten dollars down to six dollars and some change. Then the unexpected happened: I had to pay for my own lunch at the mall! Being the only cousin without a parent, I was left to do the responsible thing and pay for my own lunch. That took my six dollars down to four dollars and some change, and I still had over a week to go before I could feel financially secure with my parents again!

The worrying set in. If someone promised me a dollar—in this case it was one of my uncles—I made sure I got it. One of my cousins rebuked me for being so bold in asking for my money, but I paid her no mind—she didn't have the responsibilities that I had.

I watched every penny I spent from that point on and hid my money so no one else would get to it—not that they would try, but at that moment, I had a survival mindset. I had to provide for myself!

A funny thing happened when I got to my grandparents' farm. My grandmother noticed my attitude toward my little stash of cash, and she privately approached me and said, "You will not need that here." So she put my money away for me, and just before I left for home, I was able to buy my parents and little brother a small gift.

Even though all ended well for me, I still kept the mindset that I had to take care of myself. When I got an allowance, I saved it until my parents were borrowing from me and paying me a little extra for the loan. When my parents offered to buy me something, I did not refuse it, but I had my own cash to fall back on. That attitude spilled over into my marriage but did not register with me until I dealt with the emotional and mental aspects of money.

I'm not judging my extended family for having been on a budget or in a financial crunch, but I want you to understand how the emotional and mental aspects of money can get masked behind a habit. That's when you hear people say, "I just love to shop" or "That's just how I am." Instead of believing that change is possible when the source or root of the problem is identified, and we look to God for the wisdom and strength to overcome our problems.

Does the Heart of Your Husband Trust You?

As I said earlier, "Our financial baggage, if not dealt with, will affect us and those close to us." Therefore, I feel compelled to address the woman hiding debt from her spouse.

My sister in Christ, your financial issues most likely have nothing to do with your spouse but your own mental and emotional baggage that you have not dealt with. Take time now and determine when and why you started hiding debt from your spouse. Did it start because you did not think your spouse would understand your need for (or obsession with) certain things (e.g., status, fulfillment, attention, security, shoes, bags, and so on)?

Balancing blessing and obtaining order involves getting to the heart of your financial issues. This requires you to give your spouse the common courtesy of letting him know what is happening with the family finances.

Although most husbands and wives may be radically different when it comes to managing and spending money; genuine, Christ-centered relationships are based on honesty—which is a sign of maturity in a marriage.

Our model of virtue is a woman whose husband has confidence in her ability to manage the household finances; we are told about the Proverbs 31 woman: "The heart of her husband safely trusts her" (v. 11).

I have a friend who used to be very hurt over her husband not sharing the responsibilities of managing the household finances. He brought home his paycheck and handed it over to her. Talking with him, I noticed that it wasn't that he did not care about the family finances; he just knew without a doubt that his wife was "taking care of business." He was able to trust her to pay the bills on time and invest their money wisely so he could focus on providing for his family. She would not dare "mortgage his future" by loading him down with debt—replacing their freedom with bondage.

Proverbs 31:11 concludes by saying, "So he will have no lack of gain." Here gain represents general wealth. The virtuous woman adds financial value to her household, either by saving money from shopping wisely or using her talents to produce an income that supplements her husband's income. She is not a financial liability or a burden to her husband; like Eve, she was created to be his helpmate (see Genesis 2:18), a crown to his head (see Proverbs 12:4), and a means of obtaining favor from the Lord (see Proverbs 18:22).

As Paul suggests in Ephesians 4:25, put off falsehood and speak truthfully to one another. Reveal everything, including the emotions behind your spending. Also, have a proposal for how you plan to pay off the debt you have accumulated. If you have attained the debt without your spouse's knowledge, then in my opinion, it is up to you, not your spouse, to pay the debt. If you do not make enough or are a stay-at-home wife/mom, be creative—think of things you can sell or do to earn extra money.

Being honest with your spouse and then taking the necessary steps to live with financial integrity will produce liberating results that will far outweigh your immediate guilt, pain, and discomfort of confessing your wrong. Proverbs 20:7 reminds us that when we walk in integrity, our children are blessed.

Inspiring Investments

Now that you've gained ideas to help you start saving and your eyes have been opened to what may have been hindering your ability to save, let us turn our attention to investing.

At the risk of sounding like a newspaper ad, one of the best ways to develop an effective asset allocation plan is to consult a qualified financial planner. To adequately discuss investing would require another book and knowledge and experience beyond my degree in business and finance. However, I will encourage you to take the time to identify low-risk investment tools you can use—right now—to help you reach your financial goals and then put those tools to work for you. Some suggestions are: a certificate of deposit, a money market deposit account, a money market mutual fund, an Individual Retirement Account (IRA), or your company's 401(k) Plan.

The types of investing that we will cover in this section—beyond our responsibility to tithe—are basic ideas for investing in oneself.

Investing in Your Passion

Have you lost sight of a dream you once had to own your own business? A home-based business is widely prevalent among women. It gives them the flexibility to be more active in their children's lives and more control over their health and their careers.

Amazingly, by investing in their passions, some women have turned a home-based business into a multimillion-dollar endeavor; Julie Aigner-Clark is one of them.

When Mrs. Clark discovered no age-appropriate products were available to help her share her passion and love of art, classical music, language, and poetry with her young daughter, she set out to change that.[5]

What started as a home-based business costing $18,000 to film her first colorful, entertaining video—in the basement of her home, with borrowed equipment and a home computer—quickly led to other interactive products: DVDs, videos, music CDs, books, and toys for babies and young children. The multimillion-dollar home-based corporation was known as *The Baby Einstein Company*.[6]

Less than five years after starting her company it was acquired by the Walt Disney Company the same year the company's sales exceeded $20 million.[7]

> ▶ What is your dream job? What talent, hobby, or activity do you enjoy doing that has the potential to become something you can earn a living pursuing, or that would provide extra income for your family?

Step 9: Getting Financially Focused

With her earnings, the Proverbs 31 woman seizes the opportunity to purchase a plot of land to cultivate and plant a vineyard (v. 16). We can surmise that this wise woman had already surveyed her options and done a feasibility study—taking into account the cost of the land versus its worth; analyzing the risks associated with owning a vineyard; estimating the time and labor required to manage and maintain her investment properly; and evaluating whether the purchase will assist her in meeting her life goals and benefit her family in the years to come. She would not think about jeopardizing her family financially by acting on a whim. She had crunched the numbers and was fully prepared to negotiate. In addition, She knew that her husband had confidence in her ability to make wise decisions and to negotiate the best deals.

The Proverbs 31 Woman was able to make wise choices because of her dependency upon God. With godly wisdom, she was able to discern what she needed to do to get her business going and how to do it (v. 18).

You may be wondering where this Proverbs 31 woman gets the financial resources to invest in a plot of land. Proverbs 31:24 says, "She makes linen garments and sells them, and supplies sashes for the merchants." It is my guess that she saves the money received from her job or her other money-making ventures.

Our virtuous example planned and prepared wisely before pursuing her desire to purchase a plot of land (v.16). I hope godly wisdom encourages you to plan just as wisely.

So, how far have you gotten? I would only recommend you quit your day job to start or focus on your business once your business is earning a profit or you are financially able to do so. However, there are simple steps you can employ now to prepare you for your dream job later.

- Network, talk to people about the business you want to be in or the product or service you wish to market.

- Determine the feasibility of your product or service. Will it fill a real market need? Who are your competitors? How well are they doing? What unique quality or service will distinguish you from them?

- Know whether you want to start your own business or purchase a franchise, and whether you can operate your business from home or will you require an alternate location.

- Research whether you need an Employer Identification Number (EIN) from the IRS and a state business license.

- Get educated by attending seminars and classes. In addition, find out if your state offers free and discounted courses to potential business owners—especially in: record keeping, preparing financial statements, and your responsibility as an employer.

- Create a draft business plan to give your business ideas focus. It should outline clear objectives and goals for your business. It should specify what product or service you want to provide. In addition, it should denote how your product or service will be sold. Consider also: equipment needs, expenses you will incur, the demographics of your customers, and how you will advertise or promote your business.

- Know how much capital you need to start your business and look into various financing options: save the money yourself or get a small business loan.

- Seek out expert advice on the tax implications and state laws.

In addition to the above suggestions, visit the Small Business Administration (SBA) website at: www.sba.gov. The site offers online training courses and advice to assist you in starting and successfully managing your own business.

Investing in Your Peace of Mind

Beyond investing in your passion, an inspiring investment is also investing in your peace of mind if something should happen to your spouse—and like the prophet's widow (in 2 Kings 4:1-7), you are left with the financial responsibility of providing for your household. If your husband has made appropriate provisions for you, you may be fine, but if he hasn't and has no desire to do so, ask yourself: how will you survive?

For the single woman, what provisions have you made for yourself if you lost your job for a year or longer? What other skills can you fall back on to get you through the financial drought?

I know women who, after a divorce or losing their job, had to move in with friends or family members until they were financially able to survive on their own. The situation gets even more complicated when you add children and no child support. So, you can imagine what it was like for the prophet's widow. When the prophet died, his income died with him.

If you're married and this is a concern for you, share your concerns with your husband. Ask to see what provisions he has made to help you feel financially secure should anything happen to him. If you're not satisfied with the results of your conversation, take it to the Lord in prayer. I am convinced that if your husband refuses to make the necessary provisions for you, there is nothing wrong with setting aside money for such and such a time.

If you're single, take a look at your situation. What can you do to ease the effects of a job loss? When you're in it, that's not the time to consider your options. The time is now when you can financially do something about it.

The truth is some tough financial choices will have to be made. Is living in a gated community necessary when more affordable housing is available in a reasonably safe neighborhood outside the gates? Do you need a Sport Utility Vehicle (SUV) when a small economy car will get you from here to there cheaper?

If you can afford it, that's one thing; if you would be left in a serious financial bind if you had less or no income, then it's time to make some tough decisions to help keep the *storm at bay when the rain comes*.

Investing in Others

Philanthropy can be contagious if we see it not just as an opportunity to give (to get something in return) but, more importantly, as a responsibility to make a difference in the lives of others.

There are so many ways to invest in people. You can financially invest in your children by saving for their future. You can give to the poor by donating and contributing to charitable organizations and ministries. You can invest time in your family's emotional and spiritual well-being, or like the wise and compassionate woman of God—who takes investing in others a step further—you can find ways to actively serve those in need. Scripture says of this wise woman: "She extends her hand to the poor, yes, she reaches out her hands to the needy (Proverbs 31:20). I imagine she visited the sick and

Step 9: Getting Financially Focused

shut-in, fed the poor, helped the disabled, and comforted people in need.

I believe our generosity in investing wisely in others fuels God's generosity toward us. Every service done for us, every fortune given to us, and every opportunity opened to us is an obligation to serve, bless, and pave the way for others.

How much we sow into the lives of our family members, friends, community, and even ourselves will determine the size and quality of the heavenly harvest we will someday produce.

Leaving a Will

Preparing a will is also investing in others. Who do you want to bless with an inheritance upon your death? By leaving a will, you are telling the world exactly who gets what of your assets when you die. You are also investing in the emotional well-being of your family as they grieve and rejoice in your passing on to be with the Lord. Without a tangible will, most of your assets will likely go to probate or the IRS.

> *I believe our generosity in investing wisely in others fuels God's generosity toward us.*

Do not just assume that everything will work out. By investing the time to discuss your response to each question I have listed below with your heirs, you could ward off a host of arguments, disputes, and conflicts—that could lead to other family issues later.

Your response to these questions is the essence of most wills—which identifies who you want your beneficiaries, executors, guardians, and trustees to be upon your death. Ask yourself…

- Who will supervise the distribution of my property and carry out the desires expressed in my will?

- Who will I leave property to upon my death?

- How do I want my property to be divided?

- Where do I want to be buried, or do I want to be cremated (i.e., you may even want to describe the specific details of the service)?

- Who will I leave property to if everyone I have named in my will passes away before I do? Do I want my property to go to the remaining family members, friends, a specific organization, or to charity?

- Do I have any specific bequests (describe the property and to whom it will be given)?

- Who will be my primary beneficiary?

- Who will be my alternate beneficiary?

- Who will be the legal guardian (act as a parent for my minor child or children) of my death?

- Who will be the alternate guardian?

- Who will be my financial custodian to manage money or property I may leave to my minor child or children?

Once you have answered these questions, I highly advise you to seek counseling from someone who specializes in estate planning—to assist you in turning your responses into a legally binding document.

In addition, your will should be updated as needed to reflect major life changes (e.g., marriage, new child, death of a loved one, etc.).

The Proverbs 31 woman is able to laugh at the days ahead (v. 25) because she has made proper provisions for herself and her family. Are you able to laugh at the days ahead?

Leaving a Legacy

Leaving a will is a crucial means of investing in your loved ones. Still, I also want you to consider bestowing an intangible blessing upon each family member. Author, Greg Vaughn, uses this concept in his book *Letters from Dad*, in which he encourages men nationwide to leave a legacy of letters to their family members—especially their children—blessing, affirming, and reminding them of who they were and what they valued most.

May I encourage you—for each member of your family—to write at least one letter that will encourage them, inspire them, and comfort them upon your death? Include a life lesson you have learned, encourage them in their endeavors, speak positively of characteristics in them that you admire, and end with a prayer of blessing over them—similar to what Isaac spoke over Jacob and what Jacob spoke over his sons. Let me remind you to stay positive. If you don't have anything good to write, it's best not to write anything.

☙❧

Step 9: Your Daily Call to Order

Chapter Comments:

The motive behind this step was to help you financially position yourself to serve the Lord more readily and to help you obtain additional financial resources to invest in the kingdom of God.

In addition, it's important to remember that a healthy attitude about money can only be obtained when money is viewed from a spiritual perspective; this means money should never interfere with or take precedence over our relationship with people. Here are some helpful lessons I have learned:

> ❧ When giving money to charity, your church, and the poor, give without expecting anything in return. In the same respect, when you pay your tithes or give an offering, know that you have done what is required of you.

> ❧ When loaning money, if you do not have it to give, you do not have it to lend. If a relative or a friend needs a loan, and you can loan the money without putting yourself in a financial bind, consider making them a loan—expecting them to pay you back. However, if you do not get your money back, count it "all joy" and move on.

> ❧ Think twice before cosigning a loan for someone if you cannot afford to make the payments yourself. You never know what future circumstances will cause that person to default on the loan—sticking you with the bill and an unfavorable mark on your credit report.

> ❧ Stop comparing what you have with what someone else has, and realize that society in general (especially the media) creates within us unnecessary desires to have what we do not need.

> ❧ Pray before you invest your money. If someone has an offer that is too good to be true, it probably is.

Chapter Questions:
Group Discussion
1. What are the three criteria for acceptable debt (as discussed in this chapter)?

Step 9: Getting Financially Focused

2. What is the difference between our *feelings* about money and our *thoughts* about money?
3. Who in the Bible—besides the Prophet's Widow discussed in II Kings 4—does the Lord provide financial deliverance to?
4. What lessons have you learned about money that you want to share with your accountability partner or small group?

Personal Reflection

5. What mental or emotional issues do you have regarding money? Are you getting counseling?
6. What steps have you taken in the past to get out of debt?
7. What steps are you willing to take now to get out of debt?
8. How would your life (and your family's life) be different if you got in shape financially?

Chapter Assignments:

❑ **Challenge 1**: Write a prayer asking the Lord to forgive you for letting your spending get out of control. Then, list all your significant assets and release ownership of them to the Lord in prayer.

❑ **Challenge 2**: Respond to end of chapter questions.

❑ **Challenge 3**: Begin to track your spending.

❑ **Challenge 4**: Go on a spending fast for thirty days; buy only what you need.

❑ **Challenge 5**: List your debts and assets.

❑ **Challenge 6**: Write down your financial vision and goals, breaking long-term goals into short-term goals

❑ **Challenge 7**: Pull your credit report and obtain your FICO score.

❑ **Challenge 8**: Evaluate your spending to find ways to cut back and save.

❑ **Challenge 9**: Create an initial budget.

❑ **Challenge 10**: If you want to start your own business, use the tips listed in the "Investing in Your Passion" section to define your business objective, goals, and requirements.

❑ **Challenge 11**: If you do not have a will, answer the questions in the section: "Leaving a Will." Then, seek legal advice on making your desires official.

❑ **Challenge 12**: Write your first Legacy Letter.

❑ **Extreme Challenge**: If you still do not have peace regarding your finances after following the steps in this chapter, seek out a debt counselor or find a local church in your area that offers a financial ministries class.

❑ **Group Challenge**: Each member should write down how they feel about their current financial situation, then briefly share their thoughts with the small group—to give them a general idea of where each person may need prayer, accountability, and support—end by praying for one another.

Step 10

Being Divine by Design

> ...put on tender mercies, kindness, humility,
> meekness, longsuffering.
> —Colossians 3:12

Sometimes the most difficult thing to see is the beauty and worth in oneself. This is also true for some of the most beautiful women in the world, who walk up and down the runways in New York, Milan, and Paris, and whom the media upholds as a trophy, representing a standard of beauty for the rest of the world to admire.

Some of our daughters will pile on makeup, undergo plastic surgery, and be bound by anorexia and bulimia to be like them and look like them when there should be examples of Christ's beauty all around them. I am not just speaking of the beautiful golden glow of an early morning sunset, a colorful bouquet of assorted flowers, or freshly fallen leaves along a country road, but of godly women—mothers, grandmothers, sisters, and other Christian women whom God has made—that set a standard of excellence for beauty.

In this step, I hope to introduce you to those things that bring out the beauty and elegance in a woman of God. I will define what true beauty is, what self-worth is, what modesty is, and what is involved in walking in modesty.

The Beauty in You

Looking back over your life, can you remember what it was like during those first few years of school? Many of us found our place in society during that time when others, probably classmates, judged our cover (physical appearance)—and then tagged us as being pretty, ugly, fat, bony, gawky, stylish, short, tall, and so on—rather than combing the pages to discover that there is so much more to us.

Some of us were teased, some were accepted into certain cliques, and others may have been shunned completely.

The young girls who seemed to have finagled their way out of this labeling system were those who possessed a strong awareness of who they were. A seed of self-worth was planted in them which took root in the good soil of love, encouragement, and acceptance—which I believe was cultivated in the home.

Knowing Christ and having an intimate relationship with Him also brings out this confidence of loving and accepting who God made you to be—regardless of how others try to define you.

In my attempt to define beauty, I discovered that most dictionaries and people defined it as "something pleasurable to the eyes." This is disturbing to me because—as you and I both know—beauty is not just skin deep. External beauty does not last long without its companion, inner beauty. Without Christ's forgiveness, sin in the life of the most beautiful woman in the world makes her ugly on the inside and before God. A verse in Proverbs says, "As a ring of gold in a swine's snout, So is a lovely woman who lacks discretion" (Proverbs 11:22). In other words, that which is unbecoming (pig's snout, lousy attitude, or sin) takes away from that which is becoming (a ring of gold, a lovely woman, or righteousness).

Sarah, the wife of Abraham, was beautiful. Yet, despite her physical appearance, she was held in high esteem for her inner beauty—not her outer beauty. First Peter 3:6 interjects that she obeyed her husband and held him in high regard. I believe Sarah also had "the incorruptible beauty of a gentle and quiet spirit." Maybe that's who Peter was thinking of when he made his previous statement:

> *Do not let your adornment be merely outward— arranging the hair, wearing gold, or putting on fine apparel— rather let it be the hidden person of the heart, with the incorruptible beauty of a gentle and quiet spirit, which is very precious in the sight of God (1 Peter 3:3-4).*

It is not the reflection in the mirror that defines who you are; it is what's being reflected from your heart. I have seen women own a room because of their grace, virtue, and femininity—it had very little to do with their external beauty or how thin or petite they were.

Consider Delilah; never was her physical appearance described in the book of Judges, yet here was a Philistine woman who captured the heart of an Israelite judge named Samson.

Samson was a Nazirite, one set apart for a particular purpose; in his case it was to deliver the Israelites from the hands of the Philistines (13:5). This meant Samson could drink no wine nor strong drink, neither could he cut his hair which contained his enormous strength; strength that enabled him to tear a lion apart with his bare hands (14:6) or to defeat thousands of Philistines—without any assistance from the army of Israel (15:15).

Besides having massive physical strength, Samson was a rebellious soul who insisted on having things his way. The Bible notes Samson's promiscuous behavior of having visited a harlot in Gaza. Yet afterward, we are told, "he loved a woman in the Valley of Sorek, whose name was Delilah" (16:4).

Where they met or how they met, the Bible does not say. Yet, there was something about Delilah—beyond the physical, beyond the external sex appeal, beyond the material possessions—that drew Samson's interest.

To capture the heart of this overly confident judge, Delilah had to have self-confidence in her ability to easily charm a man. In addition, she saw Samson as a man with desires. Putting the two together, she had figured out what unique abilities she possessed that would be instrumental in providing Samson with what he needed—to get what *she* wanted.

Confrontation followed Samson most places he went, yet Delilah was able to provide him with a place of rest, relaxation, and light-hearted conversation mixed with flattery and the right amount of adulation and affirmation—all of which Samson probably didn't know he needed until he met Delilah. In short, Delilah made Samson feel good about himself (she boosted his self-esteem).

> **GOD SPECIALIZES IN TAKING THE "WEAKLINGS" OF THE WORLD AND TURNING THEM INTO STRONG BEAUTIFUL SOULS.**
>
> JUDITH COUCHMAN

Sadly, when Samson allowed himself to be transparent and vulnerable before Delilah, her charm turned to deceit, and she betrayed him—because her heart was in the wrong place.

We see from Delilah that charm may draw and fascinate people for a while, but the wrong motivation will pull out the ugliness (sin) in a person, keeping them from desiring God's best for themselves and for others—which, in my opinion, decreases a person's self-worth and inner beauty. We were not created to feel good about ourselves when we undervalue others and disregard their significance to God.

> Is there anything you are doing or that your conscience does not approve of that is affecting your inner beauty and your self-worth?

Defining Self-Worth

Paul instructs us to: "Let nothing be done through selfish ambition or conceit, but in lowliness of mind let each esteem others better than [himself or herself]" (Philippians 2:3, emphasis added).

Paul understood that self-worth in the eyes of God is attained when a person esteems others. In contrast, self-esteem is attained when a person esteems oneself.

Although self-worth and self-esteem are often used interchangeably, there is a difference. In most dictionaries, the general definition for both is "having self-respect or having self-confidence in oneself." I believe self-worth comes from being true to yourself, or living out your values. It is knowing and accepting what you know to be the absolute truth about yourself morally, culturally, and spiritually. When your values are spiritually based (or in alignment with God), your overall sense of worth as a person adds value to the lives of others, and your self-worth matures.

Self-esteem is a person's feelings about herself based on her mood, temperament, self-image, and what people think—all of which can change on a whim. Self-esteem increases when we are good at something, when goals are accomplished, when people speak highly of us, and when we have self-worth. Self-esteem diminishes when the opposite occurs: when we haven't found our niche, when we fail to complete projects or goals, when people speak badly of us, or when our values are undefined.

Lack of self-worth is essentially a spiritual problem that gets resolved when a person becomes aware of how valuable they are to God.

Self-worth that comes from having a relationship with God appreciates in value. It brings forth inner beauty which out lives, out shines, and out performs external beauty. It carries with it the understanding that we are to treat everyone (self included), as if they are worthy of God's best.

> *Charm is deceitful and beauty is passing, But a woman who fears the LORD, she shall be praised.*
>
> *—Proverbs 31:30*

Appreciating What Self-Worth Generates

As a Proverbs 31 Woman, seek to appreciate and understand what self-worth generates in the lives of those who have it and those who do not have it. Though many people will continue to judge your cover, don't allow yourself to be defined by your physical beauty. It is your inner beauty or self-worth which, like our Proverbs 31 woman, "... is far above rubies" (v. 10).

When I initially read about the Proverbs 31 Woman, I had the mindset that the author was speaking about a physically beautiful woman. However, upon further examination, never was her outward beauty mentioned. The focus had been on distinctive qualities that made her alluring to her husband, adored by her children, and an example of virtue and strength

Step 10: Being Divine By Design

for women throughout the ages. The only reference to beauty is when the author ends by saying: "Charm is deceitful and beauty is passing, But a woman who fears the LORD, she shall be praised" (v. 30).

When you are beautiful on the inside, it embodies who you are. Godly people can see the beauty in you as if your body were covered in ".. fine linen and purple" (v. 22). Men will be drawn to you, and other women will want what you have (which is Jesus).

With God's grace and the power of the Holy Spirit working in you, you can be beautiful in all the ways that reflect God's character. True beauty is a reflection of God's glory; the more you emulate Christ (in actions and attitude), the more beautiful you become. The mirror through which you see yourself will begin to unveil a beautiful woman of God who is complete in Him. This means you have self-worth, this also means you have chosen to:

- Put on the new man (2 Corinthians 5:17)
- Put on truthfulness (Ephesians 4:25)
- Put on kindness and humility (Colossians 3:12)
- Put on a gentle and quiet spirit (1 Peter 3:4)
- Put on love (Colossians 3:14)

Lay your life before God. If you will do that He will give you a true perspective of what beauty is. Without God's perspective, our view of things can easily become misconstrued. Remember, "Man looks at the outward appearance, but the LORD looks at the heart" (1 Samuel 16:7, NIV).

Before I continue, please brace yourself before reading the next section. Pray that you are able to receive what I have to say in the spirit of love and understanding.

Adorning Yourself in Modesty

In Paul's letter to young Timothy, Paul tells Timothy to tell the ladies of the congregation to:

> ... *adorn themselves in modest apparel, with propriety and moderation, not with braided hair or gold or pearls or costly clothing, but, which is proper for women professing godliness, with good works (1 Timothy 2:9-10).*

In the above passage, Paul uses the word *adorn* to describe the beautification process most women take themselves through daily. When I think of the word *adorn*, the word *decorate* comes to mind. It is not merely putting on; it is putting on with the express purpose of beautifying oneself or something.

In the process of putting on, there is a natural order in which things are done: underclothes are put on before the garment, the hair is styled before the hat is placed, stockings are slipped on before shoes, and so on. In other words, when Paul speaks of adorning oneself in modesty, he tells us that there is a godly order to how we should dress—modestly.

When you follow God's command to dress modestly, not only are you walking in obedience to God (which brings a certain level of order to your life), but your apparel reflects a woman of elegance, grace, and order.

As a representative of God, you step out of order when your dress and appearance become more important to you than your relationship with God, setting an example for other women, or the effect you may have on men—especially your sincere Christian brothers.

I realize that some women have lost a lot of weight and want to show off their beautiful new bodies; others may believe that self-worth comes from how many heads a woman turns, and still others may want to feel young, hip, stylish, and sexy. Then there are a handful of women who have become so accustomed to dressing alluring that they take no thought to who they are influencing or attracting.

Just this past week, I received an email alert from a friend that listed things a rapist looks for in a potential victim; number two on the list was clothing that was easy to take off or cut off quickly.

I wholeheartedly believe that we should feel safe in whatever we wear. However, when our dress and appearance is revealing and form-fitting, intentional or unintentional, we draw the attention of men. Matthew 5:28 reminds us that if a man looks at a woman with lust, he has committed adultery in his heart.

You might be tempted to think this is not your problem, but before you turn a deaf ear, let's consider a couple of facts.

Fact number one: men are visual. Being a woman will draw the attention of a man. Being a physically attractive woman will attract the attention of more men; and being provocatively dressed will arrest the attention of many more men.

Shaunti Feldhahn, in her book *For Women Only* says, "A man can't *not* want to look." She asked a group of men to predict their response to seeing a woman with a great body standing in a nearby line: 98% of the men could not resist looking or sneaking a peek, no matter how hard they tried.[1]

Imagine going on a job interview; would you wear a bathing suit? Hopefully not! Why? Because it's inappropriate for most job interviews. The focus would not be on what you know and why you are qualified for the job but on your body. The same holds true for a Christian woman when her attire lacks discretion or deviates too much from the acceptable norm; the focus becomes her and not God in her.

If tight, low-slung jeans, form-fitting skirts, curvaceous dresses, and other revealing styles will cause men to lust after you, do not wear them.

Fact number two: we are responsible for looking out for the interest of others. Philippians 2:4 says, "Let each of you look out not only for his own interests, but also for the interests of others." This means protecting the hearts of our brothers in Christ and men in general. It also means setting an example for our sisters in Christ. As Christian women, we have a challenge to promote and model modesty to young girls and unbelieving women and to help them acquire a healthy perspective on what modesty is.

Within the same sphere of modesty is our presentation. I know women, saved and unsaved, who will not walk out of their houses to take the trash out without makeup and a nice outfit on. At the other end of the spectrum are women who have no problem going to the corner store with rollers in their hair, T-shirt and sweat pants on, and flip-flops on their feet—and feel no shame about it.

If for some reason—other than an emergency—I had to step outside the comfort of my home in my rollers to get eggs, butter, or something I desperately needed, I doubt whether you would see me. I would be dashing here, hiding over there, or ducking behind that because—as an ambassador for Christ—I would be embarrassed by how I looked. I used rollers in this analogy, but it does not have to be rollers. It could be unkempt hair, a shirt with a plunging neckline with breasts hanging out, a skirt that rides up when you sit down, tight clothes outlining every curve, or attire symbolically saying: "Who cares" or "Look at me."

What I hoped you received from Paul's words is that you are to dress properly as a woman professing to know God. This means you care about how you present yourself as a representative of Jesus Christ. This does not mean you cannot look great and feel good. You are required to take care of yourself, look your best whenever possible, and conduct yourself in a manner that is pleasing to God.

Defining Modesty for Yourself

Only through prayer, fasting, and a study on the subject of modesty can one make an honest determination of what modesty is to them and how that will affect how they dress. But please understand that modesty is a command from God. It's not an option that we can choose to accept or not accept. The good news is that our attire does not have to be boring, bland, and lacking quality. What is modest to me may not be modest to you. Growing up, I wore pants but rarely wore jeans; I believed jeans were unbecoming on a woman—because my mother never wore jeans. My good friend in high school never wore pants because her mother thought it was inappropriate for a lady—*and this was in the late eighties.*

Some people believe you must wear skirts to your ankles, blouses buttoned all the way up, and long sleeves in every season to be modest. Then some women wear flashy and gaudy fashion that puts the focus on their outward appearance and their financial status rather than on their heart?

It's all right to have fun with fashion, but we want people to be drawn to us because of the elegance and gracefulness that God has bestowed upon us. Therefore, you should be sober in your dress and appearance by asking yourself the following questions about the clothes you wear:

- Am I representing God or myself?
- Am I dressed appropriately for the occasion?
- Are my private parts covered?

༼ What is the motivation behind how I am dressed today (e.g., am I dressed to entice men, am I trying to compete with another woman, or am I flaunting my financial status)?

There are other subtopics I could get into regarding walking in grace and modesty; the truth is, walking in grace and modesty begins in the heart. When your heart desires to please the Lord, the Holy Spirit will prompt you to make changes in areas, a week ago or yesterday, you thought were insignificant. A woman who walks in grace and modesty is not perfect; however, she understands that every area of her life should reflect God's glory—especially in those areas where her choices, attitudes, behaviors, and actions influence others.

The Attitudes of the Daughters of Zion

We discussed our need for modesty concerning looking out for others, but how does God view immodesty?

In the third chapter of Isaiah, we are introduced to the daughters of Zion. Isaiah speaks of them as arrogant women of Jerusalem who were more concerned with obtaining and adorning themselves with the latest fashion than the spiritual well-being of themselves and the people around them.

These were probably women who professed to know God, but in works, they denied Him (see Titus 1:16). They probably drew close to the Lord with their mouth and honored him with their lips, but their heart was far from Him (see Matthew 15:8).

They were described as being haughty. Haughty can be defined as "having or showing great pride in oneself and disdain, contempt, or scorn for others."[2]

When they walked, it was with overt daintiness and outstretched necks to flaunt their worldly possessions, and

Step 10: Being Divine By Design

with wantonness or "sexually loose or unrestrained eyes"[3] begging to be noticed—especially by men—for their outward beauty and the fine linen and apparel that they wore.

The way the women walked, moved, behaved, and dressed in public was explicitly to draw attention to themselves. In response to their attitude, the LORD said in Isaiah 3:16-24:

> *Because the daughters of Zion are haughty, And walk with outstretched necks And wanton eyes, Walking and mincing as they go, Making a jingling with their feet, Therefore the Lord will strike with a scab The crown of the head of the daughters of Zion, And the LORD will uncover their secret parts." In that day the Lord will take away the finery: The jingling anklets, the scarves, and the crescents; The pendants, the bracelets, and the veils; the headdresses, the leg ornaments, and the headbands; The perfume boxes, the charms, and the rings; The nose jewels, the festal apparel, and the mantles; The outer garments, the purses, and the mirrors; The fine linen, the turbans, and the robes. And so it shall be: Instead of a sweet smell there will be a stench; Instead of a sash, a rope; Instead of well-set hair, baldness; Instead of a rich robe, a girding of sackcloth; And branding instead of beauty.*

God's Word also says that a woman should dress modestly with "shamefacedness and sobriety" (1 Timothy 2:9). Shamefacedness in this passage refers to our ability to walk humbly, without arrogance, showing respect and regard for others. Sobriety could be defined as using sound judgment, controlling one's passions and desires, and how one dresses.

Whereas the women of Zion walked with outstretched necks, we should, "...walk worthy of the Lord, fully pleasing Him, being fruitful in every good work and increasing in the knowledge of God" (Colossians 1:10).

Whereas the women of Zion walked with wanton eyes, we should, "...walk by faith, not by sight" (2 Corinthians 5:7).

Whereas the women of Zion walked mincing as they go, we should, "Walk in the Spirit [so that we are not tempted to] fulfill the lust of the flesh" (Galatians 5:16, emphasis added).

I can appreciate author Anne Ortlund's observation when she analyzed the twenty-two verses describing the Proverbs 31 woman, and like me, discovered that only one verse described this woman's physical attire. Verse twenty-two says, "She makes tapestry for herself; Her clothing is fine linen and purple."

Purple at that time was considered quality fabric customarily worn by the wealthy (see Judges 8:26; Luke 16:19). Anne Ortlund prayed, "Father, I want to give 1/22 of my time to making myself as outwardly beautiful as I can; and I want to give all the rest of my time, 21/22 of my life, to becoming wise, kind, godly, hard-working, and the rest."[4]

Like the Proverbs 31 woman clothed in strength and honor, God wants us to be clothed with tender mercies, kindness, humility, meekness, long-suffering, forgiveness, and love (Colossians 3:12, paraphrased). All the qualities that make a woman beautiful.

Embracing Your Femininity

I by no means want to offend anyone, but if you are a woman, look like one! Short hair, long hair, it doesn't matter as long as your gender is defined. Feeling more comfortable in men's clothing is not an excuse to look like a man or to wear masculine clothing—if you are a woman. The Bible says: "A woman shall not wear anything that pertains to a man, nor shall a man put on a woman's garment…" (Deuteronomy 22:5).

With the variety of stores and online specialty shops, you are bound to find affordable women's clothing that exemplifies who you are and represents your softer, gentler, and refined side. Exceptions, of course, are situations that require you to wear the same clothing as a man for your personal safety or for your livelihood. Women in the military must wear the same Battle Dress Uniform (BDU) as their male counterparts, but whenever possible (off duty), they should embrace their femininity.

How Do I Look Now?

Suppose modesty is a problem for you, or you want to redefine your dress style. In that case, this section will offer some simple suggestions to help you sort through your wardrobe and refine and sharpen your look—keeping within the guidelines of modesty.

❑ **Step 1**—Seek God for yourself on a standard of modesty He is calling you to walk in. After praying and listening to God, write down what is now acceptable and unacceptable for you.

At 5'10, most skirts that fit me in the waist do not fit me in length (too short), but an appropriate skirt or dress length for me is at or below my knees. In addition, most V-necks are modest on me, but I usually wear a blazer or sweater, so my discretion is not questionable. I also try to purchase good-quality clothing because I plan to wear my purchases for years to come.

❑ **Step 2**—Think about the things you do and the places you go regularly. Then, think about where the majority of your time is being spent. Are you at home, at church, at the office, at school, at the gym, or with the kids? This will determine the type of clothes appropriate for your lifestyle (formal, casual, career, athletic, or lounge). Pick three areas you do more often than not; we will focus on refining these three areas.

❑ **Step 3**—Think about where you want to be and what you want to be doing in the near future. Are you up for a promotion at work? Will you be going back to school or reentering the workforce? Consider revamping your wardrobe for at least one of these remarkable events.

❑ **Step 4**—Select a maximum of three Christian friends or family members you trust to be lovingly honest and open with you, who have at least some fashion sense, and who can hold you accountable for complying with your new standards of modesty. These individuals will be your style guides. If you are married, consider asking your husband to be one of your style guides. Believe me when I say, "Your husband may have a better idea than most about what would look nice and elegant on you."

❑ **Step 5**—Schedule a consultation with each of your style guides individually. Have with you your new list of standards for walking in modesty. Ask each style guide the following questions:

- What do you think about how I dress (e.g., elegant, modest, provocative, or homely)?

- How would you enhance the way I dress?

- What is your opinion of my guidelines for walking in modesty?

If time permits, go through your closet with each style guide and assemble a couple of outfits for each category you defined above. Have your pen and notebook with you so you can take notes or capture suggestions with your camera phone. In addition, keep a running list of pieces or items you plan to purchase to refine and complete your wardrobe based on the advice provided by your style guides. If your budget does not permit purchasing now, set aside the funds to purchase those items later.

To get more ideas, take your pen and your spiral notebook or just your camera phone to your local shopping center with at least one of your style guides. Leave your checkbook and credit cards at home; this is a discovery trip. Do not spend money on clothing until you are comfortable with the choices you have made to redefine your wardrobe.

While at the store, stay focused on your purpose—to find modest and elegant styles that you feel comfortable wearing and that flatter you. Try on as many outfits as possible, paying close attention to the colors and styles that distinctively define you. Ask yourself:

- Does this color complement me?
- Does it fit my life-style (can I wear it to several different places like work, church, and school)?
- Does it fit within my guidelines for modesty?
- Does this item go with what I already have (jackets, purses, shoes, or other accessories)?

After you have taken the time to gather ideas to redefine your wardrobe, don't stop there. Stroll by the makeup counter at a local department store, and have someone give you some basic makeup tips. Keep in mind, however, that not a lot of makeup is needed to enhance a person's natural beauty.

Let me conclude by saying that as women of elegance and grace, our gratification should not come from shining the spotlight on ourselves but through shining the spotlight on Jesus Christ in us. In addition, remember that in all our adorning, *external beauty* is no substitute for *being divine by design*.

Step 10: Your Daily Call to Order

Chapter Comments:

The focus of this step was finding the beauty within you and the beauty of walking in elegance, grace, modesty, and as Ephesians 4:1 states: "... worthy of the calling with which [we] were called" (emphasis added).

Now, let us visit the Psalms and immerse ourselves in the beauty of God as described in the following verses:

- "One thing I have desired of the LORD, That will I seek: That I may dwell in the house of the Lord All the days of my life, To behold the beauty of the LORD, And to inquire in His temple" (Psalm 27:4).

- "Out of Zion, the perfection of beauty, God will shine forth" (Psalm 50:2).

- "And let the beauty of the Lord our God be upon us, And establish the work of our hands for us; Yes, establish the work of our hands" (Psalm 90:17).

- "Honor and majesty are before Him; Strength and beauty are in His sanctuary" (Psalm 96:6).

Chapter Questions:
Group Discussion
1. How does society's emphasis on external beauty affect most Christian women?
2. Despite all the advertising around us, what are some ways we can focus on our inner beauty without ignoring our outward appearance?
3. How would you define *modesty*?
4. How seriously should an ambassador for Christ take "the act of dressing modestly"?
5. Do you agree with the author that dressing provocatively increases our risk of being victimized or sexually assaulted?
6. Read Isaiah 3:16-24. What are your thoughts regarding Isaiah's words to the Daughters of Zion?

Personal Reflection
7. What are your feelings regarding your physical appearance? What would you change? Why?
8. How can you model Christ-like character and discretion in your dress and appearance?
9. What critical aspects of your character do you want people to be drawn to? Why?
10. Read Colossians 3:12-14. What part of God's divine wardrobe do you need to put on (i.e., if you are wearing "love," how is it being expressed to others)?

Chapter Assignments:
❑ **Challenge 1**: Respond to end of chapter questions.

❑ **Challenge 2**: Pray and study the Bible to discover more about modesty. Share your findings with your small group (or accountability partner); include how God's wisdom has influenced the way you now dress.

❑ **Challenge 3**: If modesty is an issue for you, make a couple of changes in your wardrobe to move you one step closer to being a woman of grace, elegance, and modesty (e.g., donate or refuse to buy shirts with plunging necklines, or skirts that ride up when you sit down).

❑ **Extreme Challenge**: Use the suggestions provided within this section to define or redefine your wardrobe.

Step 11

Caring for Your Castle

> UNLESS the LORD builds the house,
> They labor in vain who build it;
> —Psalm 127:1

We have heard it said often: "Home is where the heart is," and "There's no place like Home." Home is a special place for many people because it provides a place of refuge from the rest of the world. Home offers a place where we can hang up our hats, kick off our shoes, and get comfortable. It's a place where we can be ourselves and be accepted. It's a place where we can regroup and collect ourselves—receiving the nourishment needed to build us up physically, emotionally, and spiritually. In short, a home should supply its occupants with love, nourishment, comfort, warmth, and security.

I will not take you through the entire process of caring for your castle. The most important part of caring for your castle is caring for the people in it, so my goal in this step is to focus on aspects of managing your home with special emphasis placed on its occupants.

If you are single and without children, what you will glean from the following pages will be instrumental in preparing you for marriage and a family someday.

The Wise Household Manager

I have intentionally ended with this step because I cannot profess to be a "June Cleaver" or a "Martha Stewart" in the home. However, I can certainly appreciate my mother's effort in caring for her castle. As a young girl growing up, I can attest to the fact that my mother kept an incredibly clean and organized house, so I know how to clean and what clean looks like. My dilemma has been finding the time and organizing my time to keep my house as clean as my mother's. This has been a massive challenge for me with all my other responsibilities (including working outside the home).

It seemed the harder I worked, the less I accomplished until I had to admit to myself and confess to God that I could not do it all—unless His Spirit (the Holy Spirit) was working in and through me. That's when the Lord began to press on my heart about the importance of having godly priorities, discussed in step two. Next, the Lord spoke to me about decluttering and simplifying my life, which was discussed in step five, and then the significance of building relationships, discussed in step seven—all these elements, whether you see it or not, play an essential role in caring for your castle.

In chapter seven of the book of Matthew we are told of the wise man who built his house on the rock, and the foolish man who built his house on the sand. Jesus was addressing His disciples and the multitude about the blessings of obeying the Word of God and acting on the wisdom of God. He clearly illustrates in this parable the blessings of bringing something into fruition (building a house, raising a child, or strengthening a marriage) based on the solid, never-changing truth of God's Word, versus our own wisdom.

The wise man who built his house on the rock understood the wisdom and power of God—who made all things and understands all things. So he sought God for the blueprint to build his home, raise his children, or strengthen his marriage. This parable brings home the message: "Unless the Lord builds the house, they labor in vain who build it (Psalm 127:1). Let's look at ways a godly woman can wisely build her home.

> 📖 How have you been building your house? Upon a rock (the wisdom of Jesus Christ) or upon sand (the wisdom of man)?

She Fuels Her Family with Love

According to 1 John 4:12, your family and others will know that you are a woman of God by the love you show them (in the home).

By nurturing their souls you build up their self-esteem. By cultivating the attitude they should walk in and the values they should have, you create in them self-worth. Of all the negative data your husband and children receive from the world daily, you as a wife and a mother, have the opportunity in the home to counter that with positive words that encourage and uplift. Remember, "A word fitly spoken is like apples of gold" (Proverbs 25:11)

In addition, your loved ones should know that you believe they are capable, adequate, wise, and competent. Caring for your castle ushers in the spirit of hospitality, which tells your family, "I love you" and "I care about you." This spirit will thrive in your home when you consistently place yourself in prayer at the feet of Jesus.

Most of the time, this spirit of hospitality is not lived out in the home because we are being bound by what someone else is doing or not doing to appease us. Our love should be based on what is right, honorable, and just before the Lord our God.

The book of James clearly identifies the wars within us and the spirit of rift and discord among people—especially between couples. It is the desire for a person to have things their way: having their needs met, having their wants fulfilled, and having their expectations honored. He says:

> *What causes fights and quarrels among you? Don't they come from your desires that battle within you? You want something but don't get it. You kill and covet, but you cannot have what you want. You quarrel and fight. You do not have, because you do not ask God* (James 4:1-2, NIV).

The Bible also says, "Let us therefore make every effort to do what leads to peace and to mutual edification" (Romans 14:19).

My dear sister in Christ, it may take your husband and children years before they are able to respond to your acts of love, but they are definitely taking notice of whether *you* are being sincere and are probably thinking, "This too shall pass." Therefore, prepare your heart and saturate your spirit with God's love so you can go the distance. Get strength and encouragement from the Word of God. Likewise, connect with women who are willing to pray with you regularly and who will be there to help you endure the challenges you will inevitably face in your marriage, with your children, and within yourself.

Step 11: Caring for Your Castle

Yes, your husband should seek to live in love and understanding with you and make every effort to meet your needs—especially if he is a Christian. The Bible tells us that his prayers may be hindered if he treats you with little regard (1 Peter 3:7). However, thinking or expecting your husband to meet or understand all your needs is unrealistic. He is human, and as a human being, he will do things that disappoint you.

Submitting your needs to God and having the support of spirit-filled women will keep you focused on loving and what God can do, as opposed to what man can do but is not doing.

When the Shunammite woman (in 2 Kings 4:11-13) allowed God to fill her desire for a child with joy, acceptance, and contentment, her focus turned to serving others. With her focus firmly set on loving, God met her long, laid-to-rest desire for a child. With your mind firmly set on loving, God will meet your long, laid-to-rest needs. Maybe not how you expect Him to or when you expect Him to, but remember that God *is* faithful.

> *Let us therefore make every effort to do what leads to peace and to mutual edification.*
>
> *—Romans 14:19*

In the book of Proverbs, our virtuous woman is portrayed as a woman of influence: producing, inspiring, and a constant source of encouragement for her family. I do not doubt that the love, encouragement, and support this woman provided her husband—at home—enabled him to be "... known in the gates, When he sits among the elders of the land" (31:23).

As faithful and wise servants, we should serve with an attitude of love. Why? Because it is our reasonable service to the people that God has blessed us with.

She Fuels Her Family with Food

Another way to usher in hospitality in the home is by fueling your family with nutritious foods.

Before I started taking my family's health seriously, I rarely cooked. We mostly ate processed meals, fast food, or an occasional family dinner at a nice restaurant. When I did cook, my husband would ask: "What's the occasion?" To which I would respond by saying: "Gotta eat!"

Unfortunately, in my early days as a new wife and mother, cooking was not something I took pleasure in doing; honestly, it is something I still struggle with. However, after meditating on a verse in Proverbs, the significance of meal preparation hit home. The verse says:

She also rises while it is yet night, And provides food for her household, And a portion for her maidservants (Proverbs 31:15).

Our Proverbs 31 Woman had maidservants to cook for her and her family. Still, she found it necessary not to relinquish this responsibility. It was acceptable for her maids to clean, do the laundry, make the beds, and so on, but she did the cooking!

Besides wanting to serve her family, a virtuous woman realizes the importance of ensuring that her family is fed and gets the proper nutrition they need. Second, she realizes that mealtime gatherings are the perfect opportunity to find out what is going on with the people in her life (household), and probably a chance to ensure her maids (if applicable) know what is expected of them throughout the day. In addition, I would not be surprised if she uses the start of mealtime to pray with and for her family and to thank God for their "daily bread."

Step 11: Caring for Your Castle

Third, she can identify what household duties directly affect the well-being of her family, and she focuses her energy and organizes her time to serve her family in those areas. This might include: meal preparation and serving, helping her children with homework, and assisting her husband with special projects. Hear me, my sister in Christ, a virtuous woman does not allow another woman (her maidservants included) to have more position and place in her home and in her husband's and children's hearts than she has. She tries to stay connected to her family as much as possible and removes the middleman from having influential contact with her family. With a humble heart and spirit, she decides the influences her family will be subjected to in the home.

In my opinion, a passage in the book of Matthew magnifies the importance of a virtuous woman's role in the home. It says...

> *Who then is the faithful and wise servant, whom the master has put in charge of the servants in his household to give them their food at the proper time? (Matthew 24:45, NIV).*

As God's faithful and wise servant, your duty is to focus on those things necessary to capture and keep your family's heart, by doing what you were called to do by God—serve *with balance, of course.*

Meal Planning

Again, our Proverbs 31 Woman provides a wonderful example for us as we read: "She is like the merchant ships, She brings her food from afar" (v. 14). In this verse our wise example is being compared to merchant ships (filled with food items from various places). So it would be wise to assume a Proverbs 31

Woman is a selective shopper, providing her family with a variety of healthy, appetizing meals that nourish the body.

As a wise shopper—following in our wise woman's footsteps—we will start by making a master shopping list. Your shopping list should organize your food items into groups: fruits, vegetables, meats, beverages, and so on. If you need help, use past grocery receipts or walk down the aisle of your local grocery store.

Your master shopping list should also include items you buy regularly and basic items like condiments and other seasonings that you need but purchase less often. At the end of your list, leave blank lines (if typed) to add unique ingredients required for a new recipe.

I used to print multiple copies of my master shopping list and posted a copy on my refrigerator. As I discovered a need for a particular item, I highlighted the item on my list. If there was a new recipe I wanted to try and the ingredients were not already listed, I would add the ingredients in the space provided.

Whenever I went grocery shopping, I only purchased those items on my grocery list that were highlighted or written in. After shopping, a new copy of my master shopping list adorned my refrigerator. Of course, if a new recipe was a hit with my family, I would have to modify my master shopping list accordingly.

Now, the most effective way for me to maintain my grocery list is to use my smartphone and a grocery app. The app allows me to build and maintain my list by typing the product name, speaking to my phone using voice dictation, or scanning the product's barcode. I can also create my master grocery list online using a desktop computer and then sync it to my smartphone. Other benefits of using an app include: the ability to create multiple lists for stores I frequent; being able

Step 11: Caring for Your Castle

to organize my lists by grouping similar items into categories; and being able to view and maintain digital coupons.

Once your master shopping list has been created, decide on a consistent time and day each month you will grocery shop (e.g., the second and fourth Tuesday at 9:00 a.m.). Then, select a consistent day each week (or every other week) you will plan your meals. Write it in the space provided below.

- My Shopping Time: _____
- My Meal Planning Time: _____

Don't forget to add these appointments to your calendar. In addition, here are some simple suggestions to simplify meal planning:

- Designate one or two nights a week as sandwich or pizza night.

- Consider having a night in which you prepare a favorite dish of one of your family members.

- Become skilled at using leftovers; for example, Monday's main meat dish can be used for sandwich night on Wednesday.

- Introduce your family to one new healthy recipe a week or every other week.

- One night a month, introduce your family to an entrée popular in another culture.

- Consider cooking multiple meals simultaneously; freeze the extra meals and reheat them when ready to serve.

Search the internet for meal planning and nutritional facts information sites. You will find recipe ideas to liven up family meal times.

Also, in all your serving, avoid getting so caught up in the serving process that you are unable to enjoy the fruit of your labor and the people around your table.

She Fuels Herself with Breaks!

Some people get a rush of excitement the busier they are; as I stated in another chapter, I am not one of them. I get frazzled when I'm perpetually moving from one place to another or trying to meet one demand after another. Whether you are like me or the exact opposite, we all need the time and space to recoup, regroup, recharge, and rejuvenate ourselves.

God set the example for us in Genesis, where we are told that God physically rested on the seventh day from creating the world and all that is in it. He then sanctified the seventh day (the Sabbath day or Sunday). This day is considered to be a special day of worship and peaceful communion with the Body of Christ. It is also a day of rest and relaxation for God's people. ...

> THUS the heavens and the earth, and all the host of them, were finished. And on the seventh day God ended His work which He had done, and He rested on the seventh day from all His work which He had done. Then God blessed the seventh day and sanctified it, because in it He rested from all His work which God had created and made (Genesis 2:1-3).

Without adequate rest, our endurance and vitality decrease, lowering our defenses and making us more irritable and intolerant toward others. It can also contribute to mental,

Step 11: Caring for Your Castle

physical, spiritual, and emotional problems. It can also stifle our dreams and creativity and render us powerless to handle challenges within the home and elsewhere. Yet it may appear that in all your striving, the pursuit of rest and relaxation seems beyond your grasp. You can probably attest to being sleep deprived or not having that needed moment to get a grip on your day—or in some cases, to catch your breath.

As multi-taskers trying to have it all and do it all, we sometimes fail at maintaining balance. So much depends on us as women that it's no wonder it's hard for us to find rest. Yet God ordained it, and He ordained it for a reason. He knows Satan doesn't want us to rest because rest is not only about sleep. During our periods of rest (or downtime), we are also able to listen to God, hear our thoughts, meditate on decisions, or just gather our composure. This is a form of spiritual resting as we restore our souls and seek the peace of God for our lives.

> *If Satan can wear you down with exhaustion, he can lure you away from God's wisdom and will—and render you useless to God and to others.*

If Satan can wear you down with exhaustion, he can lure you away from God's wisdom and will—and render you useless to God and others.

Rest fuels us and gives us the strength to fulfill the tasks God has purposed in our hearts. Our Proverbs 31 Woman builds herself up with strength (v. 17). Her spiritual strength enabled her to balance her responsibilities and fulfill her God-given ministry. There were probably many nights she was up late working, but I also believe there were many nights she was able to get to bed early or enjoy more quiet time with the Lord, which energized her physically and enabled her to walk in spiritual strength—no matter how overwhelmed she felt. This woman of God was wise in not allowing things that needed to be done to get out of proportion with those things—seeking God, getting adequate rest, eating healthy, and exercising—that enabled her to be about her father's business of serving others.

So what should you do? Listen to your body and get the right amount of rest each night that your body requires. Most people can function reasonably well on six to eight hours of sleep per night and maybe a short nap during the day.

In addition, find ways to relax. Spend time in the presence of God, go on a nature walk, take a bubble bath, or listen to soothing music. Seek out ways to lighten your own load so you can get the rest you need and deserve. Most importantly, learn to say "no" to excessive demands on your time.

Sharing Responsibilities

I wholeheartedly believe that if you have young children or work outside the home, the household responsibilities should be shared. However, more often than not, it's still a woman's responsibility to care for the home and the people in it. If your husband refuses or can't pull his weight around the house to help lighten your load and help you get the rest you need, look for alternative solutions.

I have an acquaintance who is a stay-at-home wife and mother. She told me when she gets behind in her housework, she will hire a maid service to help her get caught up. If you can't afford to hire maid service, hire a teenager in your neighborhood to help you on a regular basis.

I have a friend who is a wife and mother and who works full-time as well as a lot of unpaid overtime. She recently started dropping her weekly laundry off at a service laundry

Step 11: Caring for Your Castle

mat. Cleaners are also available to pick up and drop off your dry-clean clothes. Groceries can be ordered online and brought to your home.

Start by listing what chores must be done daily and weekly, then prioritize them. If clean dishes are important to your husband, ensure that that task is high on your list. If keeping the floor clean is important because you have a young child crawling around the house, then that should also be high on your list.

Next, find out from your household occupants who will be responsible for what. From the youngest that can walk to the oldest that can get around, there should be something for everyone to do. At the very least (if physically able), your husband should be able to take out the trash and mow the lawn. In addition, your children should be able to keep their rooms tidy and pick up after themselves. From the remaining unassigned tasks, determine what can be outsourced so you can get the rest you need and deserve. However, if none of the above suggestions are viable for you, isolate and focus on a few chores you can do daily and weekly that would make a significant difference in the condition of your home.

Giving Grace

Between you and me, most husbands feel they've worked hard all day, and when they get home, they are due some peace and quiet, not "friction and fraction." As a wise woman of God, you should know that nagging or tossing out shrewd demands will not make your husband eager to meet your needs or in a rush to get home. The truth is, most people do not like being nagged or told what to do even if they are getting paid for it.

I overheard a male coworker—who, in my opinion, was blessed with a lovely wife and three beautiful daughters—make this comment to another male coworker: "When I step into my house and the dog is sitting in the corner ready to bolt when the door opens, that's my cue to bolt too." He was implying that the attitude in his home wasn't what he wanted to come home to.

Sometimes, a wife's attitude in the home makes matters worse. It may drive her husband to work overtime, play golf or basketball excessively, or hang out most nights with his buddies. Not that this behavior is acceptable from a husband who professes to love his wife, but consider how her unbecoming conduct might make him feel. Like the common cold, a wife's negative attitude can affect the entire family.

> 📖 How do you greet your husband when he comes home from work? How do you greet your children?

As wives, we want our husbands to want to come home to us; and as mothers, we want our children to be able to come to us if they have a need. Concerning your husband, greet him with a smile when he gets home from work, then give him time to unwind. Wait before you bombard him with what Jr. did, what little Sally did not do, why he's late, why he forgot to pick up the milk, or why he rarely takes you out. In addition, check your attitude: Are you negative, critical, or quick to find fault? Are you kind and gracious?

The classic definition of *grace* is "unmerited favor." Even though we may deserve to be punished for our sins (and at times *are* punished for our sins), God is gracious toward us and full of compassion. In response to our Lord's love and grace toward us, we should practice giving grace to others.

God's grace forgives us of our sins, wakes us up in our right mind, gives us strength when we feel weak, and is available anywhere at any time.

Giving grace requires us to have a heart that is willing to submit to the Word and Will of God. Grace toward our loved ones says, "You don't have to meet my expectations for me to love you; I accept and love you for who you are."

Giving grace is necessary in developing and maintaining any meaningful relationship. It offers love, kindness, forgiveness, compassion, sympathy, and understanding whether a person deserves it or not. It also demonstrates the presence of God in our lives.

If God's grace was sufficient for Paul (see 2 Corinthians 12:8-10), surely God's grace could equip and empower us to be gracious toward our loved ones even when they are not being considerate or gracious toward us.

> What does giving grace say about your love for the Lord and what He did on the cross for you?

I know what you are probably thinking: that the practice of giving grace will make you a pushover. If you believe that, you're mistaken. God is gracious, but never would we consider Him a pushover. Most of us believe that He is very much in control. Giving grace gives us more control as we learn to harness our emotions and allow wisdom to guide us.

Giving grace is a necessary stepping stone in developing and maintaining any meaningful relationship.

Seek God in prayer regarding the best way to approach family members about your concerns. Then, allow the Holy Spirit to guide you in giving grace. Romans 8:14 says, "For all who are led by the Spirit of God are [sons and daughters] of God" (emphasis added).

As you make a practice of giving grace in your home, may your husband "forever be captivated by your love."

Secure Your Castle with Commitment

As a woman you want to feel safe in your home, but that's not always something you have control over. If you're being abused, you should get to a safe haven. If you live in a questionable neighborhood, do what you can to feel safe and secure, but most importantly, remember that you have security in the Lord your God.

Guess what? Your children look to you to provide that same security of unconditional love, especially when they are young. When the world is cruel and their classmates are harsh, they are thankful for the security that home provides.

Security is also stability. Your children need the security of knowing that you are doing whatever you can to keep their family intact. This does not mean you condone sinful or immature behavior from your mate, nor does it mean you have to be consumed by hopelessness, loneliness, heartbreak, and despair. It does mean you are making every effort to keep your marriage strong and healthy by seeking God's wisdom and allowing God to meet your deep-seated emotional needs.

Separation and divorce grieve God, even though many preachers and teachers of the Bible concur that there are three acceptable reasons to divorce: physical abuse, adultery, or the unbelieving spouse leaves.

Whatever the case, so much is lost due to divorce—your child's security is one of those things. Studies reveal that most children blame themselves for their parents breaking up. To this, add life as they know it changing. They are forced to readjust to one parent not being around as often, and they may experience some level of neglect as the custodial parent is forced to work or work longer hours to make ends meet.

My sister in Christ, we have a responsibility in the home to assist our children in becoming all they can be in the Lord and accomplishing all they can for the kingdom of God.

Step 11: Caring for Your Castle

Psalm 127:3 reminds us that our children are a blessing from the Lord. The next verse compares our children to arrows in the hand of a warrior. It says, "Like arrows in the hand of a warrior, So are the children of one's youth" (v. 4). It's difficult as parents to aim a child in the right direction, at the right target, and at the right time if the child feels insecure in our hands.

Every ounce of effort you apply to being a godly wife and mother can be your way of honoring God and the commitment you made to your husband. It is also how God will speak to your family. Never cease to believe what God can do in your marriage and through your children when you seek Him with all your heart.

Sormie Omartian, in her book, *The Power of A Praying Wife* says:

> In every broken marriage, there is at least one person whose heart is hard against God. When a heart becomes hard, there is no vision from God's perspective. When we're miserable in a marriage, we feel that anything will be an improvement over what we're experiencing. But we don't see the whole picture. We only see the way it is, not the way God wants it to become. When we pray, however, our hearts become *soft* toward God and we get a vision. We see there is hope. We have faith that He will restore all that has been devoured, destroyed, and eaten away from the marriage.... We can trust Him to take away the pain, hopelessness, hardness, and unforgiveness. We are able to envision His ability to resurrect love and life from the deadest of places.[1]

When we operate in the spirit of hospitality, we usher in harmony and become hosts for healing and change in our home, which will eventually spill over into our church and community.

While ministering to your family, ask God to strengthen and encourage you daily. Allow Him to meet your needs and desires. Only by humbling yourself before God and allowing the Holy Spirit to instruct you do you become capable of serving in a manner that reflects God.

When you have sought the Lord and done all you can to make things work in your home, continue to stand strong in the Lord. Some people will never be satisfied with your efforts; this is not a reflection of you but of *their* failure to understand God's will and ways.

Step 11: Your Daily Call to Order

Chapter Comments:
When a person steps into your house, they should sense the presence of the Holy Spirit. Your home is a very special and intimate place; it also reflects your unique style and personality—giving welcomed guests a snapshot of who you are.

The book of Proverbs is filled with practical wisdom on building and maintaining your home; here are just a few I would like to share:

- **Stay productive**: "She watches over the ways of her household, And does not eat the bread of idleness" (31:27).
- **Get understanding**: "Through wisdom a house is built, And by understanding it is established; By knowledge

the rooms are filled with all precious and pleasant riches" (24:3-4).

ଔ **Prepare wisely**: "WISDOM has built her house, She has hewn out her seven pillars; She has slaughtered her meat, She has mixed her wine, She has also furnished her table" (9:1-2).

ଔ **Be receptive to the Holy Spirit**: "THE wise woman builds her house, But the foolish pulls it down ...." (14:1).

Chapter Questions:

Group Discussion

1. Describe the ambiance in your home (e.g., cheerful and peaceful; gloomy and noisy; a place of refuge and retreat; a pigsty; a hole in the wall; an uncomfortable place to relax; a dark and cold dungeon). What can you do to improve it?
2. Read 1 Peter 3:1-2, 8-12. What do the verses say about our attitude in the home and among others?
3. Read Genesis 2:2-3; Psalm 37:7; Matthew 11:28-29. What does the Bible say about rest?
4. What does having meals with your family allow you to do?
5. Read John 1:17; Romans 5:19-21; 6:14; Titus 2:11-12; Ephesians 2:5. Who gives grace? What is the purpose of grace?
6. Read 2 Corinthians 12:8-10; Hebrews 4:15-16. What does God's grace help us endure?
7. Read Psalm 27:1; 28:8; 46:1-2; 91:4, 14-16; Romans 8:31-32. What does the Bible teach us about who understands and meets our need for security and strength?

Personal Reflection

8. What adjustments do you need to make today in your attitude to begin the practice of giving grace?

9. What has your relationship with your husband or children encouraged or motivated them to do? What has it revealed about your character?
10. List some things that rob you of rest. What solutions can you incorporate into your life to lighten your load and help you get the rest you need or some time to unwind?
11. What are your feelings regarding your marriage?
12. If you and your husband live separate lives, how can you reconnect? Suggestion: find a common goal and work toward it.

Chapter Assignments:

❑ Challenge 1: Compile a list of ways you can show love and encourage the people in your life. Begin doing what you can on your list regularly.

❑ Challenge 2: Respond to end of chapter questions.

❑ Challenge 3: Create your master grocery list.

❑ Challenge 4: Decide on a day each week (or every other week) you will do your grocery shopping.

❑ Challenge 5: Decide on a day each week (or every other week) you will plan your family meals.

❑ Challenge 6: If married or single with children, decide on a mealtime (breakfast, lunch, or dinner) where the entire family can sit down and eat together with the television off. Commit to have dinner together at least twice a week.

❑ Challenge 7: Make a daily and weekly chores list.

❑ Challenge 8: Decide who among your able family members will do what chores around the house.

❑ Challenge 9: Decide what chores can and will be outsourced.

Step 11: Caring for Your Castle

❑ Challenge 10: Make a laundry list of things you would eventually like to do to improve the appearance and upkeep of your domain.

❑ Challenge 11: For one week, pay attention to the type of words you use to address your husband and children. How many positive words do you use versus the negative words?

❑ Group Challenge: If God has restored your marriage, prepare and share your testimony of how the Lord has resurrected your marriage—in the midst of separation or divorce—with your accountability partner or study group.

Conclusion: Bringing It Home!

I hope this book blessed you. I hope that God has taken your cluttered life and added the clarity of His Word to produce in you the courage, confidence, and commitment to contribute to what matters most (building up the kingdom of God).

I also want you to realize the importance of enjoying the people and things God has blessed you with, like your family, your home, your passion(s), your health, your ministry, your finances, and the beauty within you.

If you have completed this book, please let me know how it has blessed you or how it can be improved to bless others. Join the Balancing Blessings community at: www.facebook.com/Balancing.Blessings, visit our ministry website at: www.BalancingBlessings.org, or leave a review at: https://www.amazon.com/Balancing-Blessings-Obtaining-Order-Possessions/dp/0980009375/.

As your last challenge, I would like for you to examine yourself in light of the Proverbs 31 woman—a list of her character traits is available in Appendix A. Take time to determine whether this woman continues to elude you or whether she lives within you.

Appendix A

Forms and Worksheets

1. Combination To-Do List
2. Fitness Vision Profile
3. Clutter Analysis Worksheet
4. Identify Your Passion(s) Worksheet
5. Goal Setting Worksheet
6. Monthly Household Budget Worksheet
7. Characteristics of the Proverbs 31 Woman

Worksheet 1: Combination To-Do List

Master To-Do List	☑		Weekly Task Tracker	☑
1.	☐	*Monday*	1.	☐
2.	☐		2.	☐
3.	☐		3.	☐
4.	☐		4.	☐
5.	☐		5.	☐
6.	☐	*Tuesday*	1.	☐
7.	☐		2.	☐
8.	☐		3.	☐
9.	☐		4.	☐
10.	☐		5.	☐
11.	☐	*Wednesday*	1.	☐
12.	☐		2.	☐
13.	☐		3.	☐
14.	☐		4.	☐
15.	☐		5.	☐
16.	☐	*Thursday*	1.	☐
17.	☐		2.	☐
18.	☐		3.	☐
19.	☐		4.	☐
20.	☐		5.	☐
21.	☐	*Friday*	1.	☐
22.	☐		2.	☐
23.	☐		3.	☐
24.	☐		4.	☐
25.	☐		5.	☐
26.	☐	*Saturday/Sunday*	1.	☐
27.	☐		2.	☐
28.	☐		3.	☐
29.	☐		4.	☐
30.	☐		5.	☐

Appendix A

Worksheet 2: Fitness Vision Profile

1. What is your fitness objective (e.g., lose weight, tone up, increase endurance)?

2. What fitness area do you intend to focus on (e.g., cardiovascular, stretching, muscle strengthening)?

3. What activities do you enjoy doing?

4. Write down your fitness goal(s). Specify activities you enjoy and plan to do to help you meet your fitness objective in an area you intend to focus on.

5. Write down a personal commitment to reach your fitness goal(s) in the space provided below:

6. Visualize yourself having met your fitness goal(s). What do you look like? How do you feel? What are you doing differently? Write your vision below:

Worksheet 3: Clutter Analysis Worksheet

Circle the area evaluating: kitchen | family room | living room | dining room | home office | bathroom | laundry room | play room | master bed room | child room | other: _____.	
Possession Problem	❏ Is the clutter a possession problem—do I *have* too much stuff, or do I *have* a habit of not putting things away? ❏ If the clutter is a possession problem, what physical items or habits are causing the bulk of my clutter?
Resource Problem	❏ Is the clutter a resource problem, such as lack of time or space? ❏ If the clutter is a resource problem, what can be done to better utilize my time, space, or other available resources?

Write additional thoughts:

Appendix A

Helping You Identify Your Passion(s)

Using the "Identify Your Passion(s) Worksheet" on the next page, circle what interests you in each column. The type of people you feel compelled to help or serve, the causes you feel compelled to support financially or through active participation, and the activities or tasks you enjoy doing.

Once you have narrowed down the people, causes, and activities, start looking at where God wants you to fulfill your passion(s) at this season in your life. This could be at home, in your local church, community, or foreign country.

After completing the worksheet, if you still have difficulty finding your passion, don't fret; keep it in prayer, and continue to serve as God leads you—paying close attention to those things, tasks, causes, and people that motivate and energize you.

Worksheet 4: Identifying Your Passion(s)

People	Causes	Activities/Tasks
At-Risk Children	Cancer	Acting
Babies	Civil/Legal Rights	Administrating
Childless Couples	Domestic Violence	Advising
College Students	Drinking & Driving	Budgeting
Disabled	Drug Abuse	Building
Divorcees	Environmental:	Coaching
Elderly	Waste/Pollution	Cooking
First Ladies	Family Unity	Counseling
Homeless	Financial-steward-	Designing
Home-Makers	ship	Developing
Migrants	Freedom of Speech	Encouraging
Juveniles	Health Care Crisis	Fixing
Men/Women	HIV/AIDS	Facilitating
Nuclear family	Immigration	Fund Raising
Orphans	Media Influences	Leading
Pastors	Molestation or Rape	Lecturing
Pre-teen:	Obesity	Mentoring
Boys/Girls	Peer Pressure	Negotiating
Pregnant Teens	Pro-Life	Operating
Pregnant Women	Public Education	Organizing
Preschoolers	Religious Beliefs	Planning
Prisoners	Separation of:	Programming
Sick and Shut-in	Church and State	Serving
Single:	Sexual Immorality	Singing
Men/Women	Social Injustice	Sketching
Soldiers	Sports Awareness	Teaching
Teen:	Suicide Prevention	Traveling
Boys/Girls	Welfare Crisis	Visiting
Unborn-child	World Hunger	Writing
Widows/Widowers		

Appendix A

Worksheet 5: Goal Setting Worksheet

Circle the type of goal: career | family and home | educational | financial | spiritual | social and cultural | health and nutrition | personal		
Long Term Goals	**Long-Range** (5 to 10 years)	
	Mid-Range (1 to 5 years)	
Short Term Goals	**Short-Range** (90 days to 1 year)	
	Immediate (90 days or less) *Note: These goals should be added to your calendar and Master-Task List*	

Worksheet 6: Monthly Household Budget[1]

INCOME	$	EXPENSES CONT.	$
Net (take-home) pay		--Non Housing--	
Net (take-home) pay		Car loan	
Net overtime pay		Car insurance	
Pension, Social Security benefits		Car taxes	
		Gas and Oil	
Investment earnings		Car repairs	
Public assistance		Other transportation	
Alimony		Un-reimbursed medical	
Child support			
Other income		Other insurance	
Total Net Monthly Income		Credit Card #1	
		Credit Card #2	
EXPENSES		Credit Card #3	
Tithes (10% of Gross Pay)		Bank loan	
		Student loan	
--Housing--		Day Care/Tuition	
Rent/Mortgage		Alimony	
Property taxes		Child support	
Insurance		Telephone (Cell)	
Home maintenance		Eating out	
Home improvements		Entertainment	
HOA dues		Clothing	
Electricity		Grooming/Toiletries	
Gas/Oil		Subscriptions	
Water and Sewer		Charitable giving	
Food		Emergency savings	
Telephone (Land Line)		IRA contributions	
		Other _____	
Cable TV			
Computer/Internet		**Total Net Monthly Expenses**	
Other _____			

Monthly Household Budget (cont.)

Income After Expenses (Total Net Monthly Income - Total Net Monthly Expenses): $_____

Results: Surplus or Shortage?

---

[1]Worksheet adopted from the Fannie Mae Foundation and modified

Worksheet 7: Characteristics of the Proverbs 31 Woman

Below is a list of character traits of the Proverbs 31 Woman (vv. 10-31). As you glance through the list, you will find she is not that much different from you. You might not be all aspects of this remarkable woman, but that does not make you any less remarkable. Put an "x" in the box by those character traits you possess and a "√" by those you believe God is calling you to develop; then take steps to increase those virtues God is calling you to walk in. *She*...

❑ is a woman of godly character (walks in the fruit of the Spirit) (10)	❑ is concerned about the welfare of her family (21)
❑ is trustworthy (11)	❑ is prepared for the days ahead (21)
❑ consistently blesses (12)	❑ is a woman with skills, who regularly develops them (22)
❑ is a wise shopper (13)	❑ is a woman who positively influences the people around her (23)
❑ has selective taste in foods, clothes, and furnishings (13)	❑ is business minded (an entrepreneur) (24)
❑ is a diligent worker (13)	❑ is rooted a grounded in the Word of God, which strengthens her (25)
❑ is a great negotiator or better said, "thrifty" (14)	❑ speaks with wisdom and provides wise counsel (26)
❑ has godly priorities (15)	❑ manages her home well and stays productive (27)
❑ frequently prepares nutritious meals (15)	❑ is well thought of by her family and friends (28)
❑ is a wise investor (financially responsible) (16)	❑ pursues excellence (29)
❑ is physically fit (takes care of herself) (17)	❑ has inner beauty (30)
❑ is confident in her abilities (18)	❑ reverences God (30)
❑ is goal oriented—rarely leaves a project undone (19)	❑ reaps and sows love (31)
❑ is compassionate (20)	
❑ is charitable, gives to the poor (20)	

Appendix A

The Proverbs 31 Woman Index

31:10
284

31:11
198, 266

31:12
198

31:13
84, 251

31:14
305

31:15
76, 304

31:16
251, 269

31:17
309

31:18
77, 237, 269

31:19
58-59

31:20
198, 272-3

31:21
58-9

31:22
285, 292

31:23
303

31:24
269

31:25
18, 275

31:26
203

31:27
76-7, 81, 198, 316

31:28
176, 198

31:29
58, 176

31:30
176, 198, 285

31:31
58, 176

Bibliography

Introduction —
[1] Richard L. Strauss, "I'm in Love," www.bible.org/page.php?page_ id=1278, (accessed September 15, 2006).

Step 1 —
[1] Jim Cymbala, and Stephen Sorenson, *The Life God Blesses* (Grand Rapids, Michigan: Zondervan, 2001), 77-78.
[2] *Webster's New World College Dictionary*, 4th ed. (Cleveland, Ohio: Wiley Publishing, Inc., 2005), 1014.
[3] Ibid.

Step 2 —
[1] *The Preacher's Outline & Sermon Bible* (Chattanooga, Tennessee: Alpha-Omega Ministries, Inc., 1996), 299.
[2] Elizabeth George, *Loving God with All Your Mind* (Eugene, Oregon: Harvest House Publishers, 1994), 88.
[3] John C. Maxwell, *The Winning Attitude* (Nashville, Tennessee: Thomas Nelson Publishers, 1993), 185.

Step 3 —
[1] *Life Application Study Bible* (Wheaton, Illinois: Tyndale House Publishers, Inc., 1988), 1807.
[2] Anne Ortlund, *Disciplines of the Beautiful Woman* (Nashville, Tennessee: W Publishing Group, 1977), 110.
[3] Elizabeth George, *Loving God with All Your Mind* (Eugene, Oregon: Harvest House Publishers, 1994), 51.
[4] Ibid.

Step 4 —
[1] Michael F. Roizen, M.D. and Mehmet C. Oz, M.D., *You The Owner's Manual* (New York, New York: HarperCollins Publishers, 2005), 51.
[2] Dr. Mark Hyman, "Can Food Change Your Genes?" *Parade* (March 19, 2006), 10.
[3] Ibid.
[4] Ibid.
[5] *Simple Pledges, Building Blocks for Healthy Living*, Volume 3 (National Speaking of Women's Health Foundation, 2005), 8.
[6] Dr. Mark Hyman, 11.
[7] Braun, Ashley MPH, RD. "What Is a Folate Deficiency?" Verywell Health, 22 Mar. 2021, www.verywellhealth.com/folate-deficiency-5220432. Accessed 25 Sept. 2021.

Step 5 —
[1] *Webster's New World College Dictionary*, 4th ed. (Cleveland, OH: Wiley Publishing,

Inc., 2005), 279.
² *Life Application Study Bible*, King James Version (Wheaton, Illinois: Tyndale House Publishers, Inc., 1988), 232.
³ Kim Childress, "Simply Living," *Discovery Years* (Summer 2006), 5.
⁴ Identity Theft Resource Center: www.idtheftcenter.org, (accessed May 1, 2012).
⁵ "2012 Identity Fraud Report: Social Media and Mobile Forming the New Fraud Frontier," Javelin Strategy & Research: www.javelinstrategy.com/brochure/239, (accessed May 1, 2012).

Step 6 —
¹ Mandela, Nelson, *Long Walk to Freedom* (New York, New York: Brown and Company, 1995), 611, 619-620.
² Donald T. Phillips, *Lincoln on Leadership* (New York, New York: Warner Books, 1992), 5.
³ Ibid.
⁴ Ibid., 109.
⁵ Napoleon Hill, *Napoleon Hill's A Year of Growing RICH* (New York, New York: Penguin Books, 1993), 76.
⁶ Wikipedia, "Horatio Spafford," http://en.wikipedia.org/wiki/ Horatio_Spafford, (accessed May 15, 2006).
⁷ The Library of Congress, "The American Colony in Jerusalem," http://www.loc.gov/exhibits/americancolony/amcolony-family.html, (accessed May 15, 2006).
⁸ Dr. Henry Cloud and Dr. John Townsend, *Boundaries in Marriage* (Grand Rapids, Michigan: Zondervan, 1999), 88.
⁹ Immaculee Ilibagiza, *Left to Tell, Discovering God Amidst the Rwandan Holocaust* (Carlsbad, California: Hay House, Inc., 2006), 78.
¹⁰ Ibid, 80.
¹¹ *Life Application Study Bible*, King James Version (Wheaton, Illinois: Tyndale House Publishers, Inc., 1988), 1079.
¹² Max Lucado, *In the Grip of Grace* (Dallas: Word Publishing, 1996), 13.

Step 7 —
¹ Rick Warren, *The Purpose Driven Life* (Grand Rapids, Michigan: Zondervan, 2002), 37.
² Henry T. Blackaby and Claude V. King, *Experiencing God* (Nashville, Tennessee: LifeWay Press, 1990), 225.
³ *Webster's New World College Dictionary* (Cleveland, OH: Wiley Publishing, Inc., 2005), 1579.
⁴ John C. Maxwell, *The Winning Attitude* (Nashville, Tennessee: Thomas Nelson Publishers, 1993), 76.
⁵ H. Norman Wright, *How to Encourage the Man in Your Life* (Nashville, Tennessee: Word, Inc. 1997), 95.
⁶ John C. Maxwell and Jim Dornan, *Becoming a Person of Influence* (Nashville, Tennessee: Thomas Nelson Publishers, 1997), 107.
⁷ Ibid.
⁸ Gary Thomas, *Sacred Marriage* (Grand Rapids, Michigan: Zondervan, 2000), 49-50.

⁹ Jim Kraus, *Bloopers, Blunders, Jokes, Quips, & "Quotes"* (Wheaton, Illinois: Tyndale House Publishers, Inc., 2005), 118.

Step 8 —
[1] Mark Cahill, *One Thing You Can't Do in Heaven* (Bartlesville, Oklahoma: Genesis Publishing Group, 2004), 47-59.
[2] Ibid, 17.
[3] *Holman Illustrated Bible Dictionary* (Nashville, Tennessee: Holman Bible Publishers, 2003), 1529.

Step 9 —
[1] Howard Dayton, *Your Money Counts*, (Gainesville, Georgia: Crown Financial Ministries, Inc., 1996), 38.
[2] CNN Money, Good Debt vs. Bad Debt, http://money.cnn.com/ magazines/moneymag/money101/lesson9/index2.htm, (accessed February 22, 2007).
[3] Randy Alcorn, *Money, Possessions, and Eternity* (Wheaton, Illinois: Tyndale House Publishers, Inc., 2003), 384.
[4] Suze Orman, *The 9 Steps to Financial Freedom* (New York: Crown Publishers, Inc., 1997), 21-22.
[5] Julie Aigner-Clark, http://www.aignerclarkcreative. com/Common/Documents/biography.pdf, (accessed February 22, 2007).
[6] BlueSuitMom.com, "Talking with: Julie Aigner-Clark Founder, The Baby Einstein Company", http://www.bluesuitmom.com/career/womenbiz/babyeinstein.html, (accessed February 22, 2007).
[7] Ibid.

Step 10 —
[1] Shaunti Feldhahn, *For Women Only*, (Sisters, Oregon: Multnomah Publishers, Inc., 2004), 112-113.
[2] *Webster's New World College Dictionary*, 4th ed. (Cleveland, OH: Wiley Publishing, Inc., 2005), 652.
[3] Ibid., 1611.
[4] Anne Ortlund, *Disciplines of the Beautiful Woman*, (Eugene, Oregon: W Publishing Group, 1977), 45.

Step 11 —
[1] Stormie Omartian, *The Power of a Praying Wife*, (Eugene, Oregon: Harvest House Publishers, 1997), 18-19.

www.ingramcontent.com/pod-product-compliance
Lightning Source LLC
LaVergne TN
LVHW051543070426
835507LV00021B/2371